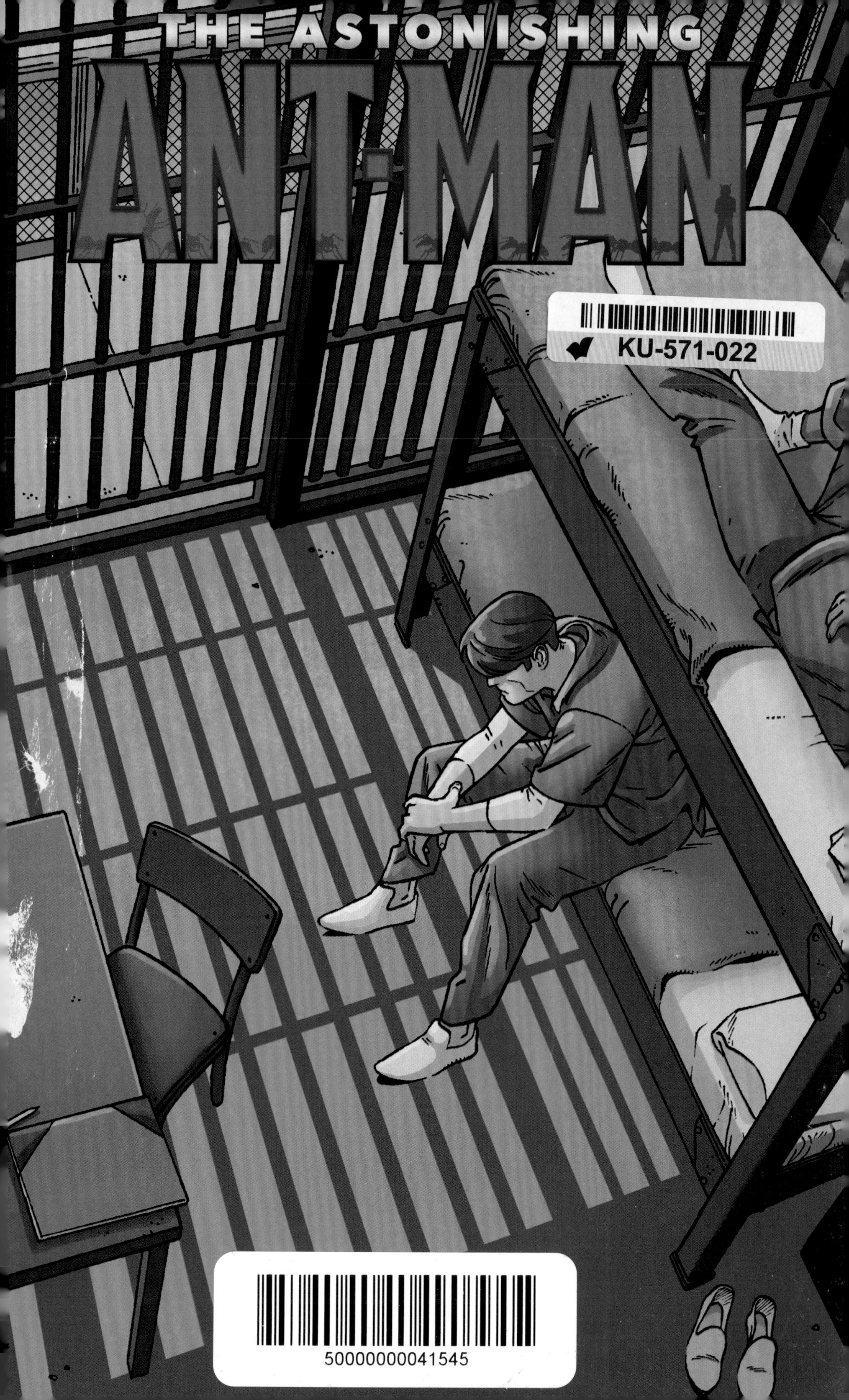
THE ASTONISHING
ANT-MAN

THE ASTONISHING ANT-MAN VOL. 3: THE TRIAL OF ANT-MAN. Contains material originally published in magazine form as THE ASTONISHING ANT-MAN #10-13 and GUARDIANS TEAM-UP #7. First printing 2⬛
ISBN# 978-0-7851-9952-6. Published by MARVEL WORLDWIDE, INC., a subsidiary of MARVEL ENTERTAINMENT, LLC. OFFICE OF PUBLICATION: 135 West 50th Street, New York, NY 10020. Copyright © 2017 MARVEL
similarity between any of the names, characters, persons, and/or institutions in this magazine with those of any living or dead person or institution is intended, and any such similarity which may exist is purely coincide
Printed in Canada. ALAN FINE, President, Marvel Entertainment; DAN BUCKLEY, President, TV, Publishing & Brand Management; JOE QUESADA, Chief Creative Officer; TOM BREVOORT, SVP of Publishing; DAVID BOG.
SVP of Business Affairs & Operations, Publishing & Partnership; C.B. CEBULSKI, VP of Brand Management & Development, Asia; DAVID GABRIEL, SVP of Sales & Marketing, Publishing; JEFF YOUNGQUIST, VP of Producti⬛
Special Projects; DAN CARR, Executive Director of Publishing Technology; ALEX MORALES, Director of Publishing Operations; SUSAN CRESPI, Production Manager; STAN LEE, Chairman Emeritus. For information regar⬛
advertising in Marvel Comics or on Marvel.com, please contact Vit DeBellis, Integrated Sales Manager, at vdebellis@marvel.com. For Marvel subscription inquiries, please call 888-511-5480. **Manufactured betw**⬛
2/3/2017 and **3/7/2017 by SOLISCO PRINTERS, SCOTT, QC, CANADA.**

10 9 8 7 6 5 4 3 2 1

THE ASTONISHING ANT-MAN

THE TRIAL OF ANT-MAN

WRITER: NICK SPENCER

ARTISTS: RAMON ROSANAS (#10-13)

& BRENT SCHOONOVER (#12-13)

COLOR ARTISTS: JORDAN BOYD WITH WIL QUINTANA (#13)

LETTERER: VC'S TRAVIS LANHAM

COVER ART: JULIAN TOTINO TEDESCO

ASSISTANT EDITOR: CHARLES BEACHAM

EDITOR: WIL MOSS

PREVIOUSLY

Scott Lang: business owner, divorced dad, ex-con...oh, and he's
Ant-Man — a super hero with the ability to shrink and talk to ants!

Needless to say, Scott leads a pretty weird life. And things have only gotten weirder
for him since he started investigating the creators of Hench and Lackey, two rival apps
that place freelance super villains at the fingertips of anyone with a smartphone.

How weird? Well, Scott's daughter Cassie (a former super hero herself) used the app
and is now mixed up with some pretty shady characters. The resulting kerfuffle has
landed Scott back in prison. But we're not quite there yet...

ANT-MAN CREATED BY **STAN LEE**, **LARRY LIEBER** & **JACK KIRBY**

COLLECTION EDITOR
JENNIFER GRÜNWALD

ASSISTANT EDITOR
CAITLIN O'CONNELL

ASSOCIATE MANAGING EDITOR
KATERI WOODY

EDITOR, SPECIAL PROJECTS
MARK D. BEAZLEY

VP PRODUCTION & SPECIAL PROJECTS
JEFF YOUNGQUIST

SVP PRINT, SALES & MARKETING
DAVID GABRIEL

EDITOR IN CHIEF
AXEL ALONSO

CHIEF CREATIVE OFFICER
JOE QUESADA

PUBLISHER
DAN BUCKLEYZ

EXECUTIVE PRODUCER
ALAN FINE

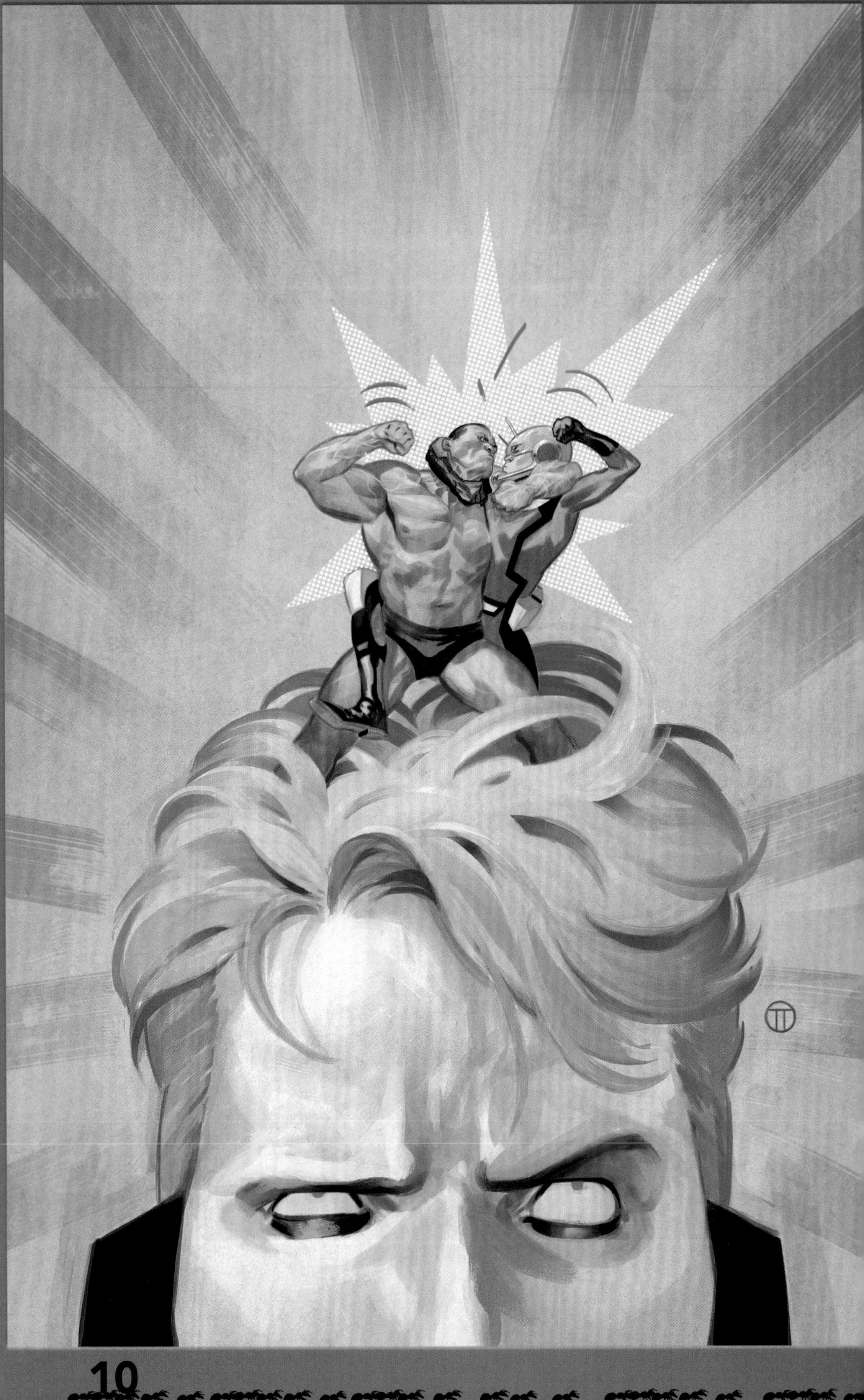

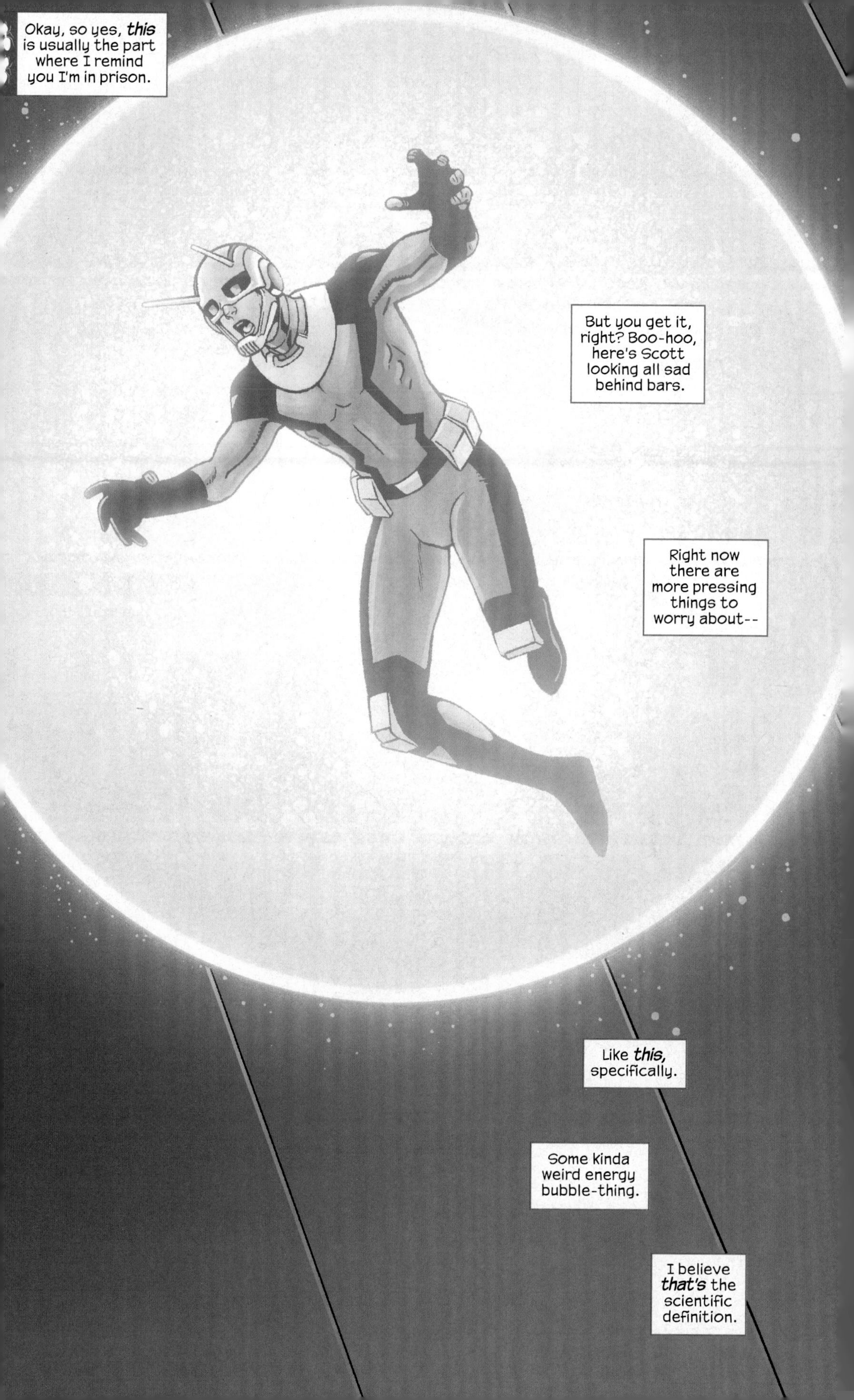
Okay, so yes, *this* is usually the part where I remind you I'm in prison.
But you get it, right? Boo-hoo, here's Scott looking all sad behind bars.
Right now there are more pressing things to worry about--
Like *this,* specifically.
Some kinda weird energy bubble-thing.
I believe *that's* the scientific definition.

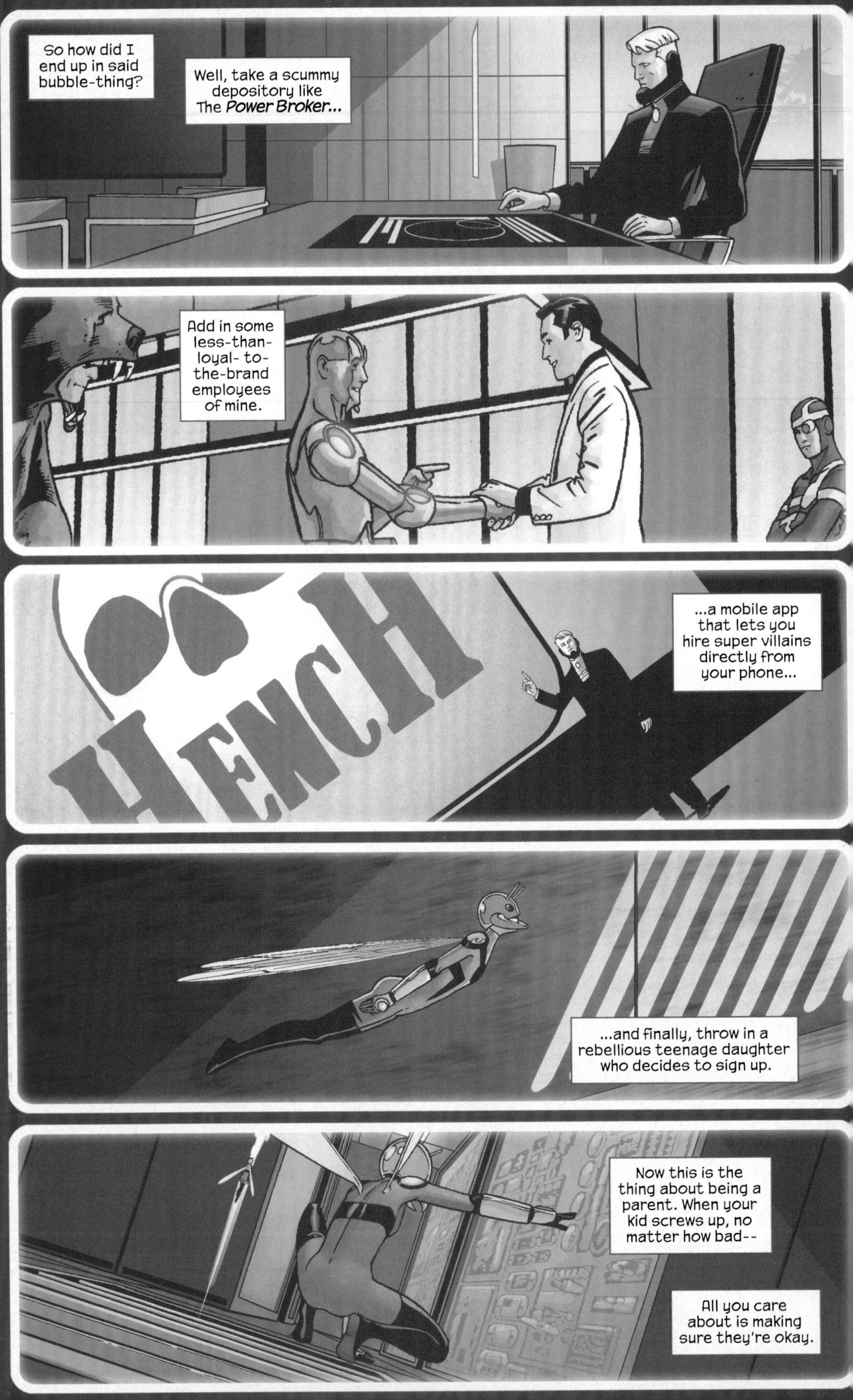

So how did I end up in said bubble-thing?
Well, take a scummy depository like The *Power Broker...*
Add in some less-than-loyal- to-the-brand employees of mine.
HENCH
...a mobile app that lets you hire super villains directly from your phone...
...and finally, throw in a rebellious teenage daughter who decides to sign up.
Now this is the thing about being a parent. When your kid screws up, no matter how bad--
All you care about is making sure they're okay.

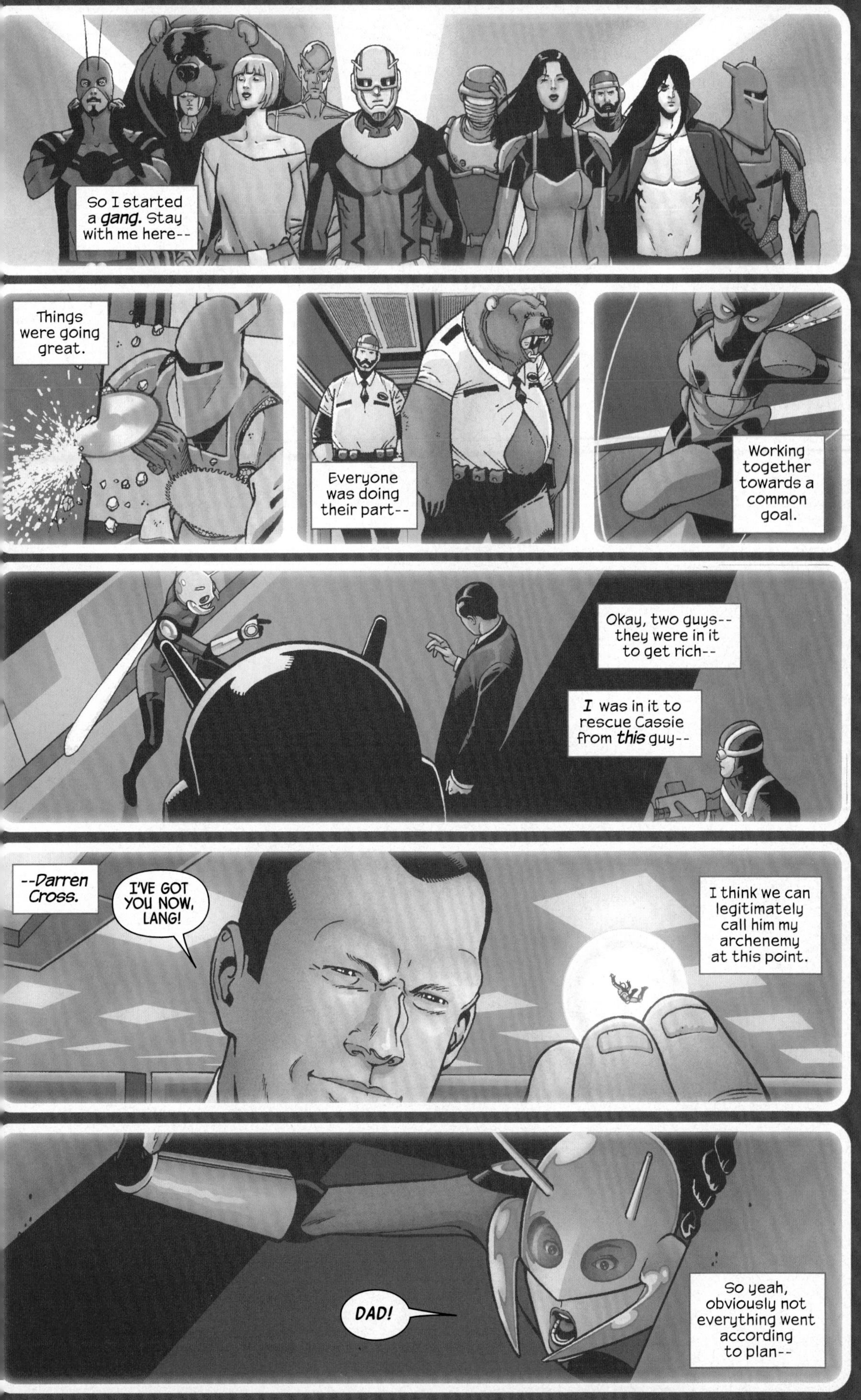
So I started a *gang.* Stay with me here--
Things were going great.
Everyone was doing their part--
Working together towards a common goal.
Okay, two guys-- they were in it to get rich--
I was in it to rescue Cassie from *this* guy--
--*Darren Cross.*
I'VE GOT YOU NOW, LANG!
I think we can legitimately call him my archenemy at this point.
DAD!
So yeah, obviously not everything went according to plan--

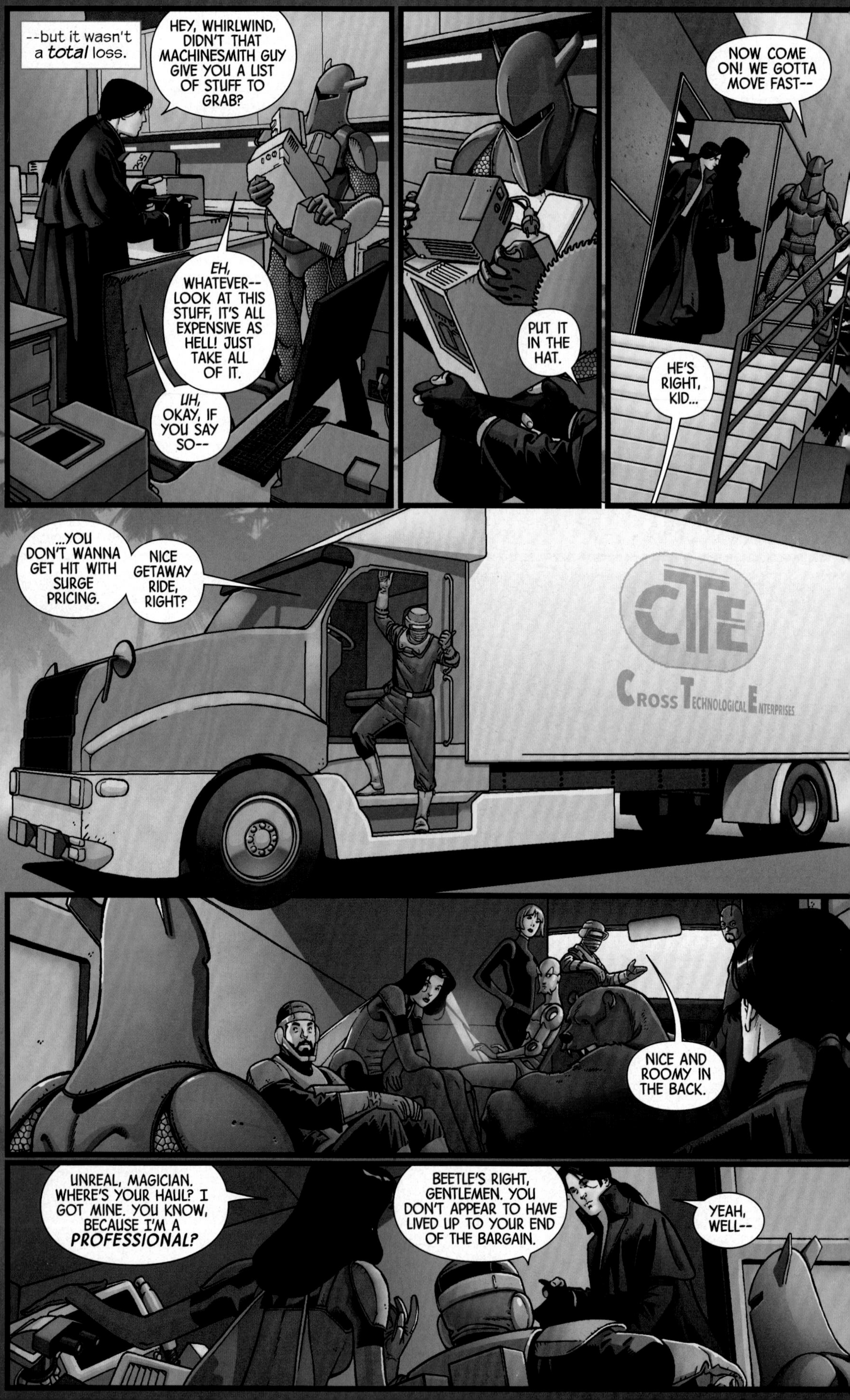
--but it wasn't a *total* loss.
HEY, WHIRLWIND, DIDN'T THAT MACHINESMITH GUY GIVE YOU A LIST OF STUFF TO GRAB?
EH, WHATEVER-- LOOK AT THIS STUFF, IT'S ALL EXPENSIVE AS HELL! JUST TAKE ALL OF IT.
UH, OKAY, IF YOU SAY SO--
PUT IT IN THE HAT.
NOW COME ON! WE GOTTA MOVE FAST--
HE'S RIGHT, KID...
...YOU DON'T WANNA GET HIT WITH SURGE PRICING.
NICE GETAWAY RIDE, RIGHT?
CTE
CROSS TECHNOLOGICAL ENTERPRISES
NICE AND ROOMY IN THE BACK.
UNREAL, MAGICIAN. WHERE'S YOUR HAUL? I GOT MINE. YOU KNOW, BECAUSE I'M A *PROFESSIONAL?*
BEETLE'S RIGHT, GENTLEMEN. YOU DON'T APPEAR TO HAVE LIVED UP TO YOUR END OF THE BARGAIN.
YEAH, WELL--

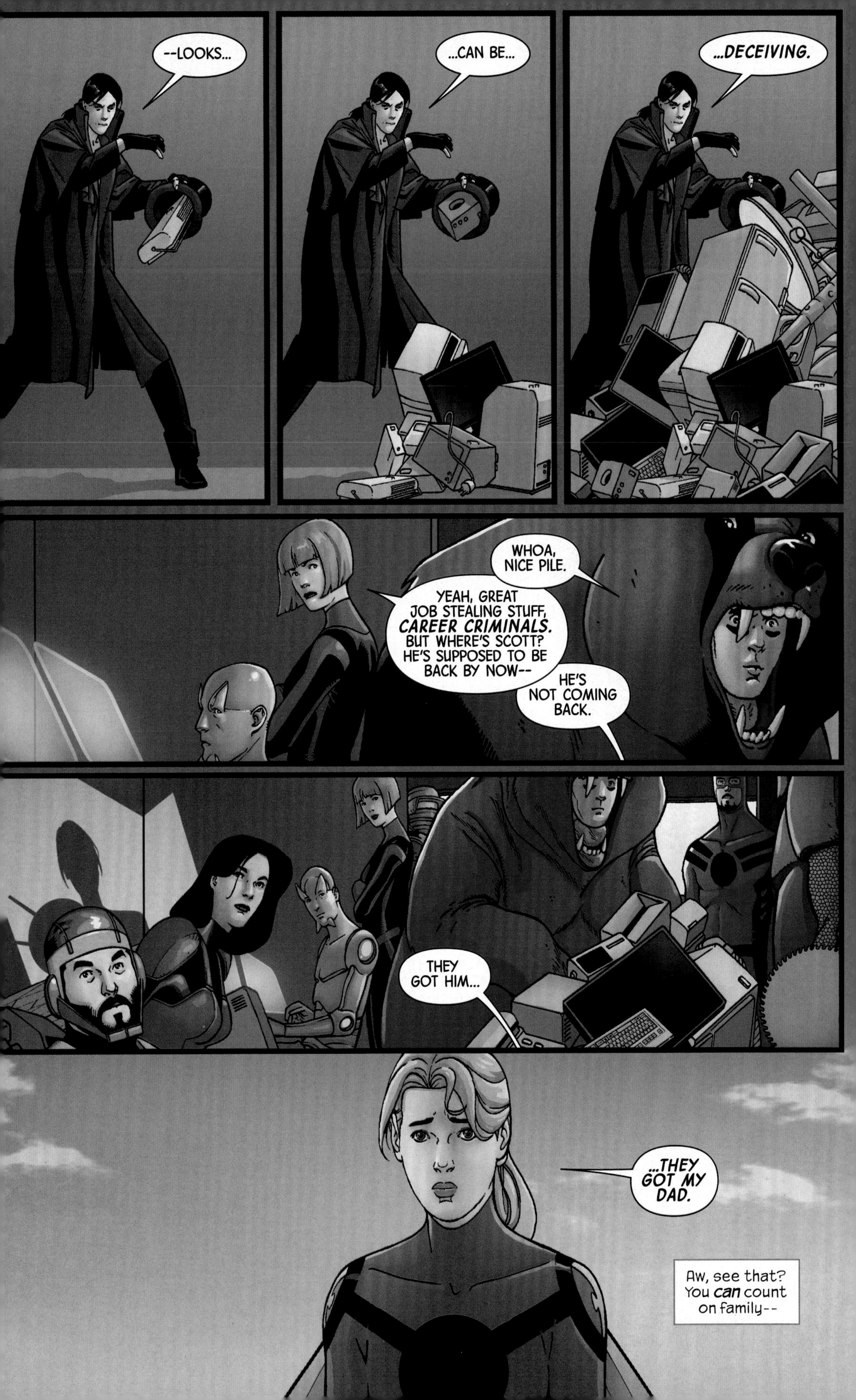
--LOOKS...
...CAN BE...
...DECEIVING.
WHOA, NICE PILE.
YEAH, GREAT JOB STEALING STUFF, CAREER CRIMINALS. BUT WHERE'S SCOTT? HE'S SUPPOSED TO BE BACK BY NOW--
HE'S NOT COMING BACK.
THEY GOT HIM...
...THEY GOT MY DAD.
Aw, see that? You can count on family--

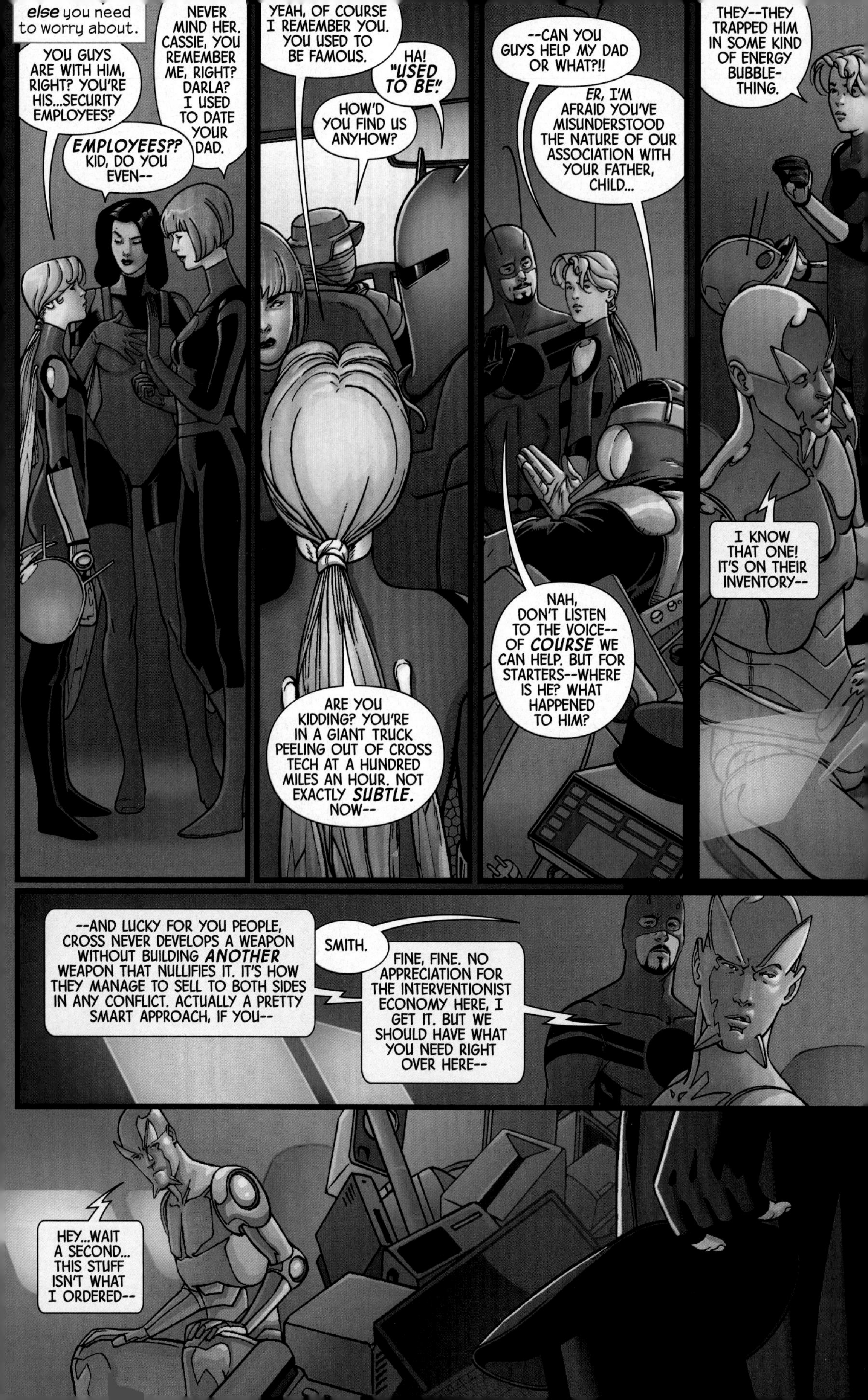

else you need to worry about.
YOU GUYS ARE WITH HIM, RIGHT? YOU'RE HIS...SECURITY EMPLOYEES?
NEVER MIND HER. CASSIE, YOU REMEMBER ME, RIGHT? DARLA? I USED TO DATE YOUR DAD.
EMPLOYEES?? KID, DO YOU EVEN--
YEAH, OF COURSE I REMEMBER YOU. YOU USED TO BE FAMOUS.
HA! *"USED TO BE!"*
HOW'D YOU FIND US ANYHOW?
ARE YOU KIDDING? YOU'RE IN A GIANT TRUCK PEELING OUT OF CROSS TECH AT A HUNDRED MILES AN HOUR. NOT EXACTLY *SUBTLE.* NOW--
--CAN YOU GUYS HELP MY DAD OR WHAT?!!
ER, I'M AFRAID YOU'VE MISUNDERSTOOD THE NATURE OF OUR ASSOCIATION WITH YOUR FATHER, CHILD...
NAH, DON'T LISTEN TO THE VOICE-- OF *COURSE* WE CAN HELP. BUT FOR STARTERS--WHERE IS HE? WHAT HAPPENED TO HIM?
THEY--THEY TRAPPED HIM IN SOME KIND OF ENERGY BUBBLE-THING.
I KNOW THAT ONE! IT'S ON THEIR INVENTORY--
--AND LUCKY FOR YOU PEOPLE, CROSS NEVER DEVELOPS A WEAPON WITHOUT BUILDING *ANOTHER* WEAPON THAT NULLIFIES IT. IT'S HOW THEY MANAGE TO SELL TO BOTH SIDES IN ANY CONFLICT. ACTUALLY A PRETTY SMART APPROACH, IF YOU--
SMITH.
FINE, FINE. NO APPRECIATION FOR THE INTERVENTIONIST ECONOMY HERE, I GET IT. BUT WE SHOULD HAVE WHAT YOU NEED RIGHT OVER HERE--
HEY...WAIT A SECOND... THIS STUFF ISN'T WHAT I ORDERED--

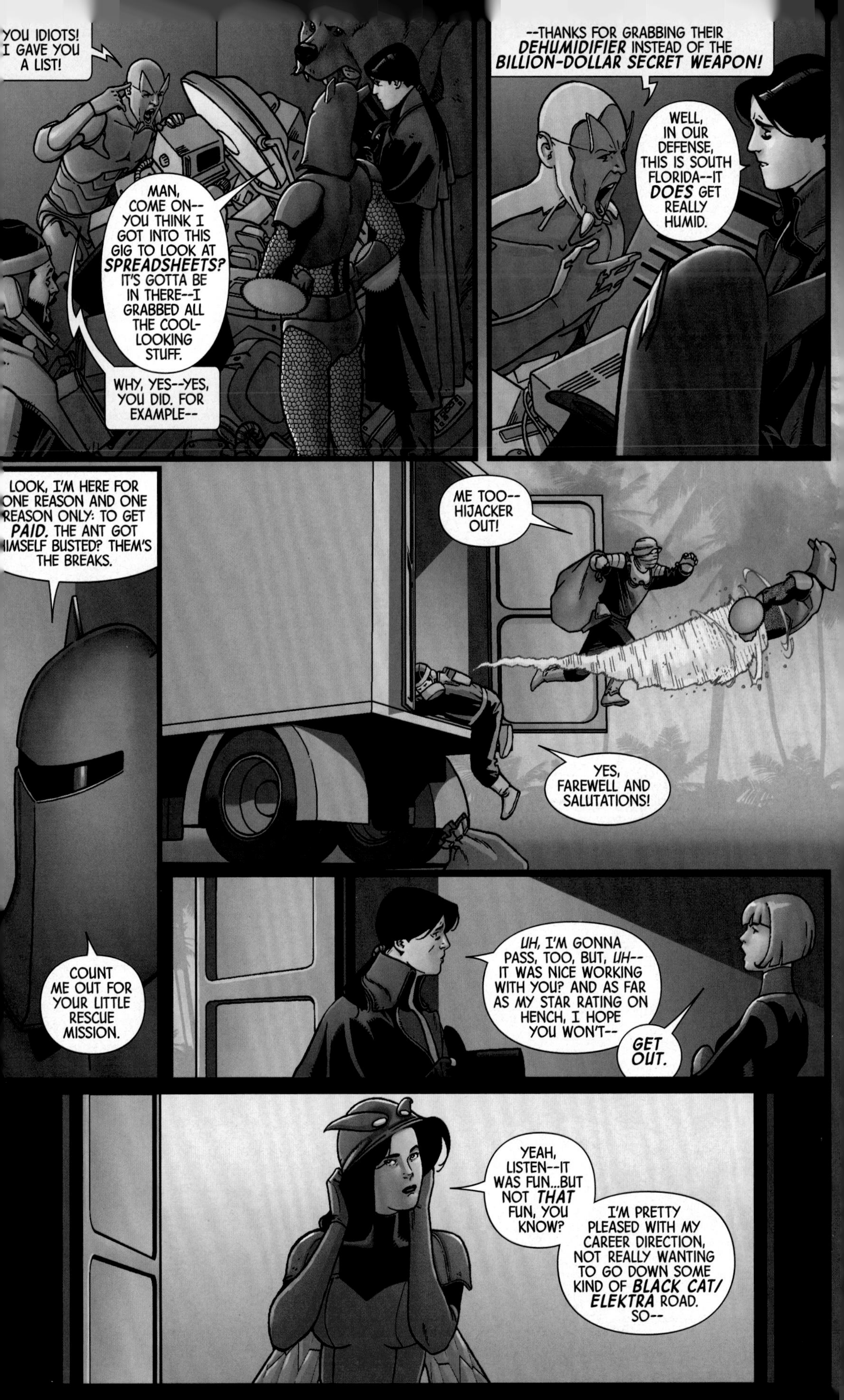
YOU IDIOTS! I GAVE YOU A LIST!
MAN, COME ON--YOU THINK I GOT INTO THIS GIG TO LOOK AT SPREADSHEETS? IT'S GOTTA BE IN THERE--I GRABBED ALL THE COOL-LOOKING STUFF.
WHY, YES--YES, YOU DID. FOR EXAMPLE--
--THANKS FOR GRABBING THEIR DEHUMIDIFIER INSTEAD OF THE BILLION-DOLLAR SECRET WEAPON!
WELL, IN OUR DEFENSE, THIS IS SOUTH FLORIDA--IT DOES GET REALLY HUMID.
LOOK, I'M HERE FOR ONE REASON AND ONE REASON ONLY: TO GET PAID. THE ANT GOT IMSELF BUSTED? THEM'S THE BREAKS.
ME TOO--HIJACKER OUT!
YES, FAREWELL AND SALUTATIONS!
COUNT ME OUT FOR YOUR LITTLE RESCUE MISSION.
UH, I'M GONNA PASS, TOO, BUT, UH--IT WAS NICE WORKING WITH YOU? AND AS FAR AS MY STAR RATING ON HENCH, I HOPE YOU WON'T--
GET OUT.
YEAH, LISTEN--IT WAS FUN...BUT NOT THAT FUN, YOU KNOW?
I'M PRETTY PLEASED WITH MY CAREER DIRECTION, NOT REALLY WANTING TO GO DOWN SOME KIND OF BLACK CAT/ELEKTRA ROAD. SO--

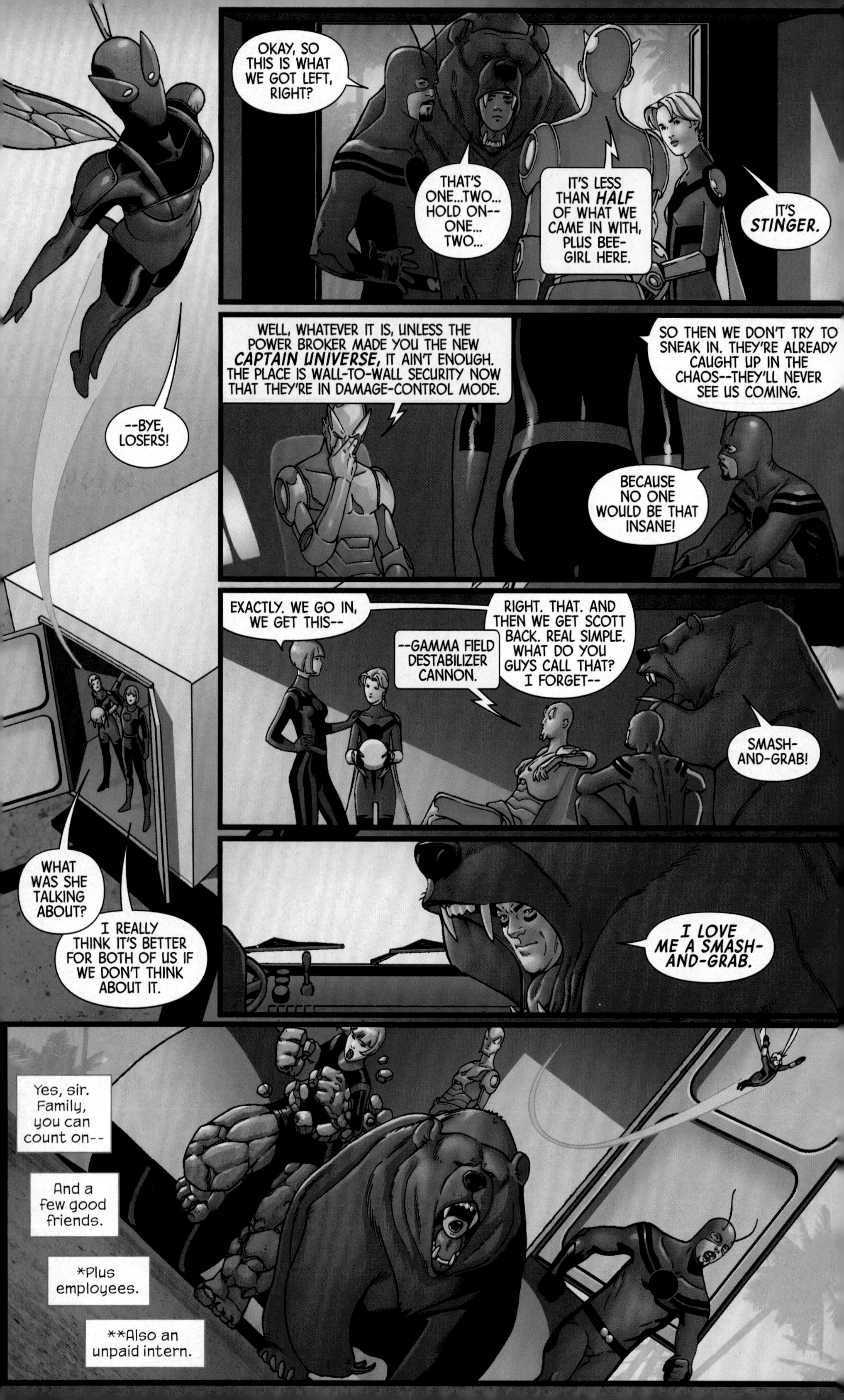
OKAY, SO THIS IS WHAT WE GOT LEFT, RIGHT?
THAT'S ONE...TWO... HOLD ON-- ONE... TWO...
IT'S LESS THAN HALF OF WHAT WE CAME IN WITH, PLUS BEE-GIRL HERE.
IT'S STINGER.
WELL, WHATEVER IT IS, UNLESS THE POWER BROKER MADE YOU THE NEW CAPTAIN UNIVERSE, IT AIN'T ENOUGH. THE PLACE IS WALL-TO-WALL SECURITY NOW THAT THEY'RE IN DAMAGE-CONTROL MODE.
SO THEN WE DON'T TRY TO SNEAK IN. THEY'RE ALREADY CAUGHT UP IN THE CHAOS--THEY'LL NEVER SEE US COMING.
BECAUSE NO ONE WOULD BE THAT INSANE!
EXACTLY. WE GO IN, WE GET THIS--
--GAMMA FIELD DESTABILIZER CANNON.
RIGHT. THAT. AND THEN WE GET SCOTT BACK. REAL SIMPLE. WHAT DO YOU GUYS CALL THAT? I FORGET--
SMASH-AND-GRAB!
I LOVE ME A SMASH-AND-GRAB.
--BYE, LOSERS!
WHAT WAS SHE TALKING ABOUT?
I REALLY THINK IT'S BETTER FOR BOTH OF US IF WE DON'T THINK ABOUT IT.
Yes, sir. Family, you can count on--
And a few good friends.
*Plus employees.
**Also an unpaid intern.

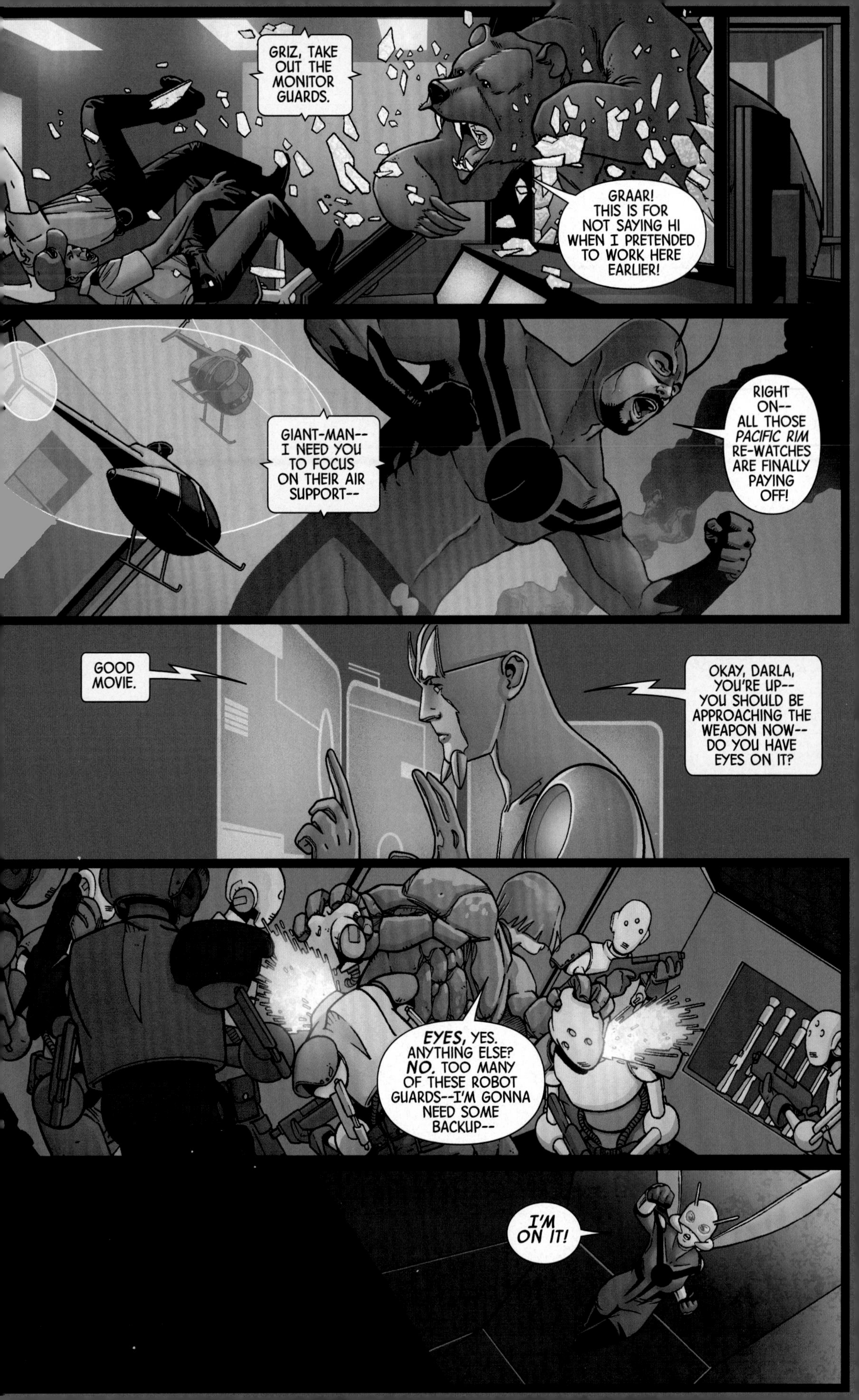
GRIZ, TAKE OUT THE MONITOR GUARDS.
GRAAR! THIS IS FOR NOT SAYING HI WHEN I PRETENDED TO WORK HERE EARLIER!
GIANT-MAN-- I NEED YOU TO FOCUS ON THEIR AIR SUPPORT--
RIGHT ON-- ALL THOSE *PACIFIC RIM* RE-WATCHES ARE FINALLY PAYING OFF!
GOOD MOVIE.
OKAY, DARLA, YOU'RE UP-- YOU SHOULD BE APPROACHING THE WEAPON NOW-- DO YOU HAVE EYES ON IT?
EYES, YES. ANYTHING ELSE? ***NO.*** TOO MANY OF THESE ROBOT GUARDS--I'M GONNA NEED SOME BACKUP--
I'M ON IT!

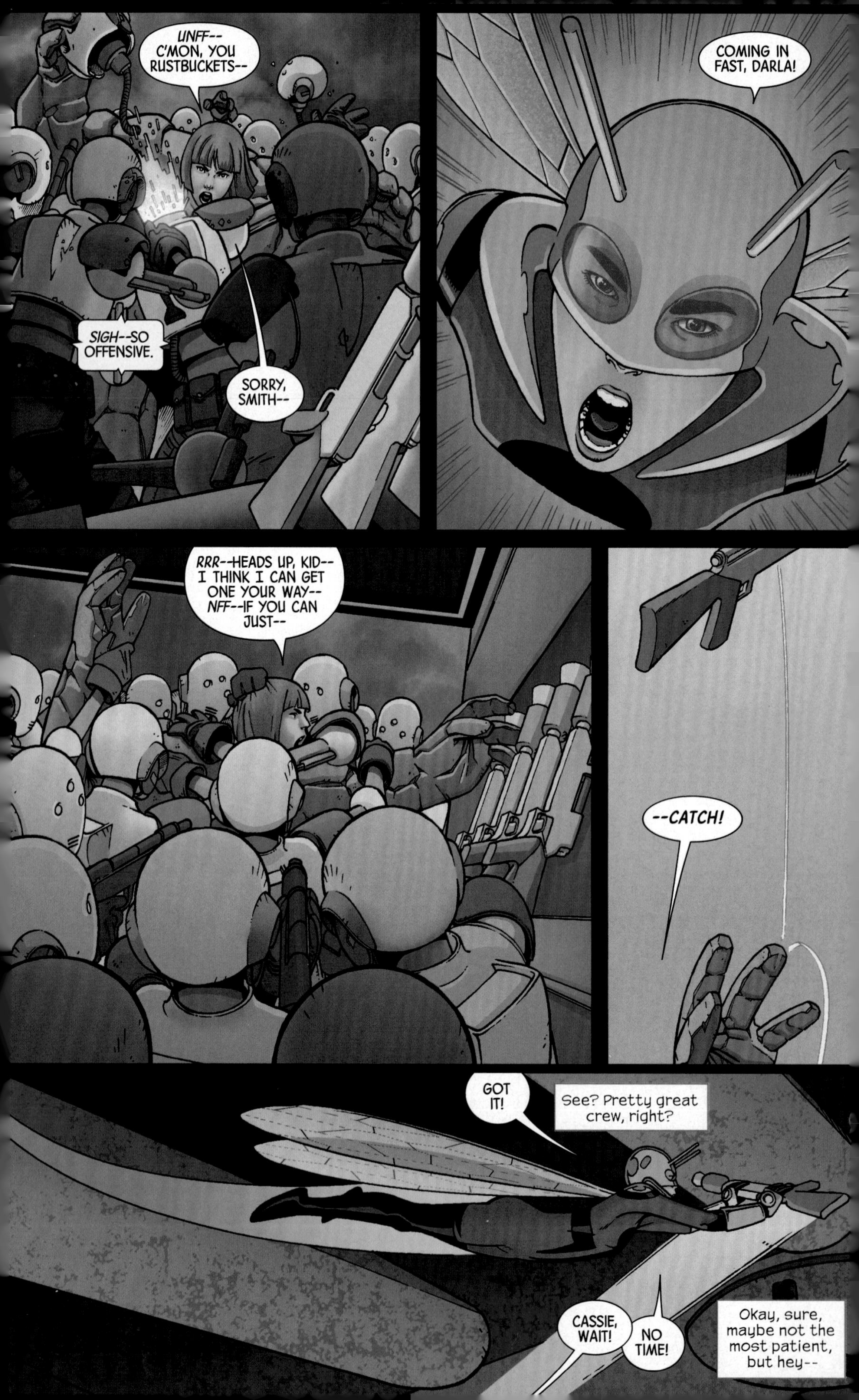
UNFF-- C'MON, YOU RUSTBUCKETS--
SIGH--SO OFFENSIVE.
SORRY, SMITH--
COMING IN FAST, DARLA!
RRR--HEADS UP, KID-- I THINK I CAN GET ONE YOUR WAY-- NFF--IF YOU CAN JUST--
--CATCH!
GOT IT!
See? Pretty great crew, right?
CASSIE, WAIT!
NO TIME!
Okay, sure, maybe not the most patient, but hey--

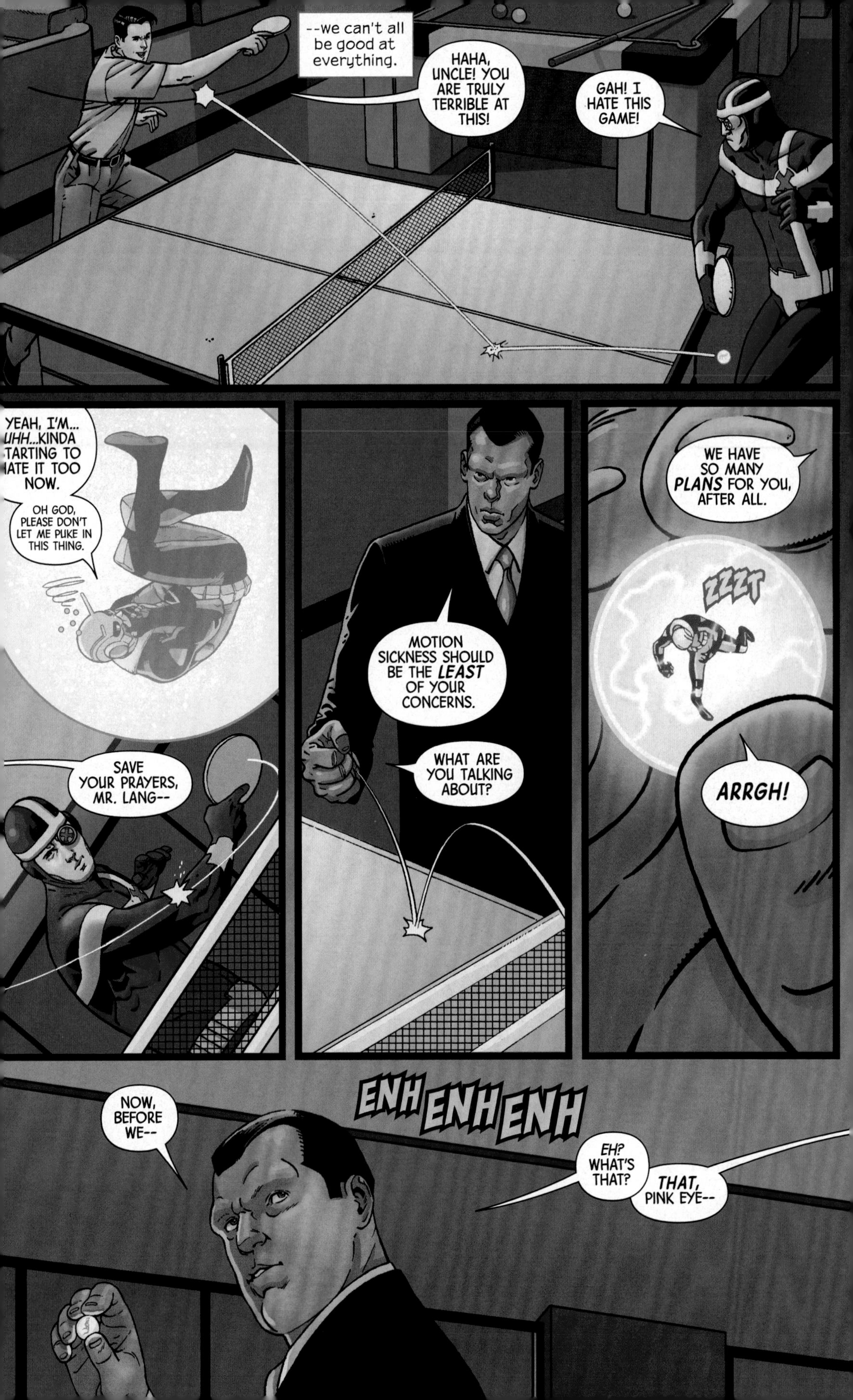
--we can't all be good at everything.
HAHA, UNCLE! YOU ARE TRULY TERRIBLE AT THIS!
GAH! I HATE THIS GAME!
YEAH, I'M... UHH...KINDA TARTING TO ATE IT TOO NOW.
OH GOD, PLEASE DON'T LET ME PUKE IN THIS THING.
SAVE YOUR PRAYERS, MR. LANG--
MOTION SICKNESS SHOULD BE THE LEAST OF YOUR CONCERNS.
WHAT ARE YOU TALKING ABOUT?
WE HAVE SO MANY PLANS FOR YOU, AFTER ALL.
ZZZT
ARRGH!
NOW, BEFORE WE--
ENH ENH ENH
EH? WHAT'S THAT?
THAT, PINK EYE--

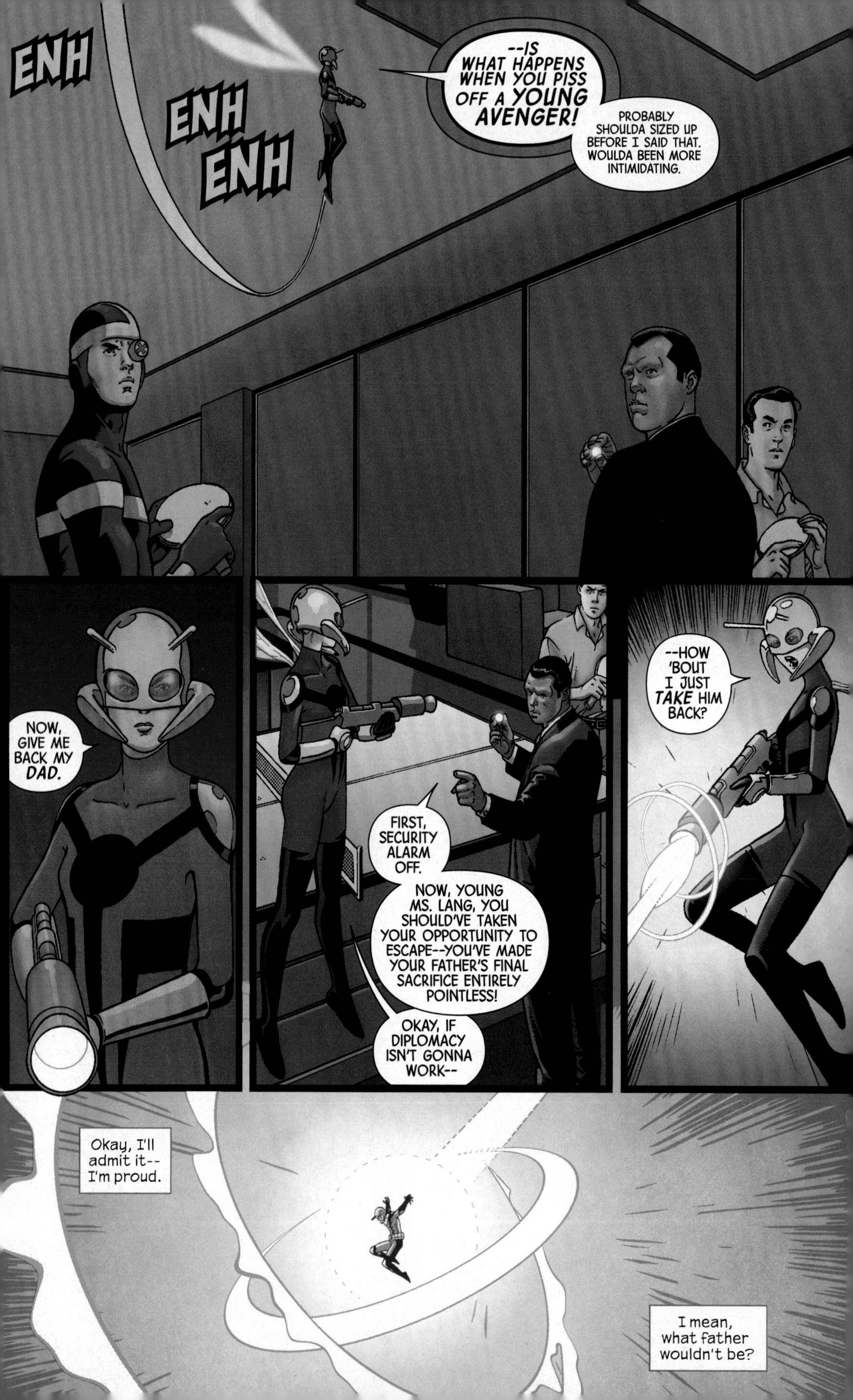
ENH
ENH
ENH
--IS WHAT HAPPENS WHEN YOU PISS OFF A YOUNG AVENGER!
PROBABLY SHOULDA SIZED UP BEFORE I SAID THAT. WOULDA BEEN MORE INTIMIDATING.
NOW, GIVE ME BACK MY DAD.
FIRST, SECURITY ALARM OFF.
NOW, YOUNG MS. LANG, YOU SHOULD'VE TAKEN YOUR OPPORTUNITY TO ESCAPE--YOU'VE MADE YOUR FATHER'S FINAL SACRIFICE ENTIRELY POINTLESS!
OKAY, IF DIPLOMACY ISN'T GONNA WORK--
--HOW 'BOUT I JUST TAKE HIM BACK?
Okay, I'll admit it-- I'm proud.
I mean, what father wouldn't be?

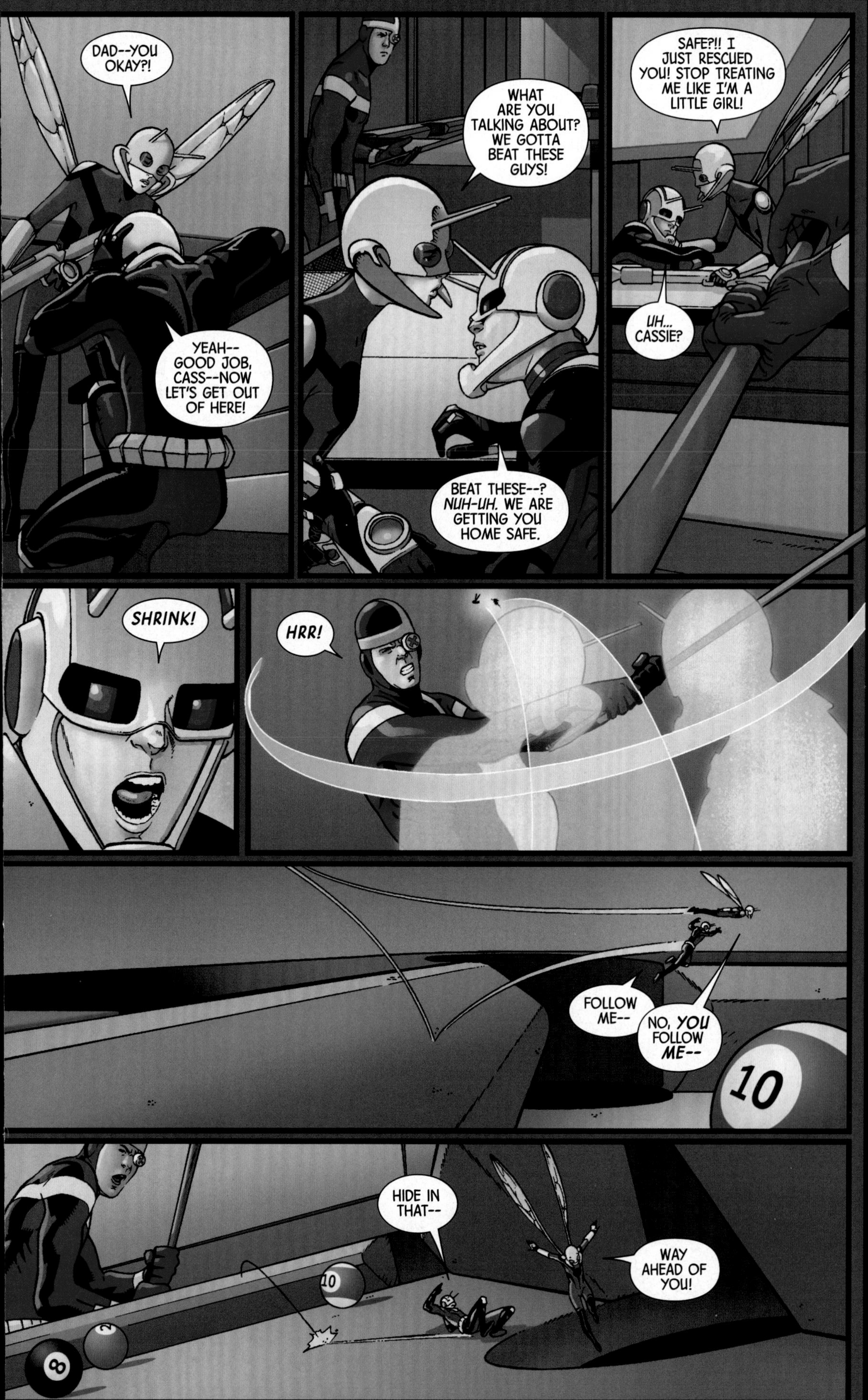
DAD--YOU OKAY?!
YEAH-- GOOD JOB, CASS--NOW LET'S GET OUT OF HERE!
WHAT ARE YOU TALKING ABOUT? WE GOTTA BEAT THESE GUYS!
BEAT THESE--? *NUH-UH.* WE ARE GETTING YOU HOME SAFE.
SAFE?!! I JUST RESCUED YOU! STOP TREATING ME LIKE I'M A LITTLE GIRL!
UH... CASSIE?
SHRINK!
HRR!
FOLLOW ME--
NO, *YOU* FOLLOW *ME--*
10
HIDE IN THAT--
WAY AHEAD OF YOU!
10
2
8

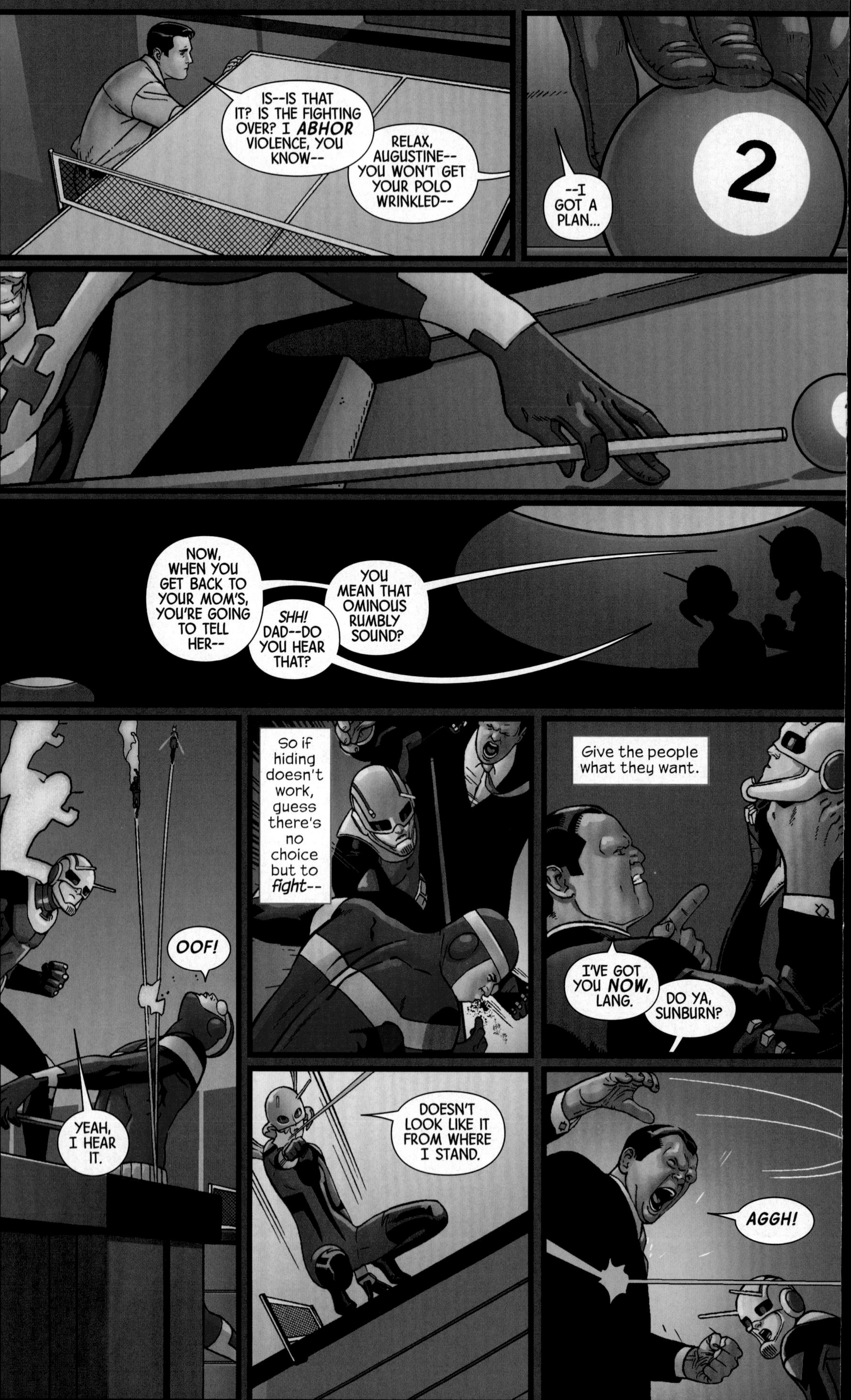
IS--IS THAT IT? IS THE FIGHTING OVER? I ABHOR VIOLENCE, YOU KNOW--
RELAX, AUGUSTINE--YOU WON'T GET YOUR POLO WRINKLED--
--I GOT A PLAN...
2
NOW, WHEN YOU GET BACK TO YOUR MOM'S, YOU'RE GOING TO TELL HER--
SHH! DAD--DO YOU HEAR THAT?
YOU MEAN THAT OMINOUS RUMBLY SOUND?
OOF!
YEAH, I HEAR IT.
So if hiding doesn't work, guess there's no choice but to fight--
Give the people what they want.
I'VE GOT YOU NOW, LANG.
DO YA, SUNBURN?
DOESN'T LOOK LIKE IT FROM WHERE I STAND.
AGGH!

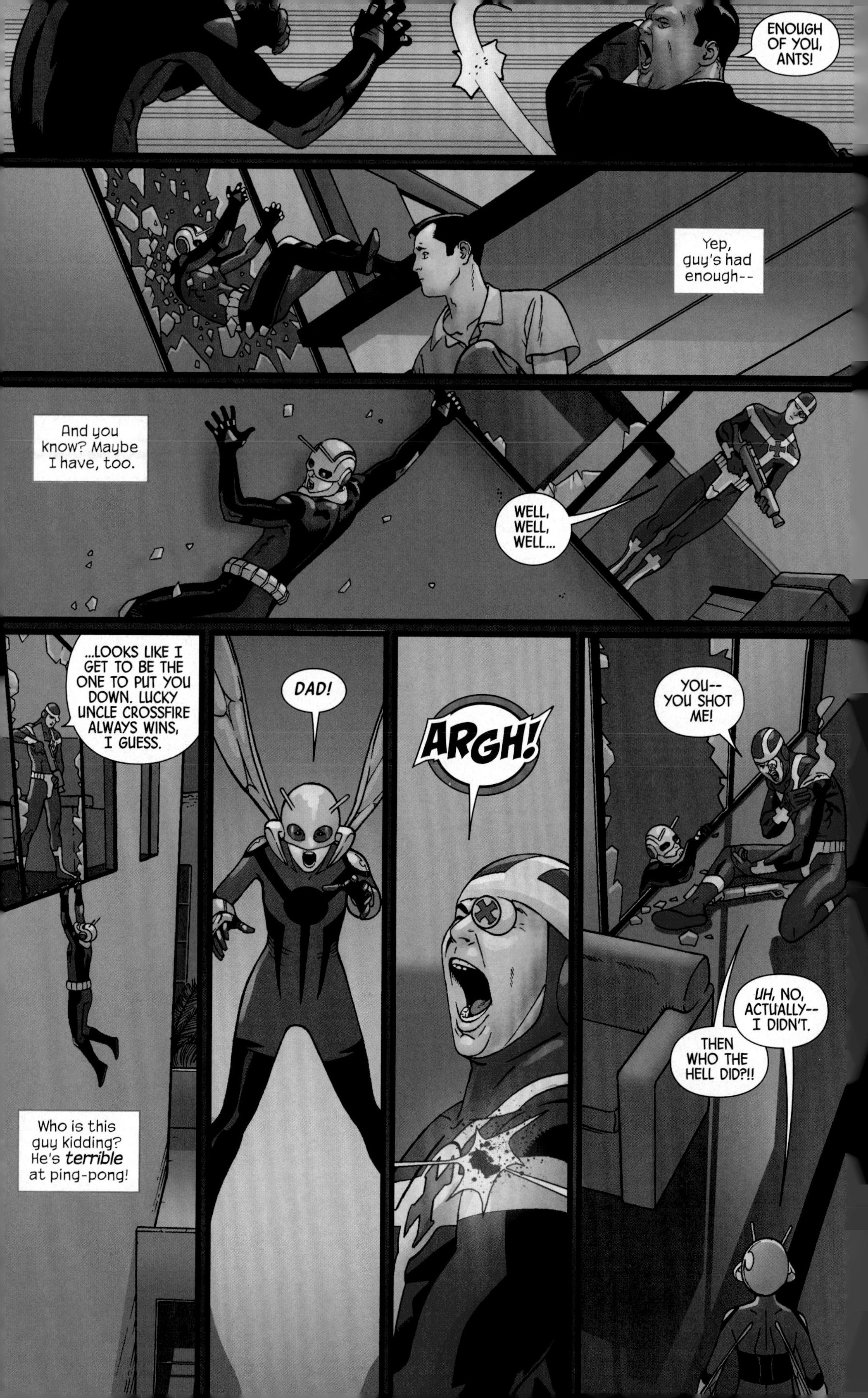
ENOUGH OF YOU, ANTS!
Yep, guy's had enough--
And you know? Maybe I have, too.
WELL, WELL, WELL...
...LOOKS LIKE I GET TO BE THE ONE TO PUT YOU DOWN. LUCKY UNCLE CROSSFIRE ALWAYS WINS, I GUESS.
Who is this guy kidding? He's *terrible* at ping-pong!
DAD!
ARGH!
YOU-- YOU SHOT ME!
UH, NO, ACTUALLY-- I DIDN'T.
THEN WHO THE HELL DID?!!

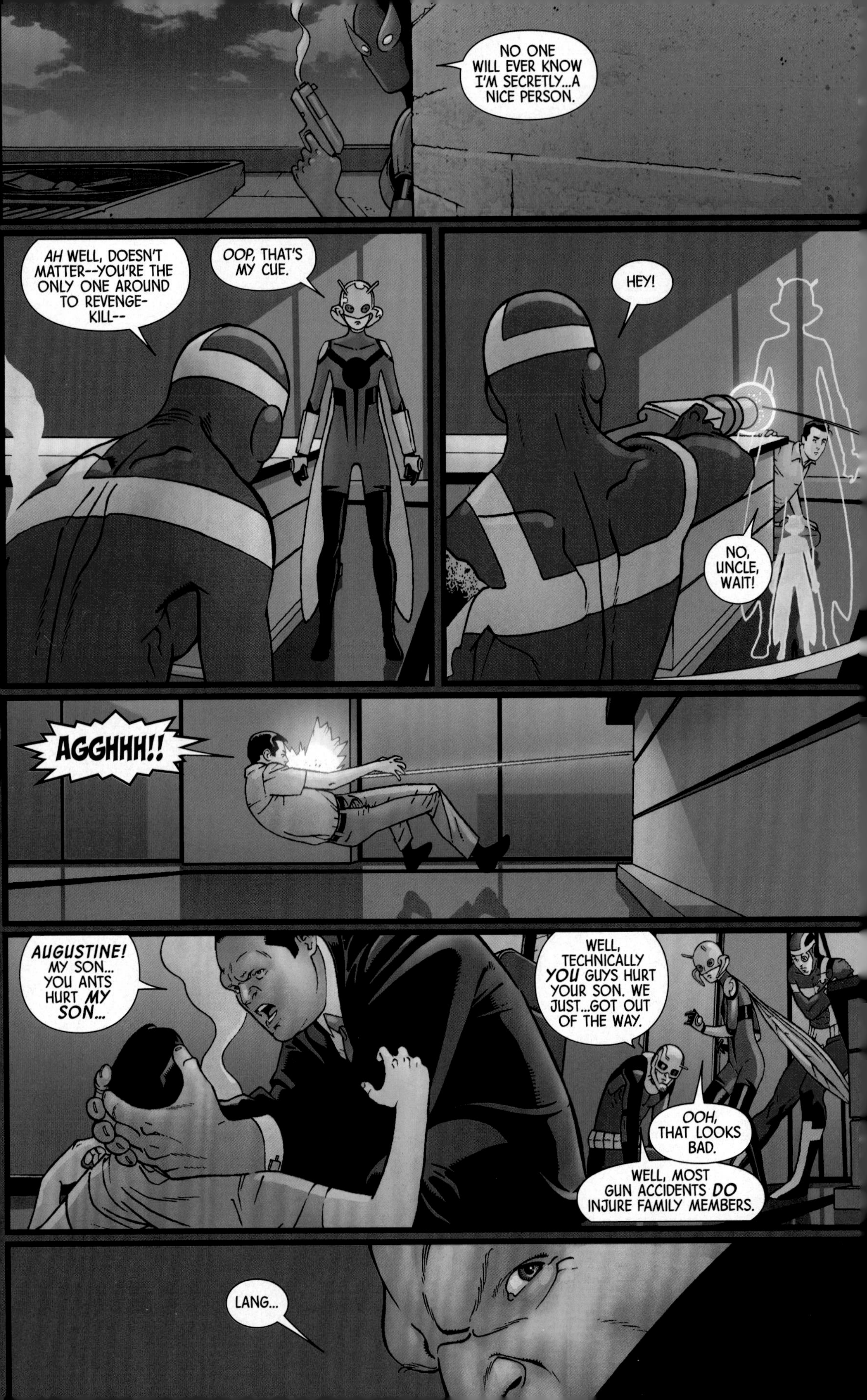
NO ONE WILL EVER KNOW I'M SECRETLY...A NICE PERSON.
AH WELL, DOESN'T MATTER--YOU'RE THE ONLY ONE AROUND TO REVENGE-KILL--
OOP, THAT'S MY CUE.
HEY!
NO, UNCLE, WAIT!
AGGHHH!!
AUGUSTINE! MY SON... YOU ANTS HURT MY SON...
WELL, TECHNICALLY YOU GUYS HURT YOUR SON. WE JUST...GOT OUT OF THE WAY.
OOH, THAT LOOKS BAD.
WELL, MOST GUN ACCIDENTS DO INJURE FAMILY MEMBERS.
LANG...

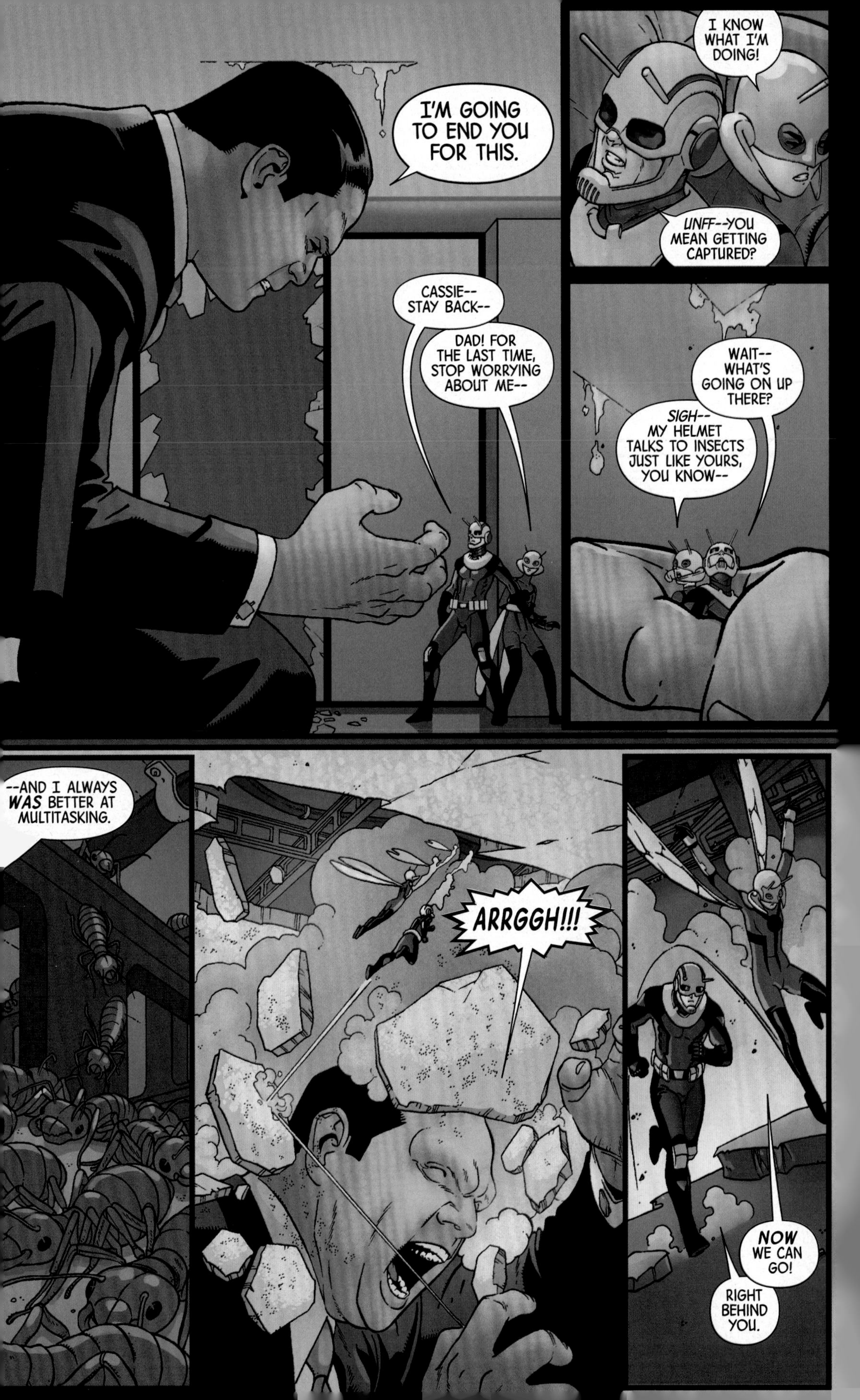
I'M GOING TO END YOU FOR THIS.
I KNOW WHAT I'M DOING!
UNFF--YOU MEAN GETTING CAPTURED?
CASSIE-- STAY BACK--
DAD! FOR THE LAST TIME, STOP WORRYING ABOUT ME--
WAIT-- WHAT'S GOING ON UP THERE?
SIGH-- MY HELMET TALKS TO INSECTS JUST LIKE YOURS, YOU KNOW--
--AND I ALWAYS WAS BETTER AT MULTITASKING.
ARRGGH!!!
NOW WE CAN GO!
RIGHT BEHIND YOU.

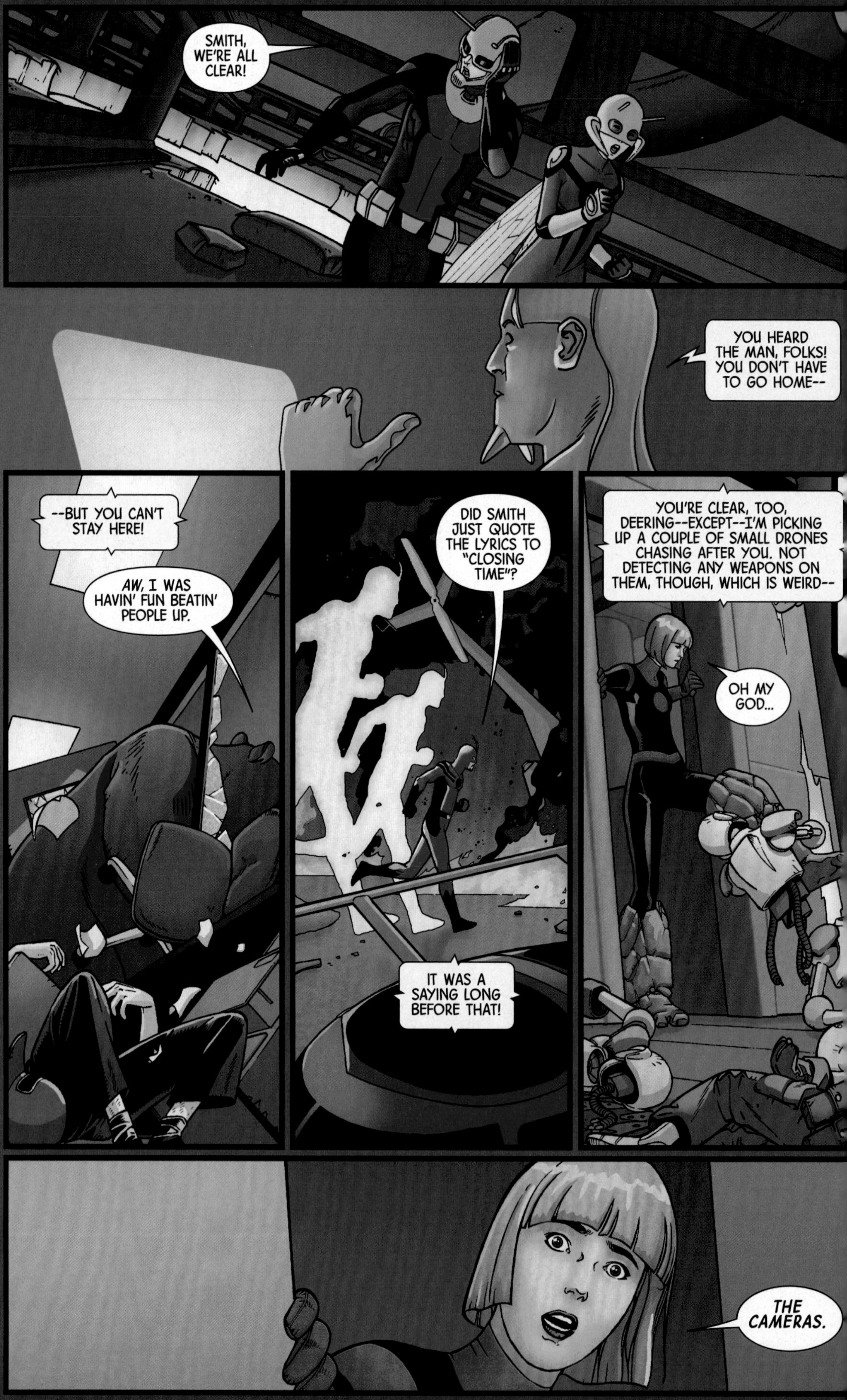
SMITH, WE'RE ALL CLEAR!
YOU HEARD THE MAN, FOLKS! YOU DON'T HAVE TO GO HOME--
--BUT YOU CAN'T STAY HERE!
AW, I WAS HAVIN' FUN BEATIN' PEOPLE UP.
DID SMITH JUST QUOTE THE LYRICS TO "CLOSING TIME"?
IT WAS A SAYING LONG BEFORE THAT!
YOU'RE CLEAR, TOO, DEERING--EXCEPT--I'M PICKING UP A COUPLE OF SMALL DRONES CHASING AFTER YOU. NOT DETECTING ANY WEAPONS ON THEM, THOUGH, WHICH IS WEIRD--
OH MY GOD...
THE CAMERAS.

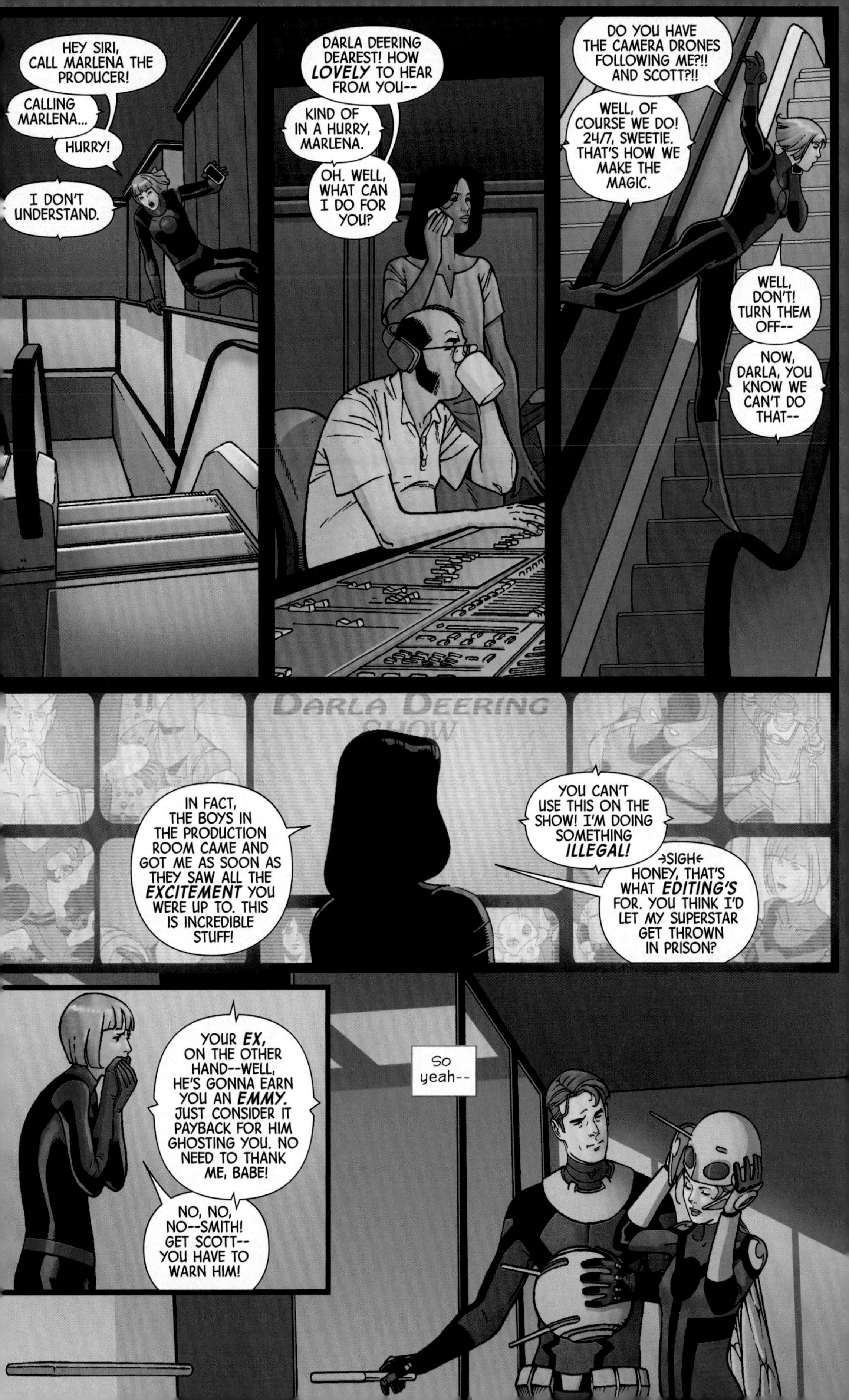
HEY SIRI, CALL MARLENA THE PRODUCER!
CALLING MARLENA...
HURRY!
I DON'T UNDERSTAND.
DARLA DEERING DEAREST! HOW LOVELY TO HEAR FROM YOU--
KIND OF IN A HURRY, MARLENA.
OH. WELL, WHAT CAN I DO FOR YOU?
DO YOU HAVE THE CAMERA DRONES FOLLOWING ME?!! AND SCOTT?!!
WELL, OF COURSE WE DO! 24/7, SWEETIE. THAT'S HOW WE MAKE THE MAGIC.
WELL, DON'T! TURN THEM OFF--
NOW, DARLA, YOU KNOW WE CAN'T DO THAT--
DARLA DEERING SHOW
IN FACT, THE BOYS IN THE PRODUCTION ROOM CAME AND GOT ME AS SOON AS THEY SAW ALL THE EXCITEMENT YOU WERE UP TO. THIS IS INCREDIBLE STUFF!
YOU CAN'T USE THIS ON THE SHOW! I'M DOING SOMETHING ILLEGAL!
→SIGH← HONEY, THAT'S WHAT EDITING'S FOR. YOU THINK I'D LET MY SUPERSTAR GET THROWN IN PRISON?
YOUR EX, ON THE OTHER HAND--WELL, HE'S GONNA EARN YOU AN EMMY. JUST CONSIDER IT PAYBACK FOR HIM GHOSTING YOU. NO NEED TO THANK ME, BABE!
NO, NO, NO--SMITH! GET SCOTT--YOU HAVE TO WARN HIM!
So yeah--

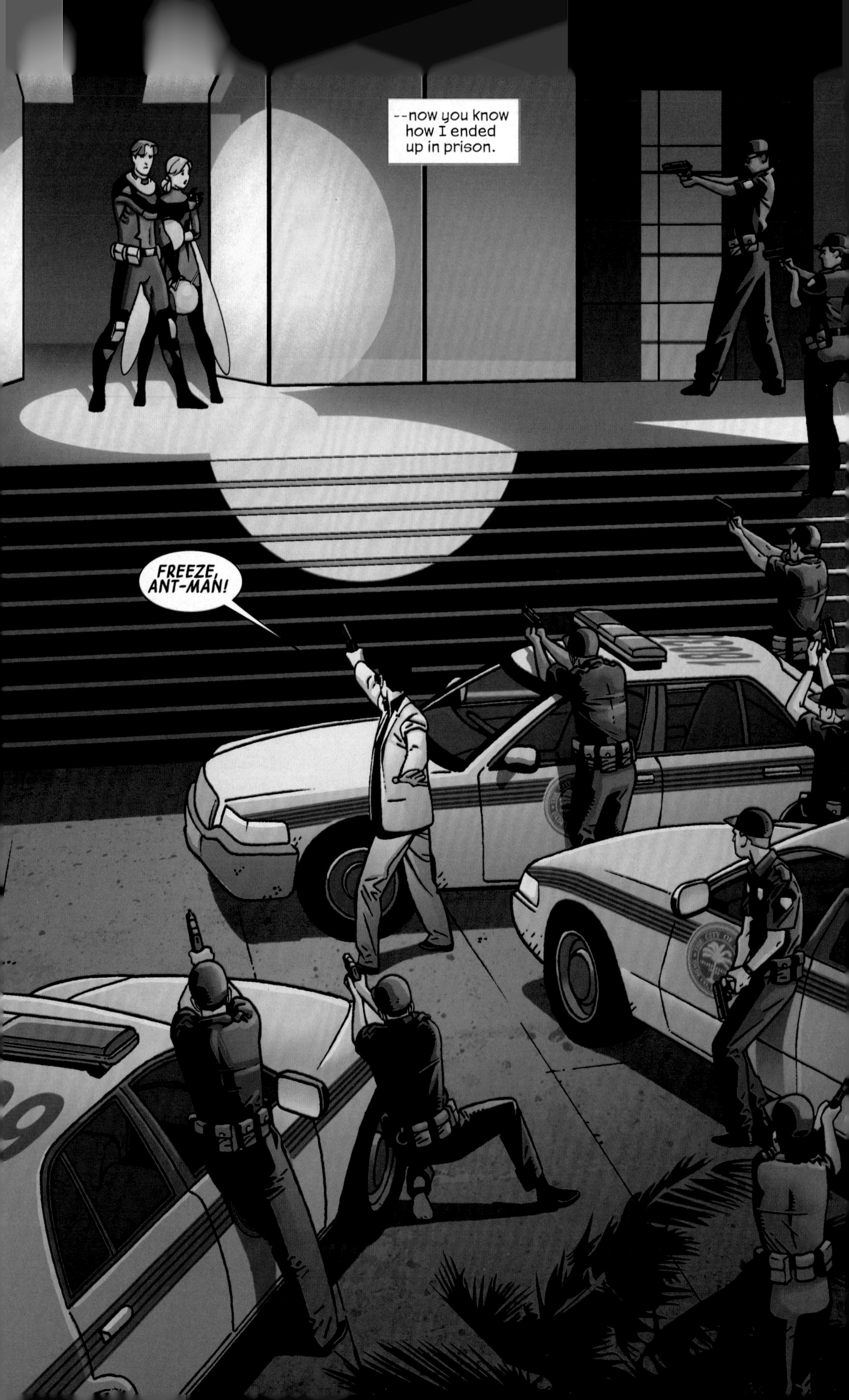
--now you know how I ended up in prison.
FREEZE, ANT-MAN!

There's this bad-guy tech developer--the *Power Broker*. He started up an app that allows you to hire super villains on demand.

Called it *Hench*.

So then the Cross family hired a couple of my employees to steal it from him...

That led Power Broker to double down and launch *Hench X*, which offers to turn anyone into a super villain.

Which, of course, my daughter Cassie couldn't wait to sign up for.

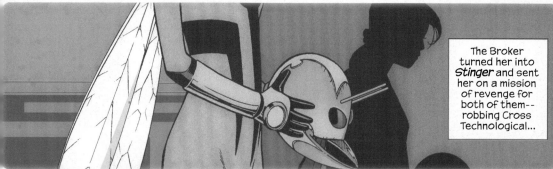

Personal Information:

First Name :
CASSIE

Last Name :
LANG

Phone:

Contact Information:

Email Address :

Retype E-mail :

Account Information:

Enter Username:

Withdraw Code:

Retype Code:

Define Password (Letters and Numbers):

Retype Password:

The Broker turned her into *Stinger* and sent her on a mission of revenge for both of them-- robbing Cross Technological...

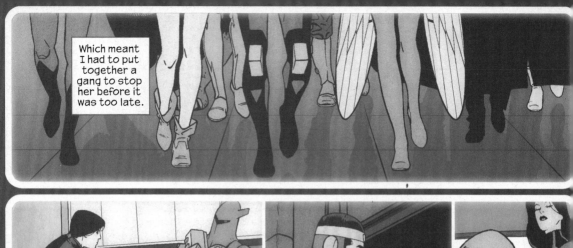

Which meant I had to put together a gang to stop her before it was too late.

And the whole operation actually went pretty well...

...until it, um...didn't.

Eventually, me and Cassie got away from those jerks, though, and we were in the clear--

--'til the cops showed up, I mean.

FREEZE!

Now, don't get me wrong-- getting arrested is always terrible-- well, unless it's by the *hotness* police--

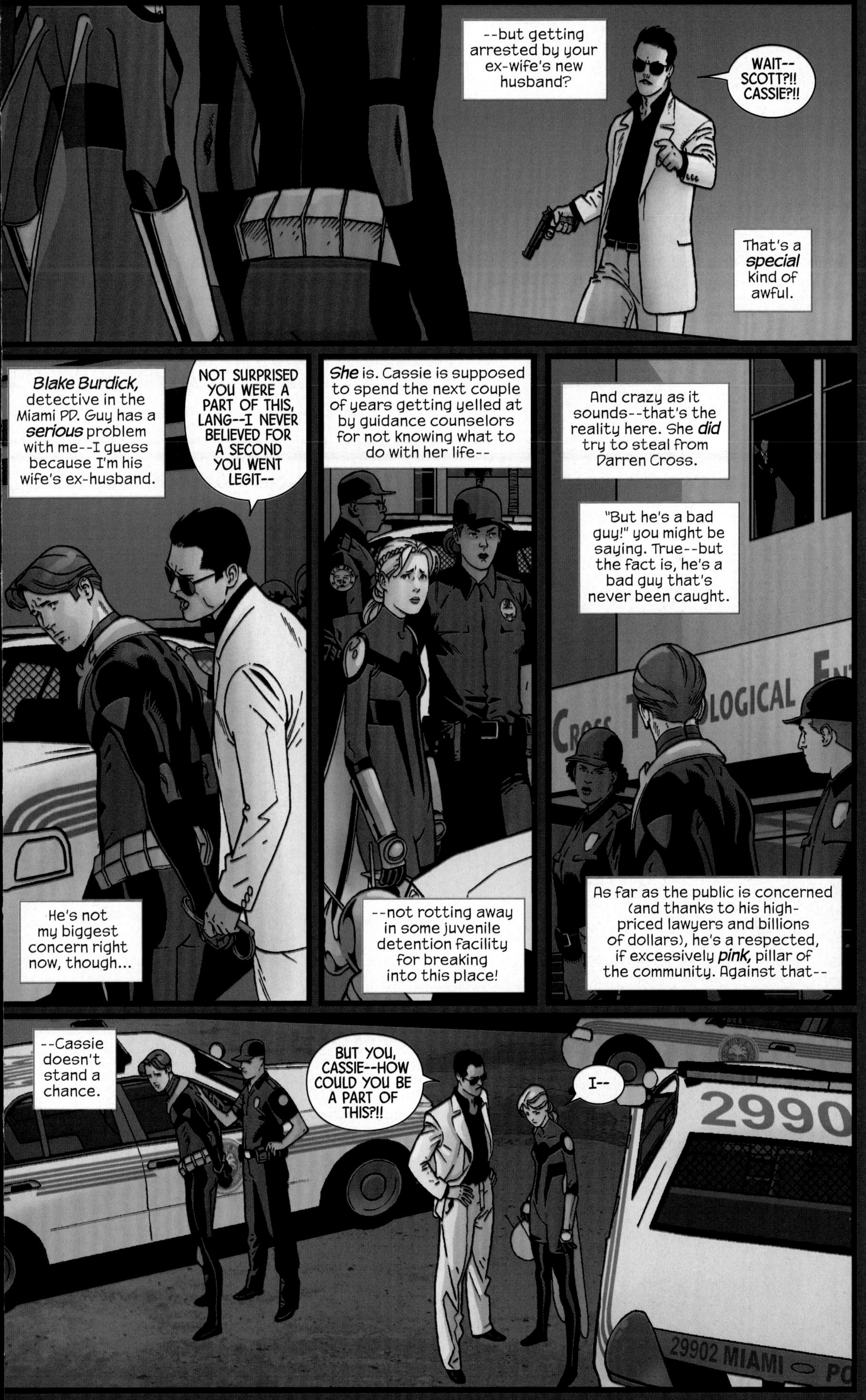
--but getting arrested by your ex-wife's new husband?
WAIT-- SCOTT?!! CASSIE?!!
That's a *special* kind of awful.
Blake Burdick, detective in the Miami PD. Guy has a *serious* problem with me--I guess because I'm his wife's ex-husband.
NOT SURPRISED YOU WERE A PART OF THIS, LANG--I NEVER BELIEVED FOR A SECOND YOU WENT LEGIT--
He's not my biggest concern right now, though...
She is. Cassie is supposed to spend the next couple of years getting yelled at by guidance counselors for not knowing what to do with her life--
--not rotting away in some juvenile detention facility for breaking into this place!
And crazy as it sounds--that's the reality here. She *did* try to steal from Darren Cross.
"But he's a bad guy!" you might be saying. True--but the fact is, he's a bad guy that's never been caught.
CROSS TECHNOLOGICAL ENT
As far as the public is concerned (and thanks to his high-priced lawyers and billions of dollars), he's a respected, if excessively *pink,* pillar of the community. Against that--
--Cassie doesn't stand a chance.
BUT YOU, CASSIE--HOW COULD YOU BE A PART OF THIS?!!
I--
2990
29902 MIAMI

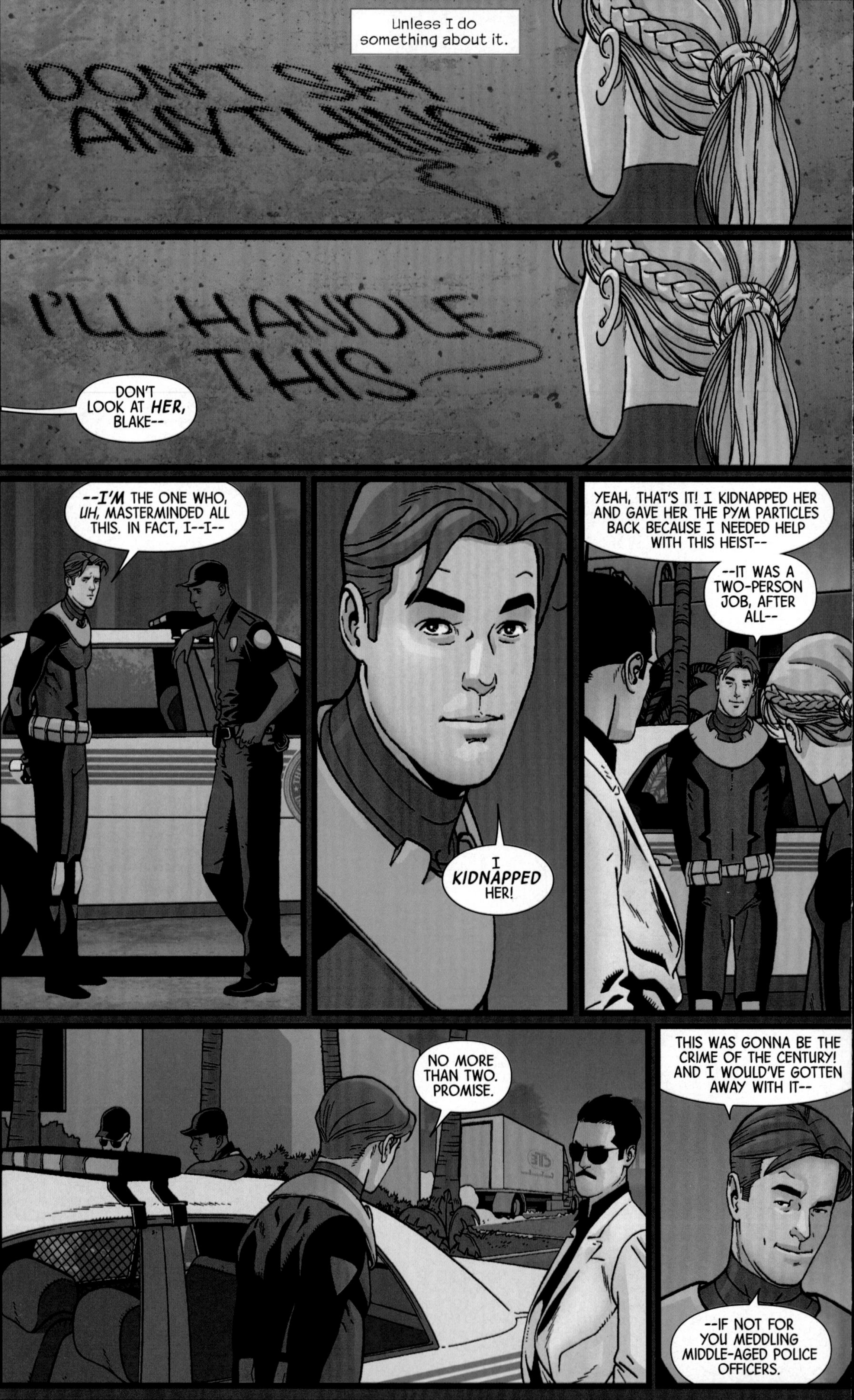
Unless I do something about it.
DON'T SAY ANYTHING
I'LL HANDLE THIS
DON'T LOOK AT HER, BLAKE--
--I'M THE ONE WHO, UH, MASTERMINDED ALL THIS. IN FACT, I--I--
I KIDNAPPED HER!
YEAH, THAT'S IT! I KIDNAPPED HER AND GAVE HER THE PYM PARTICLES BACK BECAUSE I NEEDED HELP WITH THIS HEIST--
--IT WAS A TWO-PERSON JOB, AFTER ALL--
NO MORE THAN TWO. PROMISE.
THIS WAS GONNA BE THE CRIME OF THE CENTURY! AND I WOULD'VE GOTTEN AWAY WITH IT--
--IF NOT FOR YOU MEDDLING MIDDLE-AGED POLICE OFFICERS.

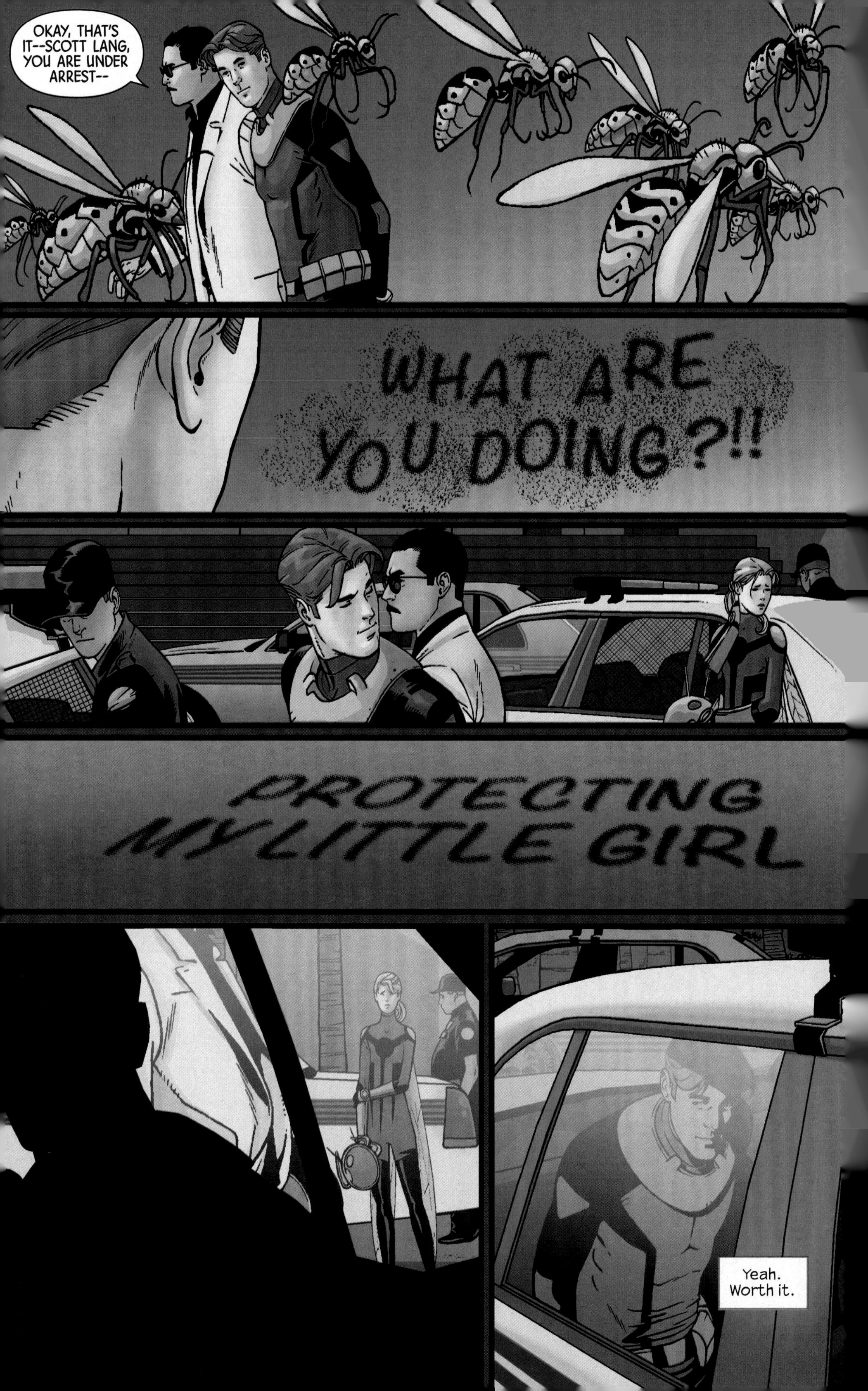
OKAY, THAT'S IT--SCOTT LANG, YOU ARE UNDER ARREST--
WHAT ARE YOU DOING?!!
PROTECTING MY LITTLE GIRL
Yeah. Worth it.

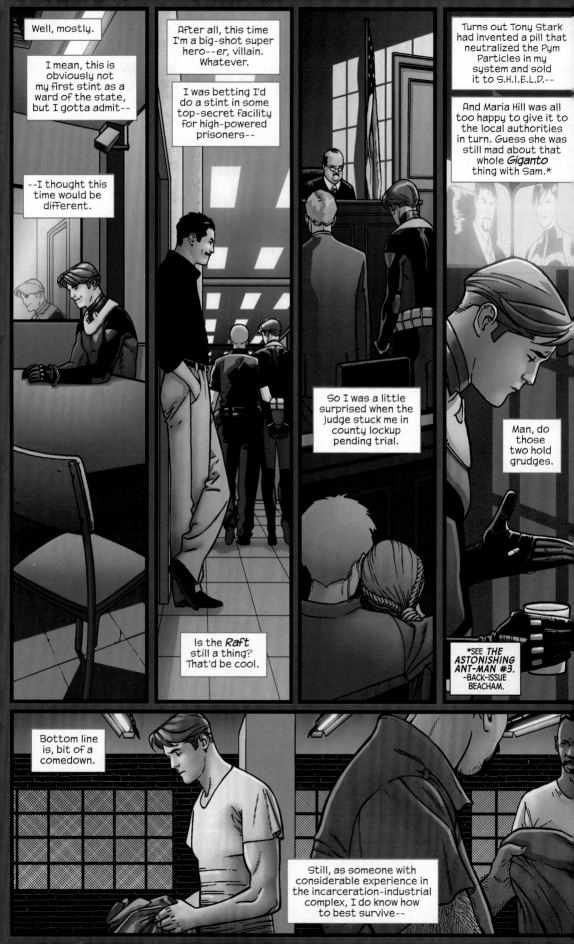

Well, mostly.

I mean, this is obviously not my first stint as a ward of the state, but I gotta admit--

--I thought this time would be different.

After all, this time I'm a big-shot super hero--er, villain. Whatever.

I was betting I'd do a stint in some top-secret facility for high-powered prisoners--

Is the *Raft* still a thing? That'd be cool.

So I was a little surprised when the judge stuck me in county lockup pending trial.

Turns out Tony Stark had invented a pill that neutralized the Pym Particles in my system and sold it to S.H.I.E.L.D.--

And Maria Hill was all too happy to give it to the local authorities in turn. Guess she was still mad about that whole *Giganto* thing with Sam.*

Man, do those two hold grudges.

*SEE *THE ASTONISHING ANT-MAN #3.* –BACK-ISSUE BEACHAM.

Bottom line is, bit of a comedown.

Still, as someone with considerable experience in the incarceration-industrial complex, I do know how to best survive--

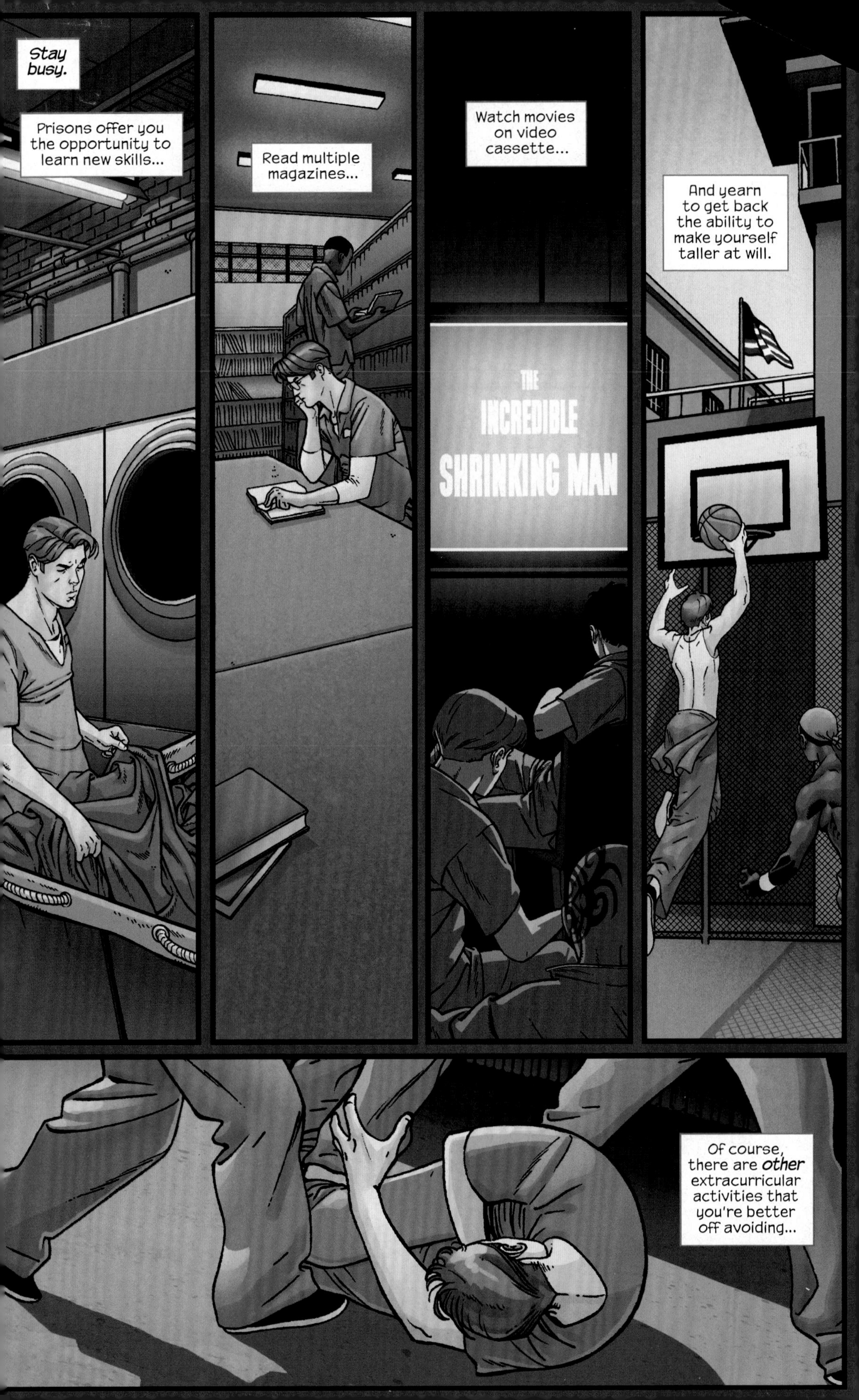
Stay busy.
Prisons offer you the opportunity to learn new skills...
Read multiple magazines...
Watch movies on video cassette...
THE INCREDIBLE SHRINKING MAN
And yearn to get back the ability to make yourself taller at will.
Of course, there are *other* extracurricular activities that you're better off avoiding...

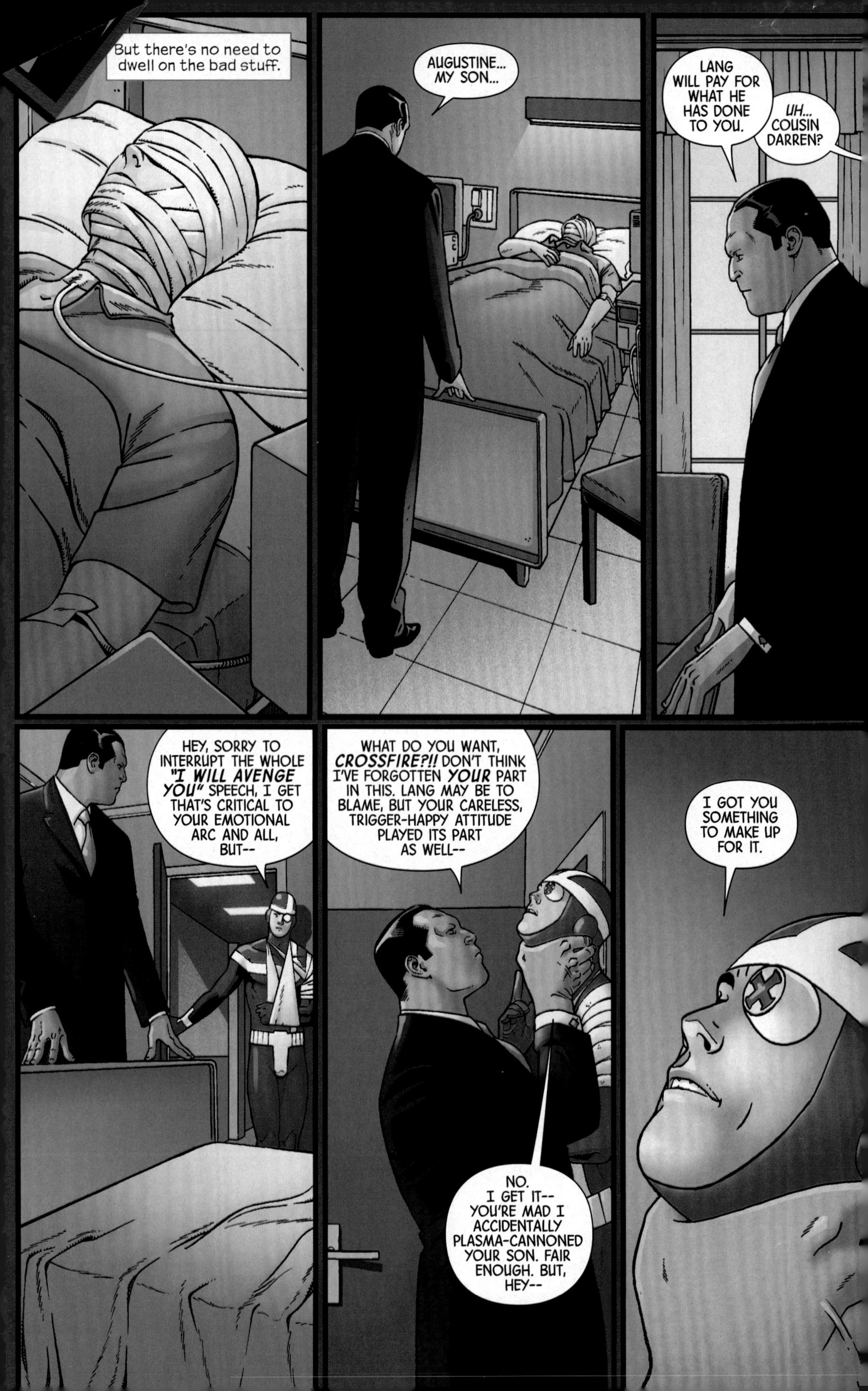
But there's no need to dwell on the bad stuff.
AUGUSTINE... MY SON...
LANG WILL PAY FOR WHAT HE HAS DONE TO YOU.
UH... COUSIN DARREN?
HEY, SORRY TO INTERRUPT THE WHOLE "I WILL AVENGE YOU" SPEECH, I GET THAT'S CRITICAL TO YOUR EMOTIONAL ARC AND ALL, BUT--
WHAT DO YOU WANT, CROSSFIRE?!! DON'T THINK I'VE FORGOTTEN YOUR PART IN THIS. LANG MAY BE TO BLAME, BUT YOUR CARELESS, TRIGGER-HAPPY ATTITUDE PLAYED ITS PART AS WELL--
NO. I GET IT-- YOU'RE MAD I ACCIDENTALLY PLASMA-CANNONED YOUR SON. FAIR ENOUGH. BUT, HEY--
I GOT YOU SOMETHING TO MAKE UP FOR IT.

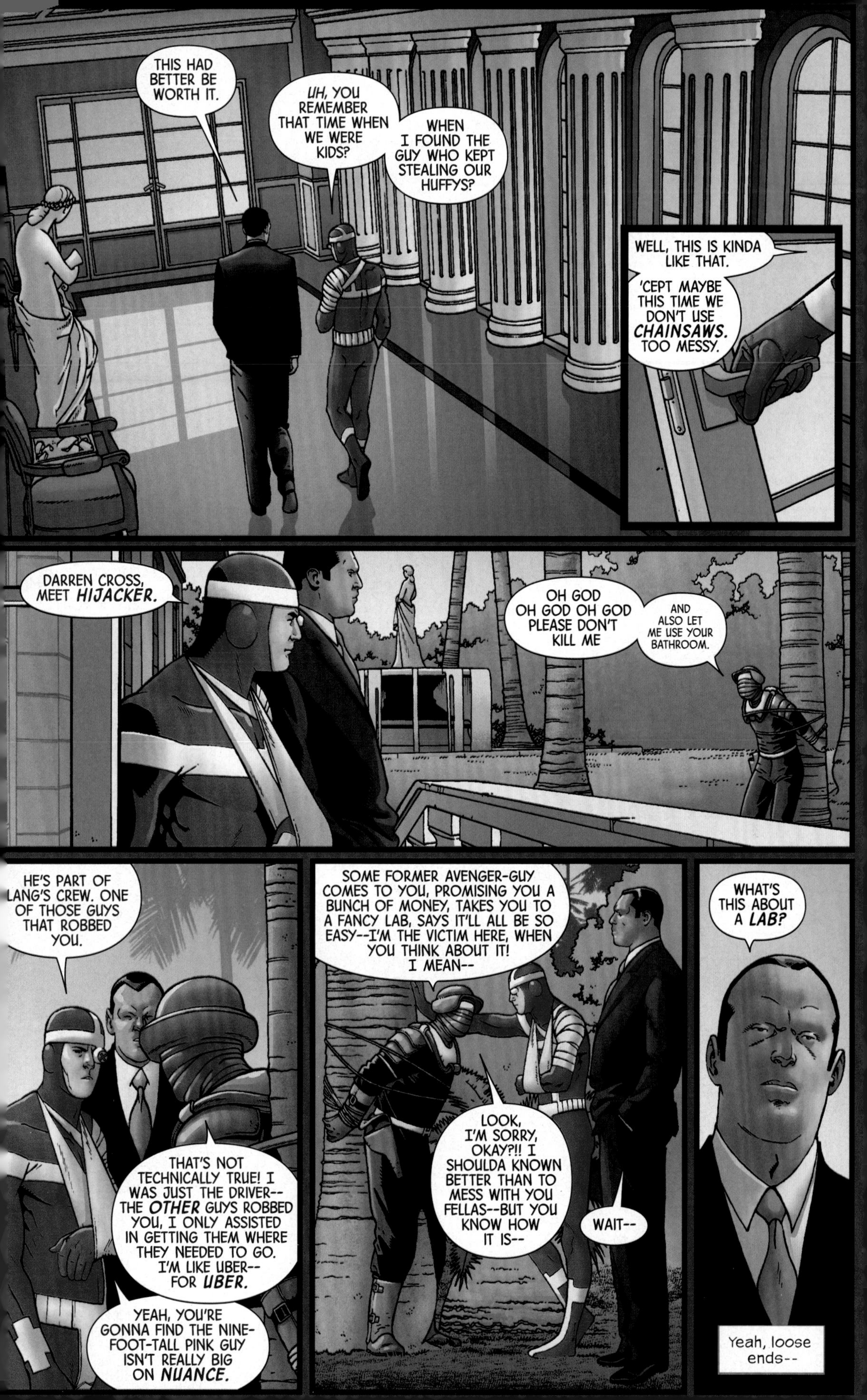
THIS HAD BETTER BE WORTH IT.
UH, YOU REMEMBER THAT TIME WHEN WE WERE KIDS?
WHEN I FOUND THE GUY WHO KEPT STEALING OUR HUFFYS?
WELL, THIS IS KINDA LIKE THAT.
'CEPT MAYBE THIS TIME WE DON'T USE CHAINSAWS. TOO MESSY.
DARREN CROSS, MEET HIJACKER.
OH GOD OH GOD OH GOD PLEASE DON'T KILL ME
AND ALSO LET ME USE YOUR BATHROOM.
HE'S PART OF LANG'S CREW. ONE OF THOSE GUYS THAT ROBBED YOU.
THAT'S NOT TECHNICALLY TRUE! I WAS JUST THE DRIVER-- THE OTHER GUYS ROBBED YOU, I ONLY ASSISTED IN GETTING THEM WHERE THEY NEEDED TO GO. I'M LIKE UBER-- FOR UBER.
YEAH, YOU'RE GONNA FIND THE NINE-FOOT-TALL PINK GUY ISN'T REALLY BIG ON NUANCE.
SOME FORMER AVENGER-GUY COMES TO YOU, PROMISING YOU A BUNCH OF MONEY, TAKES YOU TO A FANCY LAB, SAYS IT'LL ALL BE SO EASY--I'M THE VICTIM HERE, WHEN YOU THINK ABOUT IT! I MEAN--
LOOK, I'M SORRY, OKAY?!! I SHOULDA KNOWN BETTER THAN TO MESS WITH YOU FELLAS--BUT YOU KNOW HOW IT IS--
WAIT--
WHAT'S THIS ABOUT A LAB?
Yeah, loose ends--

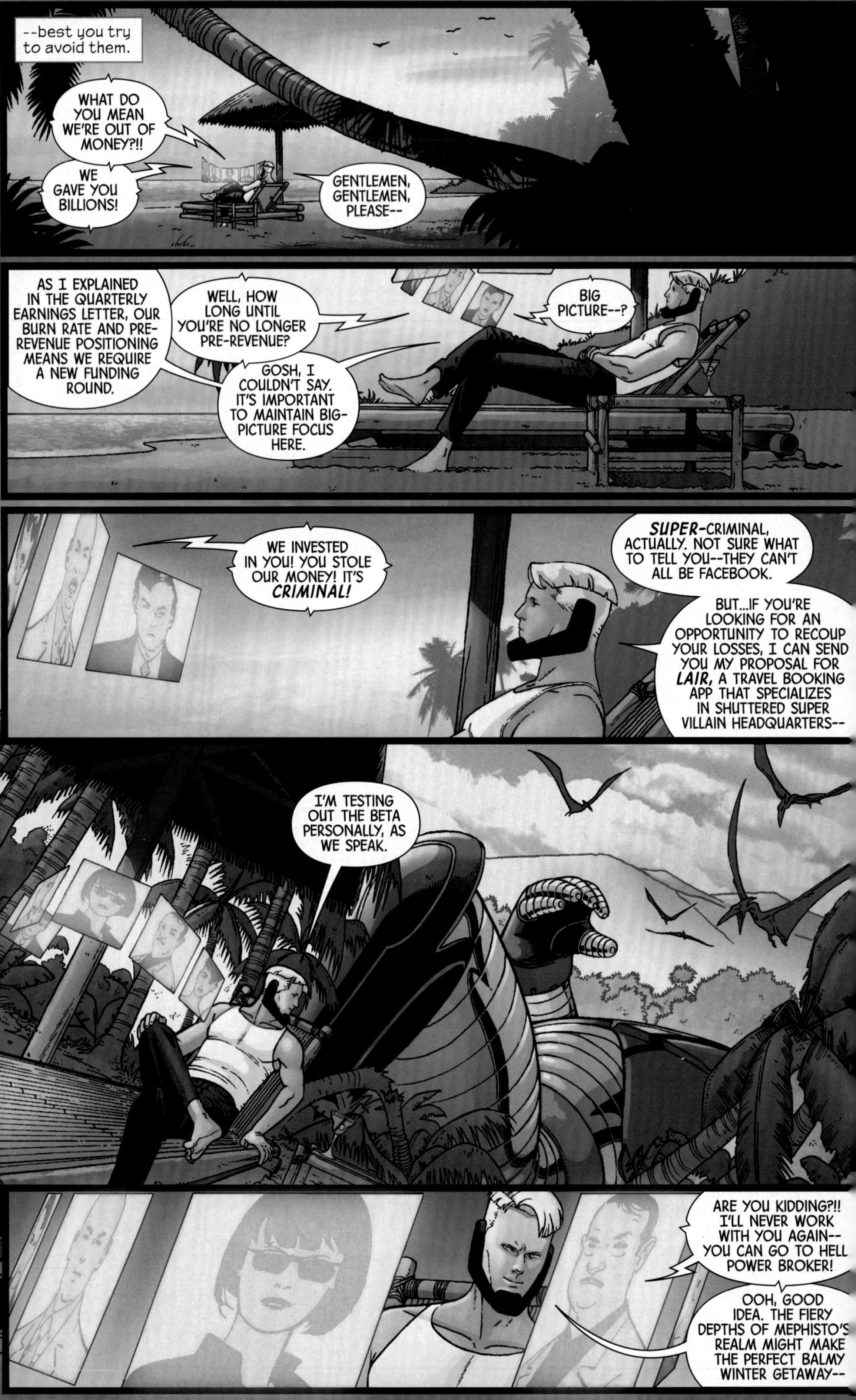
--best you try to avoid them.
WHAT DO YOU MEAN WE'RE OUT OF MONEY?!!
WE GAVE YOU BILLIONS!
GENTLEMEN, GENTLEMEN, PLEASE--
AS I EXPLAINED IN THE QUARTERLY EARNINGS LETTER, OUR BURN RATE AND PRE-REVENUE POSITIONING MEANS WE REQUIRE A NEW FUNDING ROUND.
WELL, HOW LONG UNTIL YOU'RE NO LONGER PRE-REVENUE?
GOSH, I COULDN'T SAY. IT'S IMPORTANT TO MAINTAIN BIG-PICTURE FOCUS HERE.
BIG PICTURE--?
WE INVESTED IN YOU! YOU STOLE OUR MONEY! IT'S CRIMINAL!
SUPER-CRIMINAL, ACTUALLY. NOT SURE WHAT TO TELL YOU--THEY CAN'T ALL BE FACEBOOK.
BUT...IF YOU'RE LOOKING FOR AN OPPORTUNITY TO RECOUP YOUR LOSSES, I CAN SEND YOU MY PROPOSAL FOR LAIR, A TRAVEL BOOKING APP THAT SPECIALIZES IN SHUTTERED SUPER VILLAIN HEADQUARTERS--
I'M TESTING OUT THE BETA PERSONALLY, AS WE SPEAK.
ARE YOU KIDDING?!! I'LL NEVER WORK WITH YOU AGAIN--YOU CAN GO TO HELL POWER BROKER!
OOH, GOOD IDEA. THE FIERY DEPTHS OF MEPHISTO'S REALM MIGHT MAKE THE PERFECT BALMY WINTER GETAWAY--

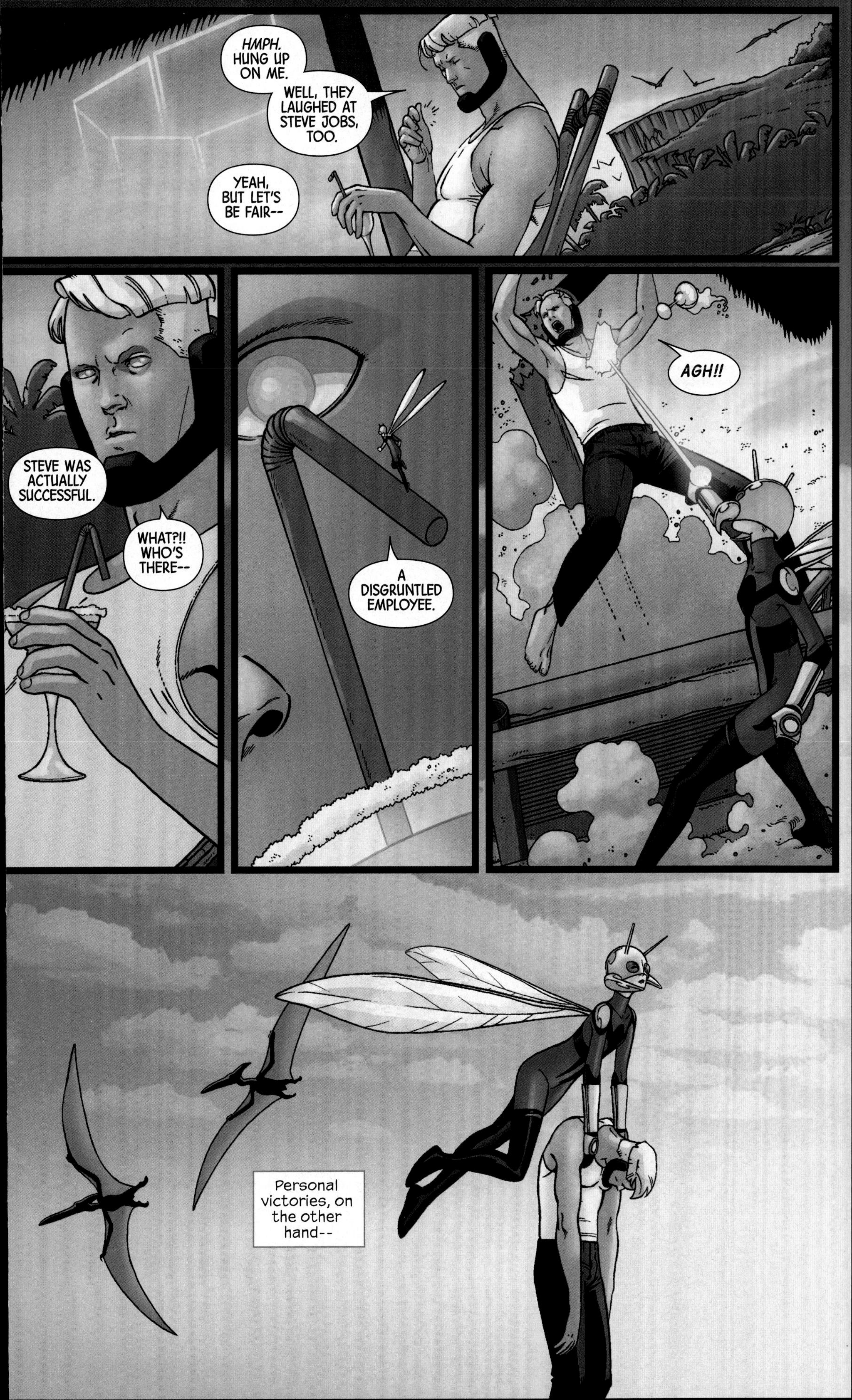
HMPH. HUNG UP ON ME.
WELL, THEY LAUGHED AT STEVE JOBS, TOO.
YEAH, BUT LET'S BE FAIR--
STEVE WAS ACTUALLY SUCCESSFUL.
WHAT?!! WHO'S THERE--
A DISGRUNTLED EMPLOYEE.
AGH!!
Personal victories, on the other hand--

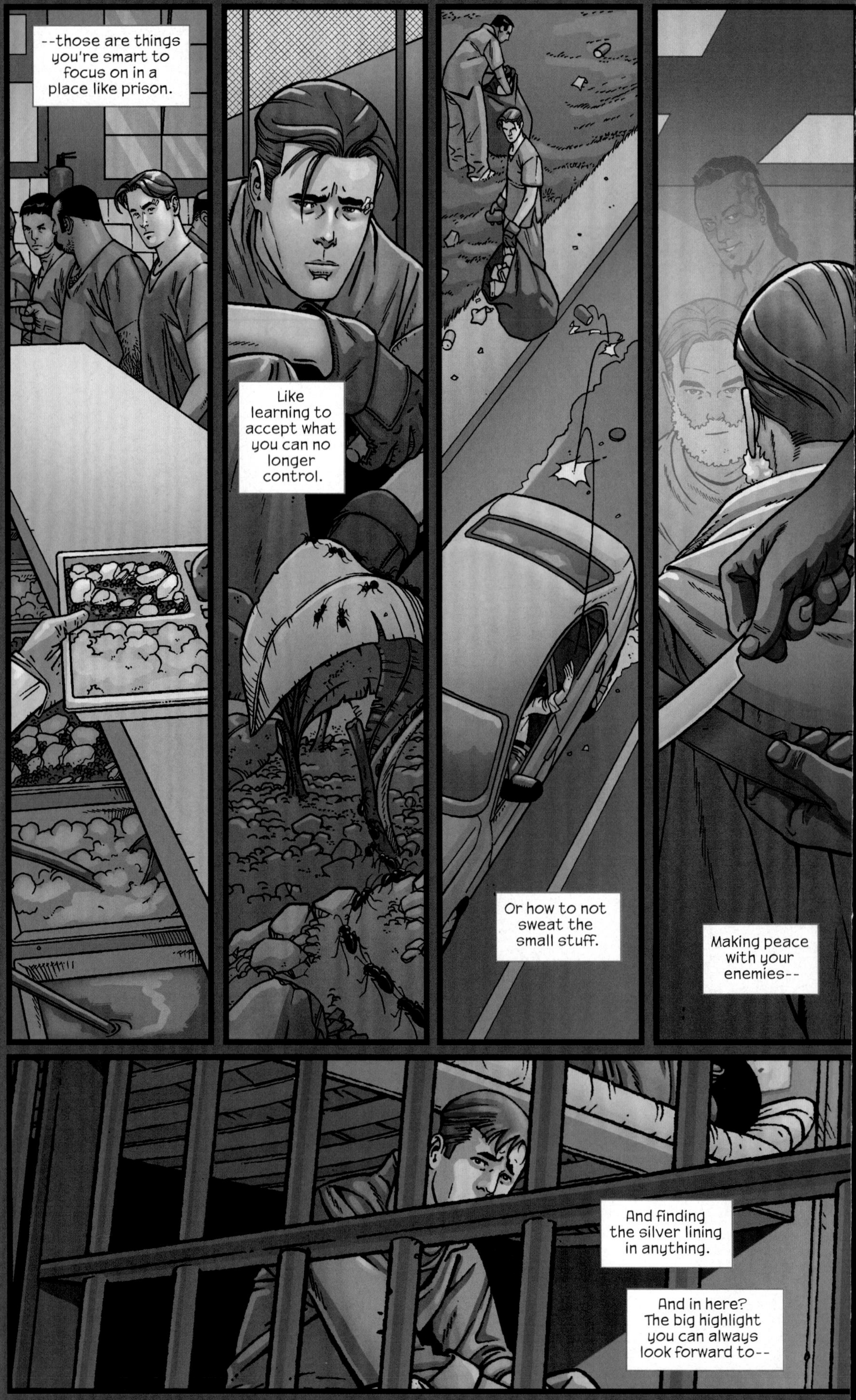
--those are things you're smart to focus on in a place like prison.
Like learning to accept what you can no longer control.
Or how to not sweat the small stuff.
Making peace with your enemies--
And finding the silver lining in anything.
And in here? The big highlight you can always look forward to--

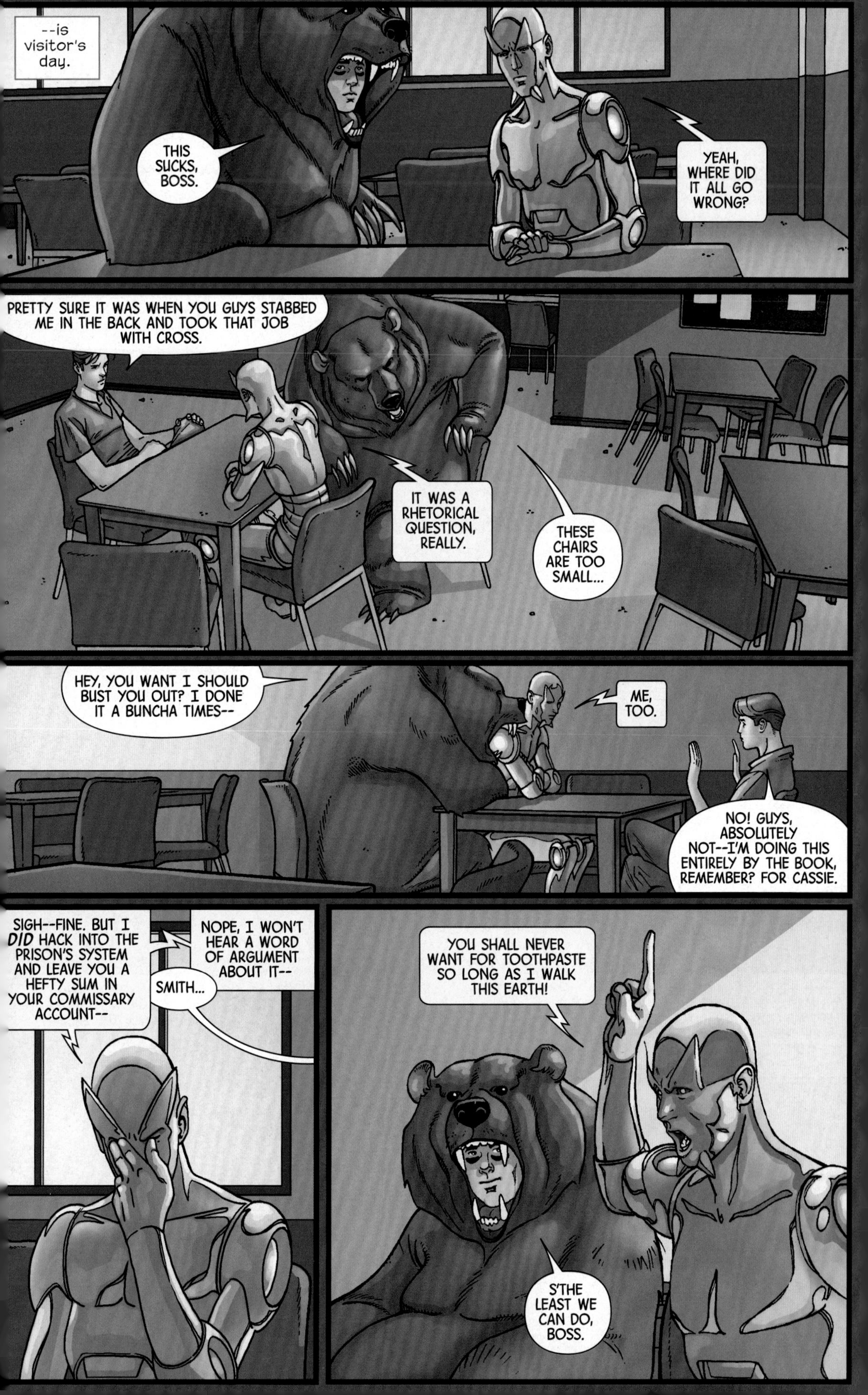
--is visitor's day.
THIS SUCKS, BOSS.
YEAH, WHERE DID IT ALL GO WRONG?
PRETTY SURE IT WAS WHEN YOU GUYS STABBED ME IN THE BACK AND TOOK THAT JOB WITH CROSS.
IT WAS A RHETORICAL QUESTION, REALLY.
THESE CHAIRS ARE TOO SMALL...
HEY, YOU WANT I SHOULD BUST YOU OUT? I DONE IT A BUNCHA TIMES--
ME, TOO.
NO! GUYS, ABSOLUTELY NOT--I'M DOING THIS ENTIRELY BY THE BOOK, REMEMBER? FOR CASSIE.
SIGH--FINE. BUT I DID HACK INTO THE PRISON'S SYSTEM AND LEAVE YOU A HEFTY SUM IN YOUR COMMISSARY ACCOUNT--
NOPE, I WON'T HEAR A WORD OF ARGUMENT ABOUT IT--
SMITH...
YOU SHALL NEVER WANT FOR TOOTHPASTE SO LONG AS I WALK THIS EARTH!
S'THE LEAST WE CAN DO, BOSS.

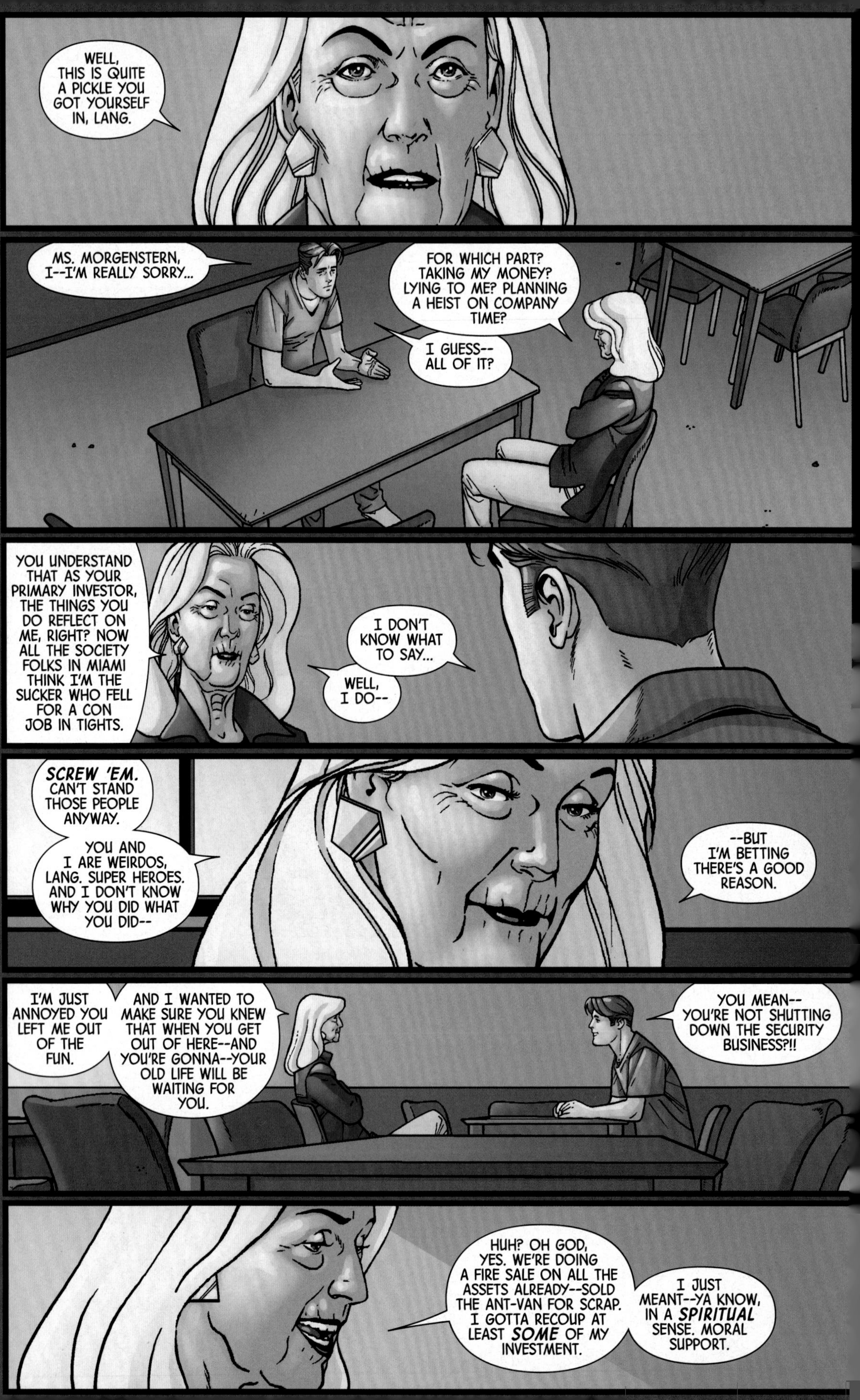
WELL, THIS IS QUITE A PICKLE YOU GOT YOURSELF IN, LANG.
MS. MORGENSTERN, I--I'M REALLY SORRY...
FOR WHICH PART? TAKING MY MONEY? LYING TO ME? PLANNING A HEIST ON COMPANY TIME?
I GUESS-- ALL OF IT?
YOU UNDERSTAND THAT AS YOUR PRIMARY INVESTOR, THE THINGS YOU DO REFLECT ON ME, RIGHT? NOW ALL THE SOCIETY FOLKS IN MIAMI THINK I'M THE SUCKER WHO FELL FOR A CON JOB IN TIGHTS.
I DON'T KNOW WHAT TO SAY...
WELL, I DO--
SCREW 'EM. CAN'T STAND THOSE PEOPLE ANYWAY.
YOU AND I ARE WEIRDOS, LANG. SUPER HEROES. AND I DON'T KNOW WHY YOU DID WHAT YOU DID--
--BUT I'M BETTING THERE'S A GOOD REASON.
I'M JUST ANNOYED YOU LEFT ME OUT OF THE FUN.
AND I WANTED TO MAKE SURE YOU KNEW THAT WHEN YOU GET OUT OF HERE--AND YOU'RE GONNA--YOUR OLD LIFE WILL BE WAITING FOR YOU.
YOU MEAN-- YOU'RE NOT SHUTTING DOWN THE SECURITY BUSINESS?!!
HUH? OH GOD, YES. WE'RE DOING A FIRE SALE ON ALL THE ASSETS ALREADY--SOLD THE ANT-VAN FOR SCRAP. I GOTTA RECOUP AT LEAST SOME OF MY INVESTMENT.
I JUST MEANT--YA KNOW, IN A SPIRITUAL SENSE. MORAL SUPPORT.

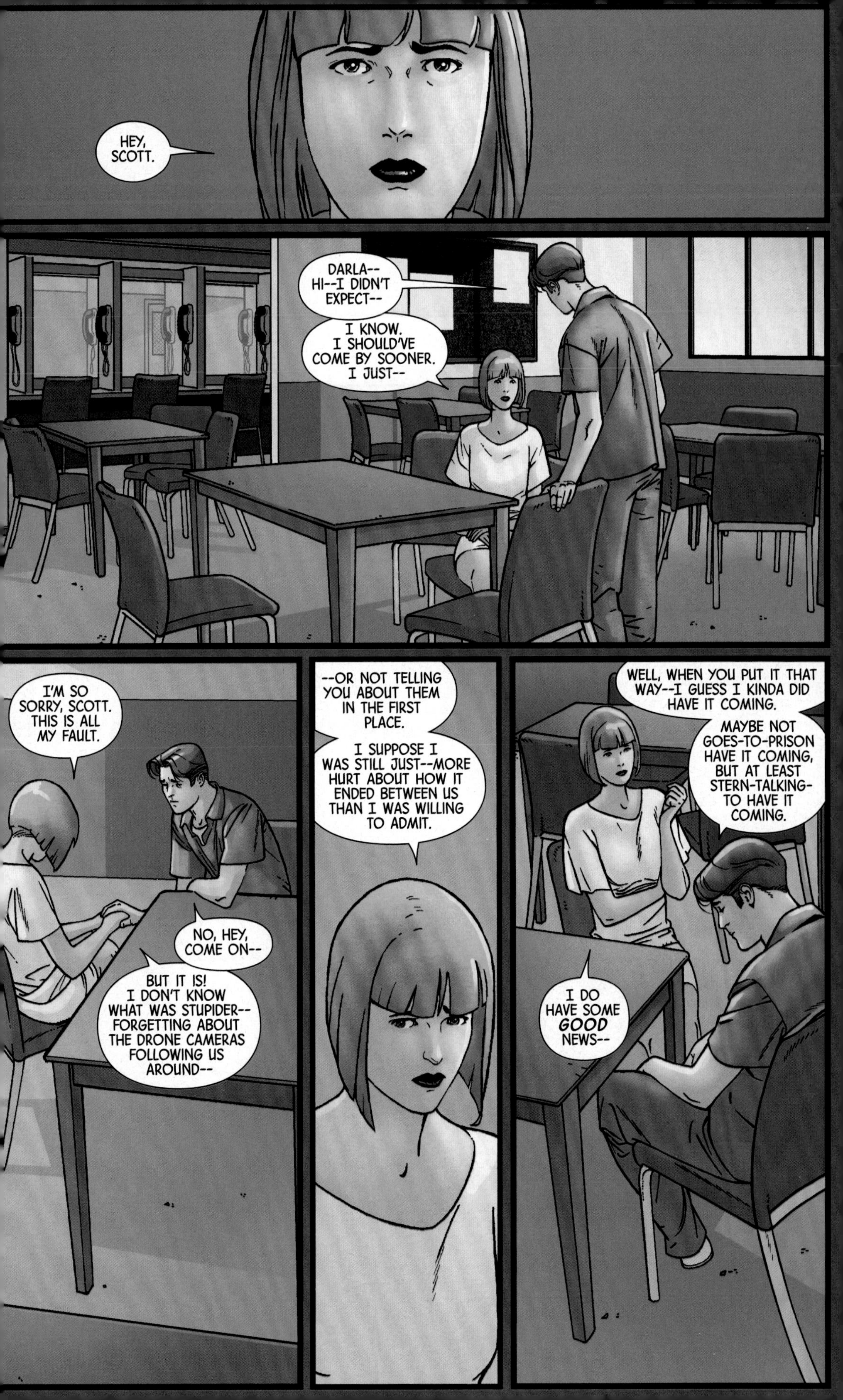
HEY, SCOTT.
DARLA-- HI--I DIDN'T EXPECT--
I KNOW. I SHOULD'VE COME BY SOONER. I JUST--
I'M SO SORRY, SCOTT. THIS IS ALL MY FAULT.
NO, HEY, COME ON--
BUT IT IS! I DON'T KNOW WHAT WAS STUPIDER-- FORGETTING ABOUT THE DRONE CAMERAS FOLLOWING US AROUND--
--OR NOT TELLING YOU ABOUT THEM IN THE FIRST PLACE.
I SUPPOSE I WAS STILL JUST--MORE HURT ABOUT HOW IT ENDED BETWEEN US THAN I WAS WILLING TO ADMIT.
WELL, WHEN YOU PUT IT THAT WAY--I GUESS I KINDA DID HAVE IT COMING.
MAYBE NOT GOES-TO-PRISON HAVE IT COMING, BUT AT LEAST STERN-TALKING-TO HAVE IT COMING.
I DO HAVE SOME GOOD NEWS--

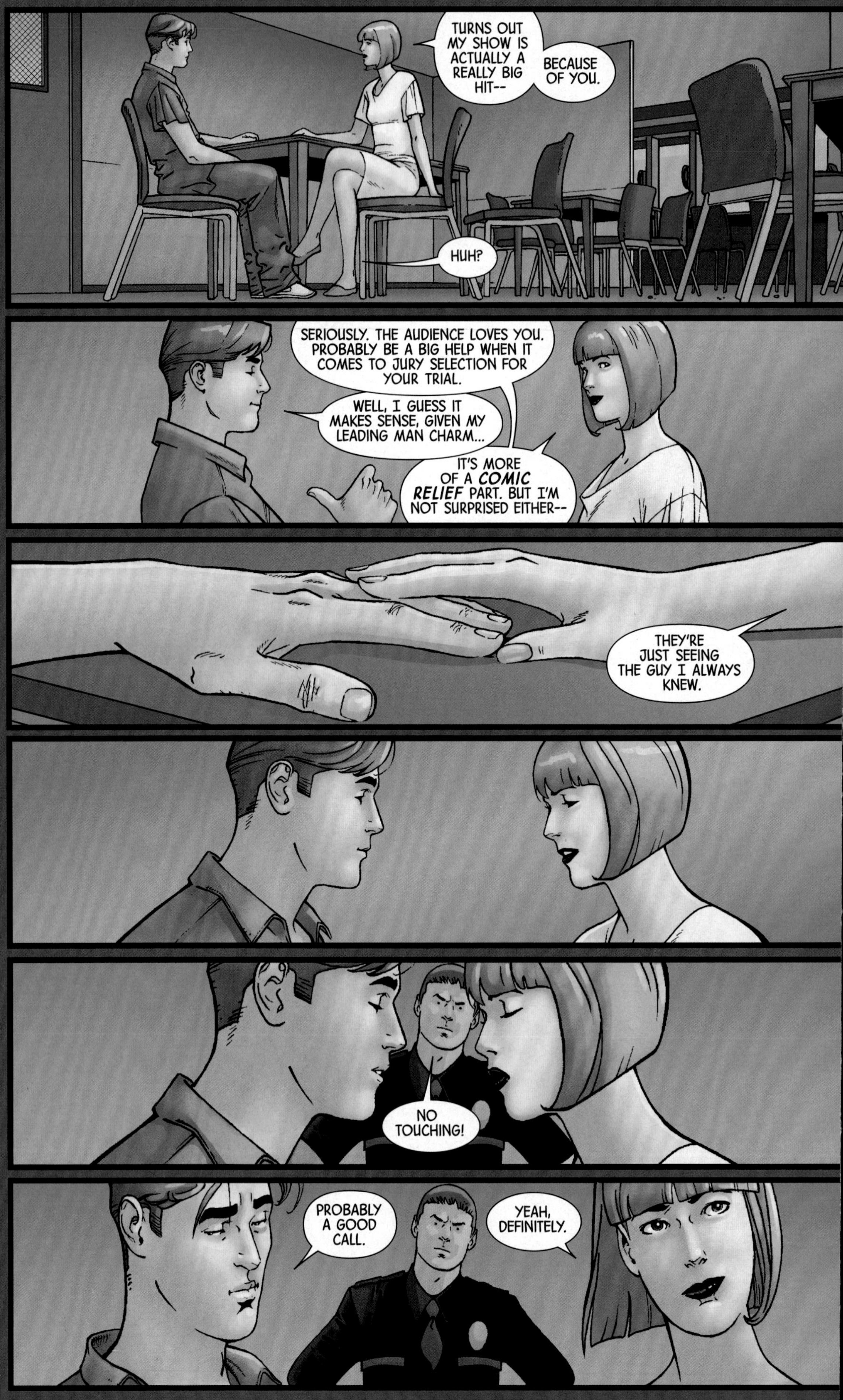
TURNS OUT MY SHOW IS ACTUALLY A REALLY BIG HIT--
BECAUSE OF YOU.
HUH?
SERIOUSLY. THE AUDIENCE LOVES YOU. PROBABLY BE A BIG HELP WHEN IT COMES TO JURY SELECTION FOR YOUR TRIAL.
WELL, I GUESS IT MAKES SENSE, GIVEN MY LEADING MAN CHARM...
IT'S MORE OF A COMIC RELIEF PART. BUT I'M NOT SURPRISED EITHER--
THEY'RE JUST SEEING THE GUY I ALWAYS KNEW.
NO TOUCHING!
PROBABLY A GOOD CALL.
YEAH, DEFINITELY.

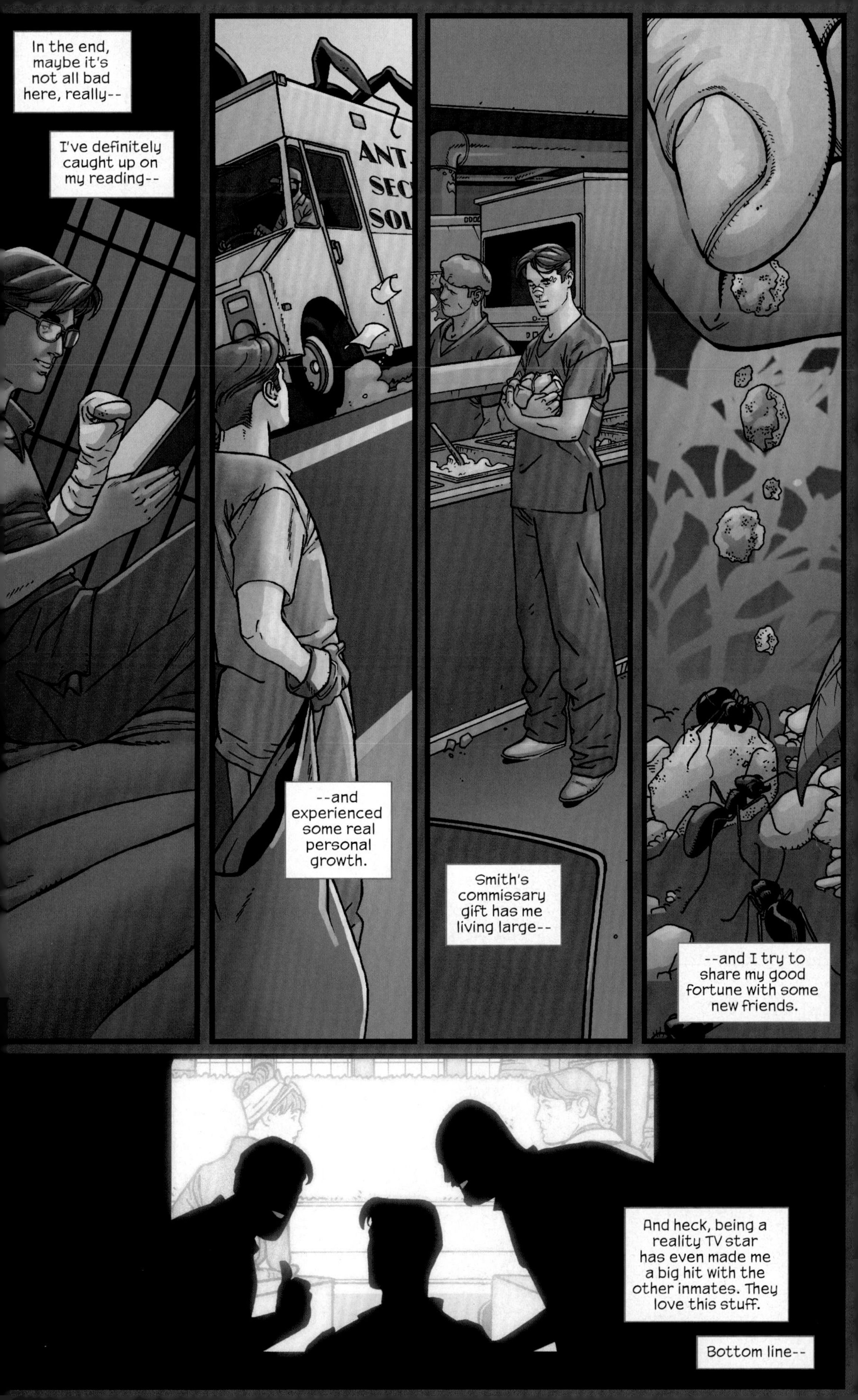
In the end, maybe it's not all bad here, really--
I've definitely caught up on my reading--
ANT
SEC
SOL
--and experienced some real personal growth.
Smith's commissary gift has me living large--
--and I try to share my good fortune with some new friends.
And heck, being a reality TV star has even made me a big hit with the other inmates. They love this stuff.
Bottom line--

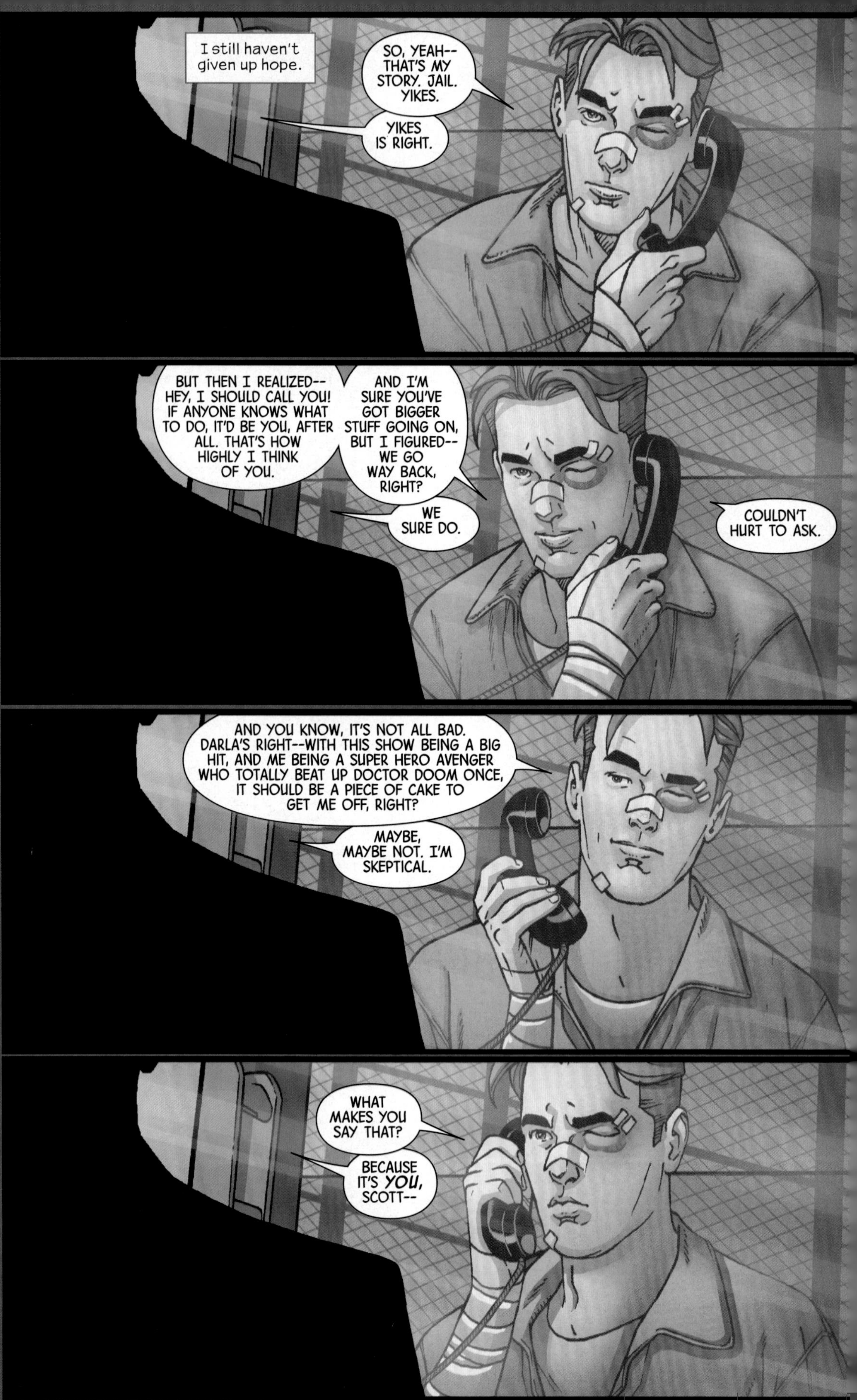
I still haven't given up hope.
SO, YEAH-- THAT'S MY STORY. JAIL. YIKES.
YIKES IS RIGHT.
BUT THEN I REALIZED-- HEY, I SHOULD CALL YOU! IF ANYONE KNOWS WHAT TO DO, IT'D BE YOU, AFTER ALL. THAT'S HOW HIGHLY I THINK OF YOU.
AND I'M SURE YOU'VE GOT BIGGER STUFF GOING ON, BUT I FIGURED-- WE GO WAY BACK, RIGHT?
WE SURE DO.
COULDN'T HURT TO ASK.
AND YOU KNOW, IT'S NOT ALL BAD. DARLA'S RIGHT--WITH THIS SHOW BEING A BIG HIT, AND ME BEING A SUPER HERO AVENGER WHO TOTALLY BEAT UP DOCTOR DOOM ONCE, IT SHOULD BE A PIECE OF CAKE TO GET ME OFF, RIGHT?
MAYBE, MAYBE NOT. I'M SKEPTICAL.
WHAT MAKES YOU SAY THAT?
BECAUSE IT'S *YOU*, SCOTT--

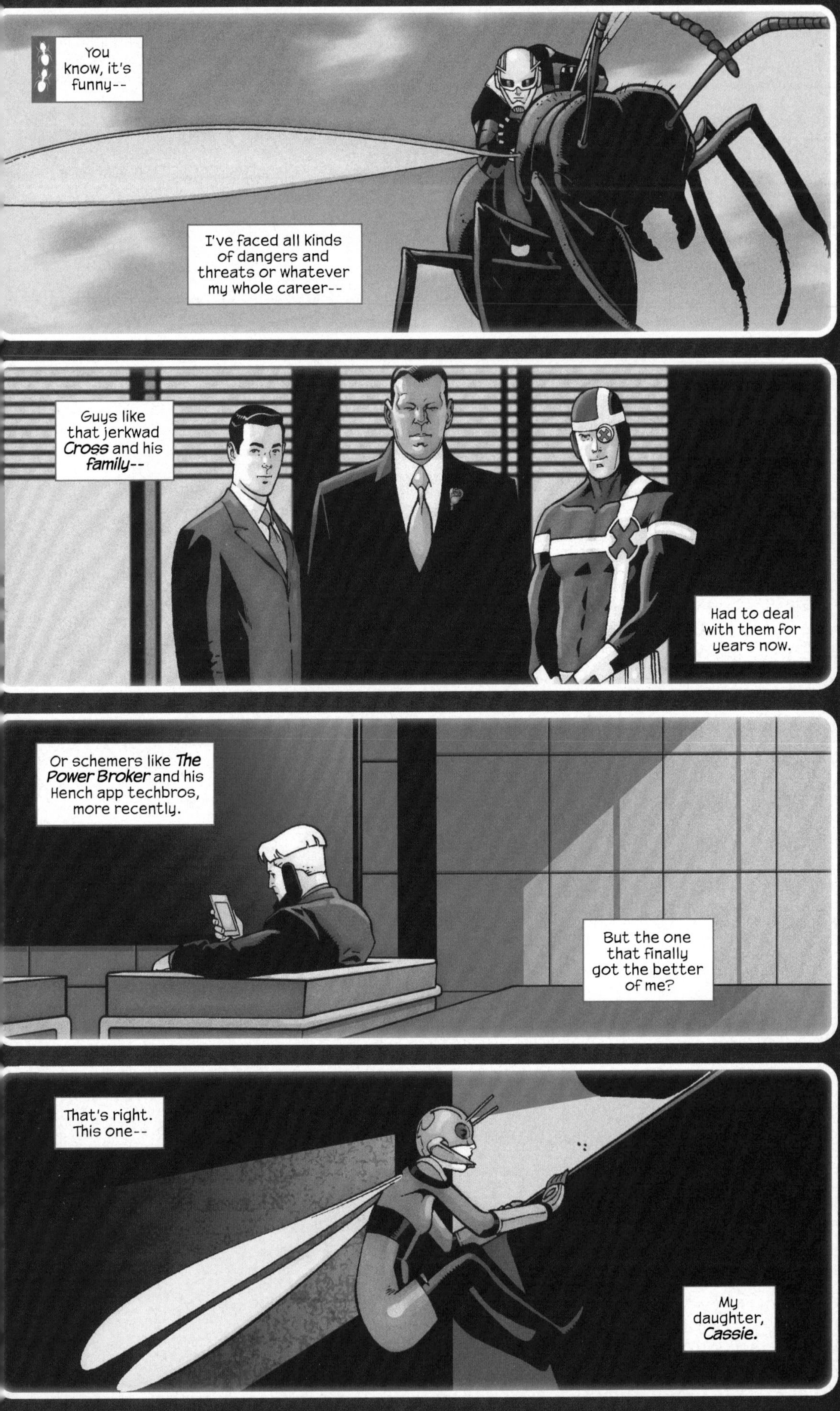

You know, it's funny--
I've faced all kinds of dangers and threats or whatever my whole career--
Guys like that jerkwad *Cross* and his *family*--
Had to deal with them for years now.
Or schemers like ***The Power Broker*** and his Hench app techbros, more recently.
But the one that finally got the better of me?
That's right. This one--
My daughter, ***Cassie.***

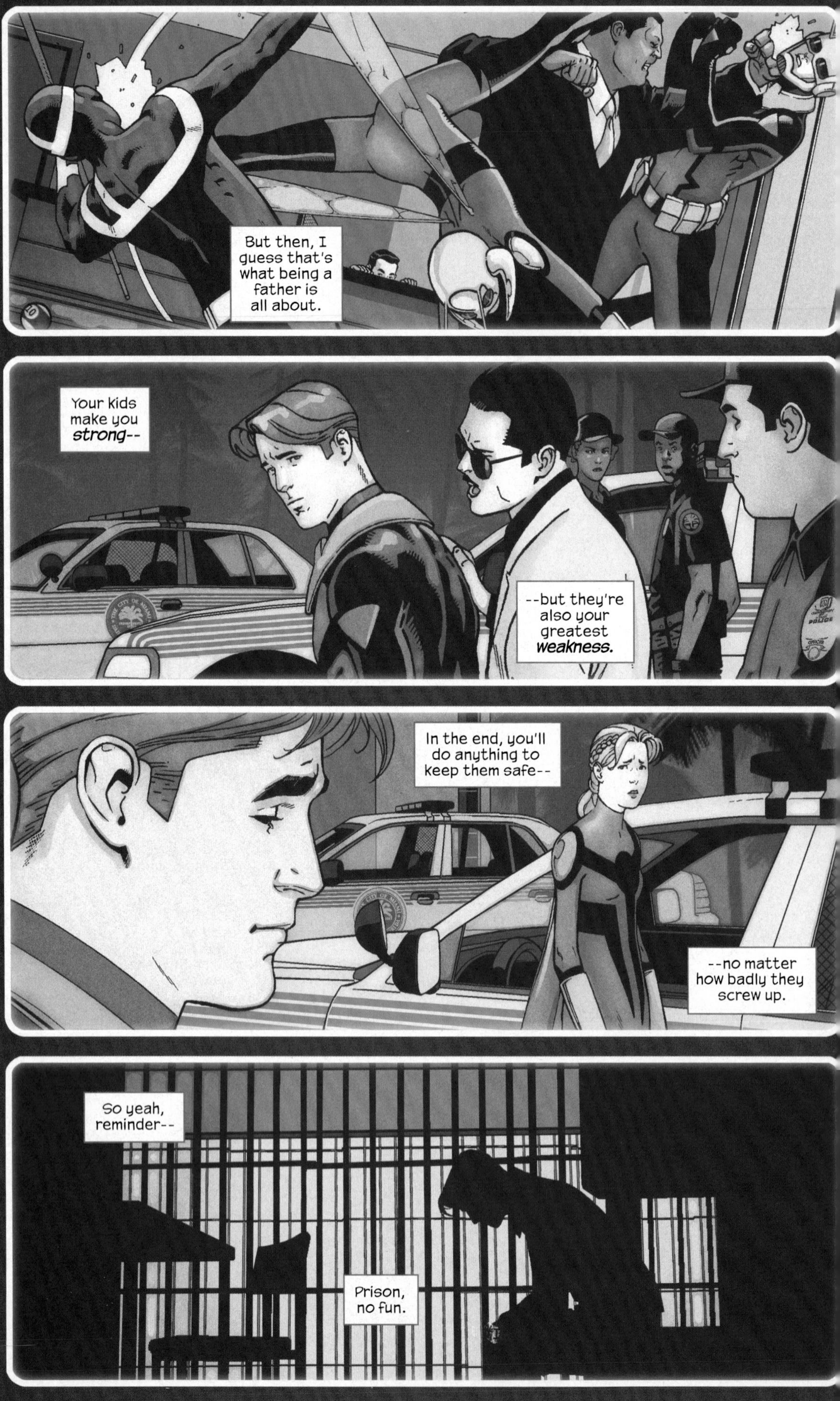
But then, I guess that's what being a father is all about.
Your kids make you *strong*--
--but they're also your greatest *weakness.*
In the end, you'll do anything to keep them safe--
--no matter how badly they screw up.
So yeah, reminder--
Prison, no fun.

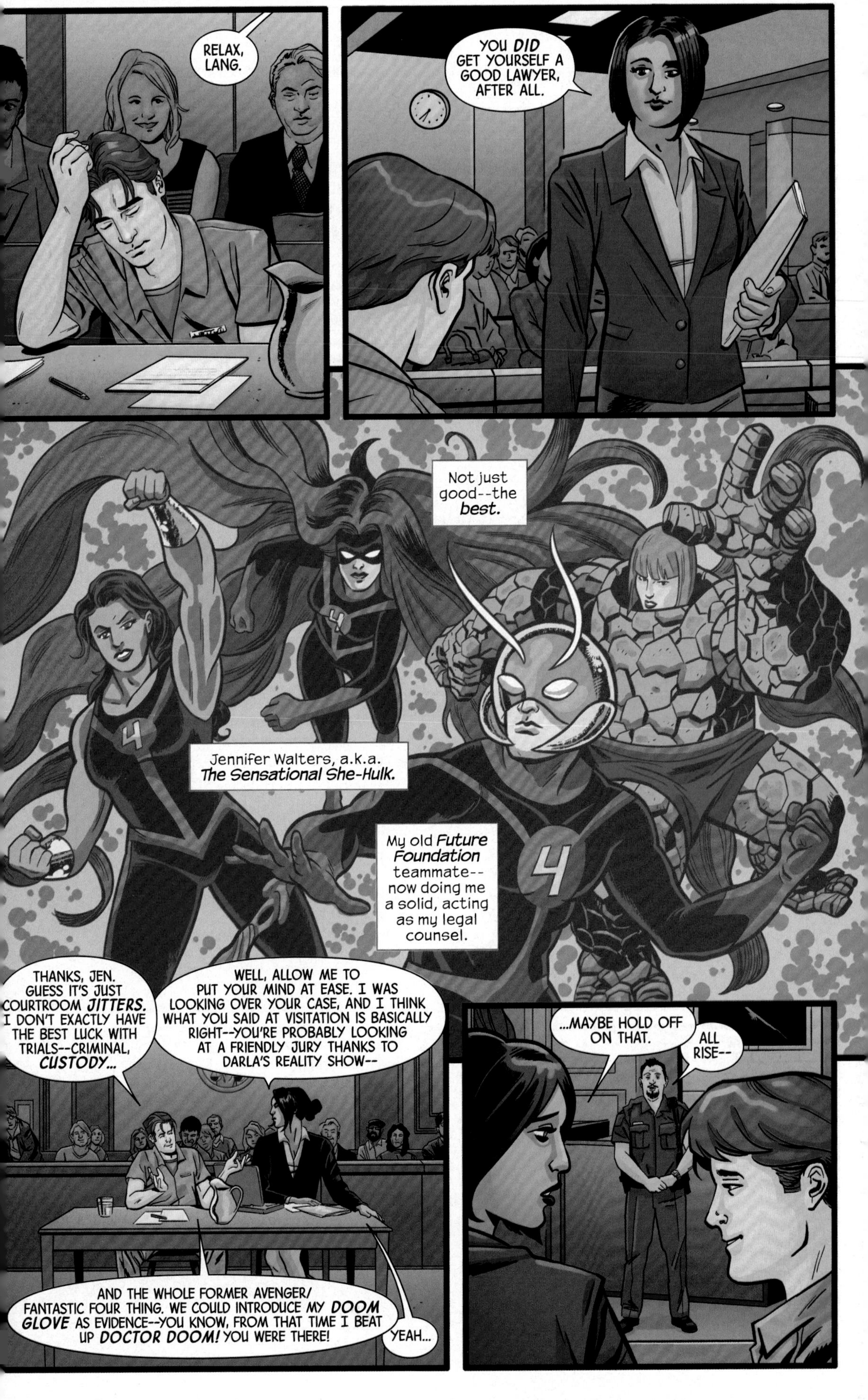
RELAX, LANG.
YOU DID GET YOURSELF A GOOD LAWYER, AFTER ALL.
Not just good--the best.
Jennifer Walters, a.k.a. The Sensational She-Hulk.
My old Future Foundation teammate--now doing me a solid, acting as my legal counsel.
THANKS, JEN. GUESS IT'S JUST COURTROOM JITTERS. I DON'T EXACTLY HAVE THE BEST LUCK WITH TRIALS--CRIMINAL, CUSTODY...
WELL, ALLOW ME TO PUT YOUR MIND AT EASE. I WAS LOOKING OVER YOUR CASE, AND I THINK WHAT YOU SAID AT VISITATION IS BASICALLY RIGHT--YOU'RE PROBABLY LOOKING AT A FRIENDLY JURY THANKS TO DARLA'S REALITY SHOW--
AND THE WHOLE FORMER AVENGER/ FANTASTIC FOUR THING. WE COULD INTRODUCE MY DOOM GLOVE AS EVIDENCE--YOU KNOW, FROM THAT TIME I BEAT UP DOCTOR DOOM! YOU WERE THERE!
YEAH...
...MAYBE HOLD OFF ON THAT.
ALL RISE--

THE HONORABLE JUDGE RONALD WILCOX PRESIDING.

BE SEATED, BE SEATED...

NOW, BEFORE WE BEGIN--I UNDERSTAND THIS TRIAL HAS ATTRACTED A LOT OF ATTENTION, PARTICULARLY FROM THOSE FOLKS IN THE *MEDIA* WHO I SEE HAVE FILLED UP THE GALLERY SEATS HERE TODAY--AND WHILE THIS IS INDEED A BIT MORE OF A... *COLORFUL* CASE--

JUDGE WILCOX

--I EXPECT IT TO BE HANDLED WITH THE SAME DECORUM AND DIGNITY AS ANY OF OUR PROCEEDINGS HERE.

THERE WILL BE NO ALIEN INVASIONS OR TIME-TRAVELING SCOTT LANGS COMING BACK TO WARN US ABOUT THE FUTURE. THE FIRST PERSON WHO PUTS ON *TIGHTS* WITHOUT MY EXPRESSED CONSENT IS GOING TO FIND THEMSELVES IN *CONTEMPT*--

IS THAT UNDERSTOOD, MS. WALTERS, MR. LANG?

AW, NO, WE GOT THE *GHOSTBUSTERS II* JUDGE.

LOUD AND CLEAR, YOUR HONOR.

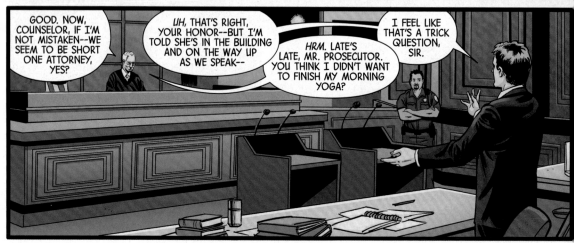

GOOD. NOW, COUNSELOR, IF I'M NOT MISTAKEN--WE SEEM TO BE SHORT ONE ATTORNEY, YES?

UH, THAT'S RIGHT, YOUR HONOR--BUT I'M TOLD SHE'S IN THE BUILDING AND ON THE WAY UP AS WE SPEAK--

HRM. LATE'S LATE, MR. PROSECUTOR. YOU THINK I DIDN'T WANT TO FINISH MY MORNING YOGA?

I FEEL LIKE THAT'S A TRICK QUESTION, SIR.

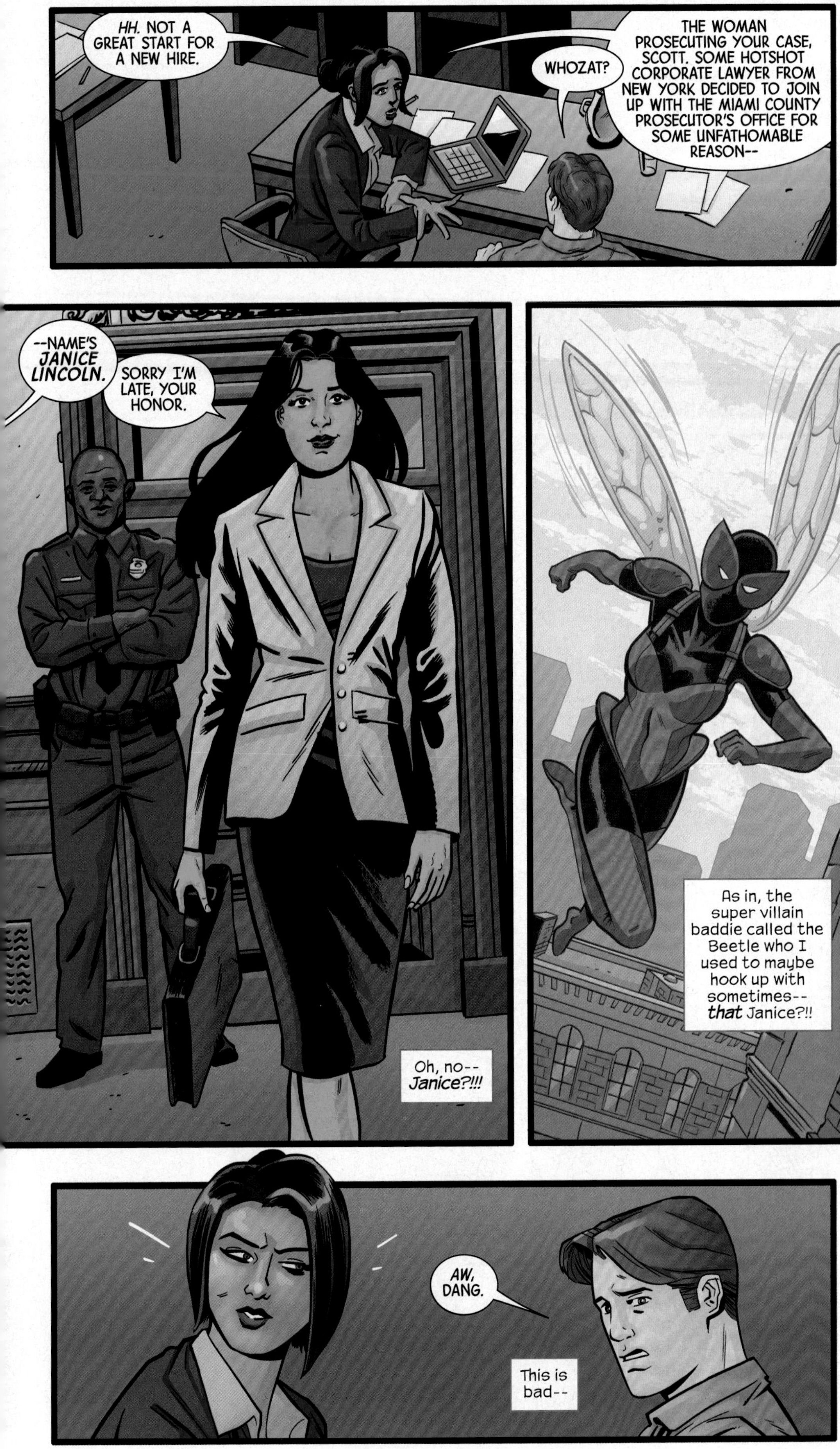
HH. NOT A GREAT START FOR A NEW HIRE.
WHOZAT?
THE WOMAN PROSECUTING YOUR CASE, SCOTT. SOME HOTSHOT CORPORATE LAWYER FROM NEW YORK DECIDED TO JOIN UP WITH THE MIAMI COUNTY PROSECUTOR'S OFFICE FOR SOME UNFATHOMABLE REASON--
--NAME'S JANICE LINCOLN.
SORRY I'M LATE, YOUR HONOR.
Oh, no-- Janice?!!!
As in, the super villain baddie called the Beetle who I used to maybe hook up with sometimes-- that Janice?!!
AW, DANG.
This is bad--

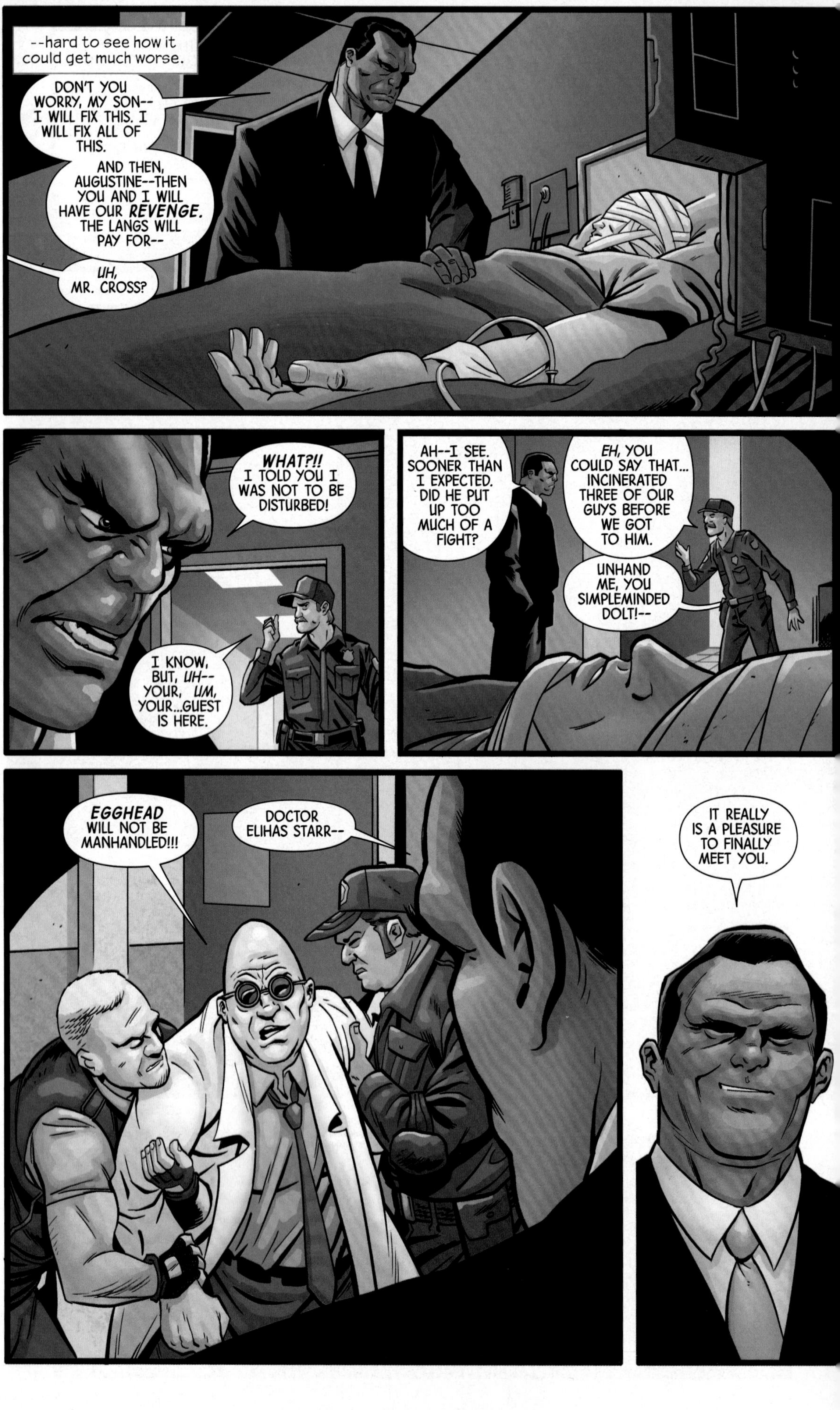
--hard to see how it could get much worse.
DON'T YOU WORRY, MY SON-- I WILL FIX THIS. I WILL FIX ALL OF THIS.
AND THEN, AUGUSTINE--THEN YOU AND I WILL HAVE OUR *REVENGE.* THE LANGS WILL PAY FOR--
UH, MR. CROSS?
WHAT?!! I TOLD YOU I WAS NOT TO BE DISTURBED!
I KNOW, BUT, *UH*-- YOUR, *UM*, YOUR...GUEST IS HERE.
AH--I SEE. SOONER THAN I EXPECTED. DID HE PUT UP TOO MUCH OF A FIGHT?
EH, YOU COULD SAY THAT... INCINERATED THREE OF OUR GUYS BEFORE WE GOT TO HIM.
UNHAND ME, YOU SIMPLEMINDED DOLT!--
EGGHEAD WILL NOT BE MANHANDLED!!!
DOCTOR ELIHAS STARR--
IT REALLY IS A PLEASURE TO FINALLY MEET YOU.

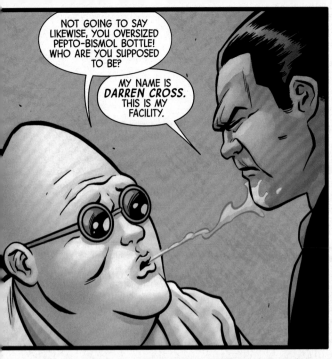

NOT GOING TO SAY LIKEWISE, YOU OVERSIZED PEPTO-BISMOL BOTTLE! WHO ARE YOU SUPPOSED TO BE?

MY NAME IS DARREN CROSS. THIS IS MY FACILITY.

WAIT A MOMENT--CROSS? AS IN CROSS TECHNOLOGICAL?

ONE AND THE SAME.

WHAT THE DEVIL DOES CROSS TECH WANT WITH ME?!! THIS BETTER NOT BE ABOUT PATENT INFRINGEMENT, BECAUSE I DO NOT BELIEVE IN LOBBYIST-DRIVEN I.P. LAWS!

HARDLY, DOCTOR STARR. I ACTUALLY SOUGHT YOU OUT FOR YOUR VERY SPECIFIC TALENTS--

THIS POOR SOUL ON THE BED HERE IS MY SON, AUGUSTINE. YOU SEE--

HM. LOOKS LIKE HE TOOK A NASTY SPILL, BUT I AM NOT THAT TYPE OF DOCTOR.

OF COURSE NOT. BUT YOU ARE AN EXPERT ON THE INNOVATIONS AND INVENTIONS OF A MAN OF INTEREST TO US BOTH--

--HANK PYM.

PYM?!! WHAT DOES HE HAVE TO DO WITH THIS?!!

COME WITH ME, STARR--

I THINK YOU'LL LIKE WHERE THIS IS "HEAD"-ED...

OH, THAT IS AWFUL. JUST AWFUL.

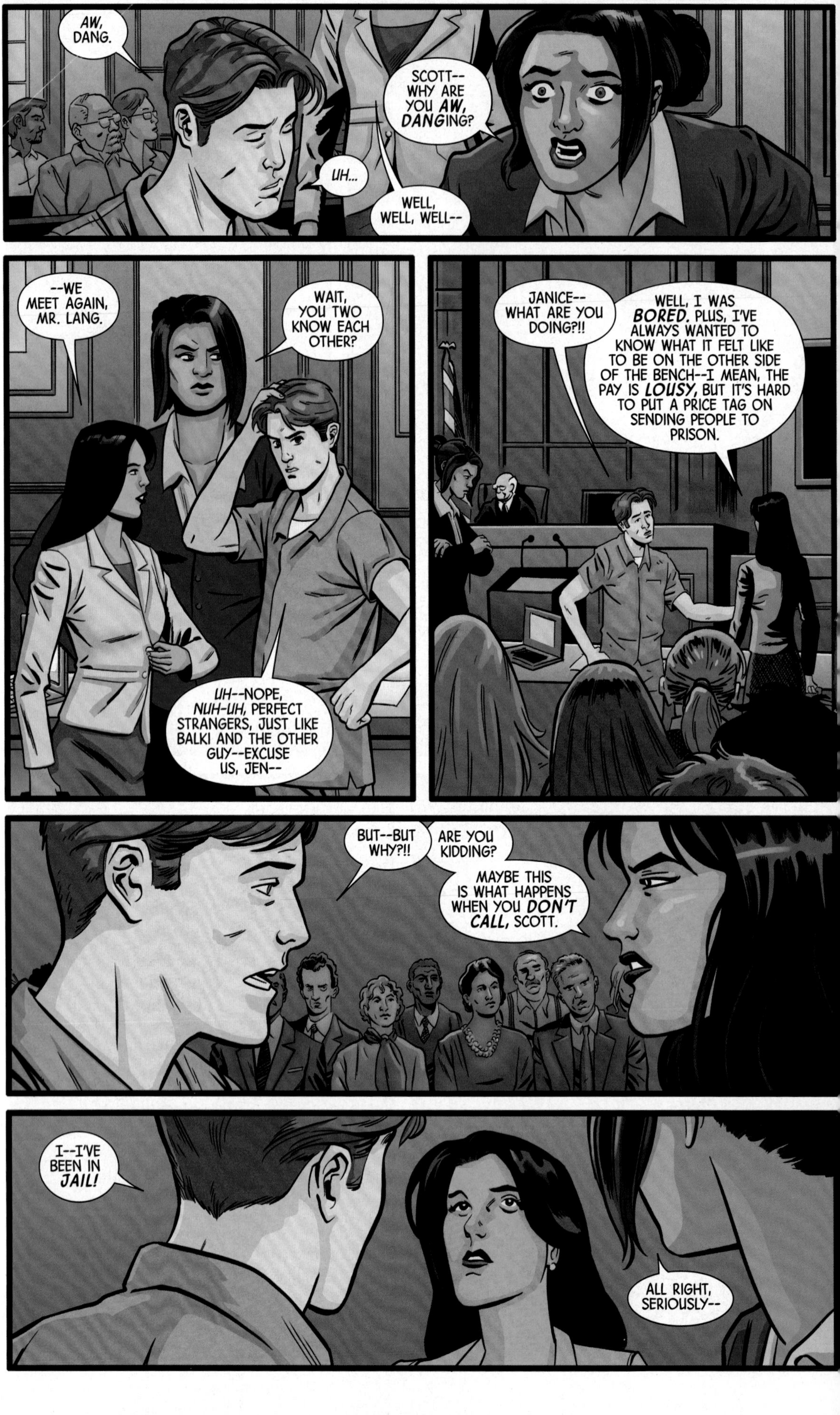
AW, DANG.
SCOTT-- WHY ARE YOU AW, DANGING?
UH...
WELL, WELL, WELL--
--WE MEET AGAIN, MR. LANG.
WAIT, YOU TWO KNOW EACH OTHER?
UH--NOPE, NUH-UH, PERFECT STRANGERS, JUST LIKE BALKI AND THE OTHER GUY--EXCUSE US, JEN--
JANICE-- WHAT ARE YOU DOING?!!
WELL, I WAS BORED. PLUS, I'VE ALWAYS WANTED TO KNOW WHAT IT FELT LIKE TO BE ON THE OTHER SIDE OF THE BENCH--I MEAN, THE PAY IS LOUSY, BUT IT'S HARD TO PUT A PRICE TAG ON SENDING PEOPLE TO PRISON.
BUT--BUT WHY?!!
ARE YOU KIDDING?
MAYBE THIS IS WHAT HAPPENS WHEN YOU DON'T CALL, SCOTT.
I--I'VE BEEN IN JAIL!
ALL RIGHT, SERIOUSLY--

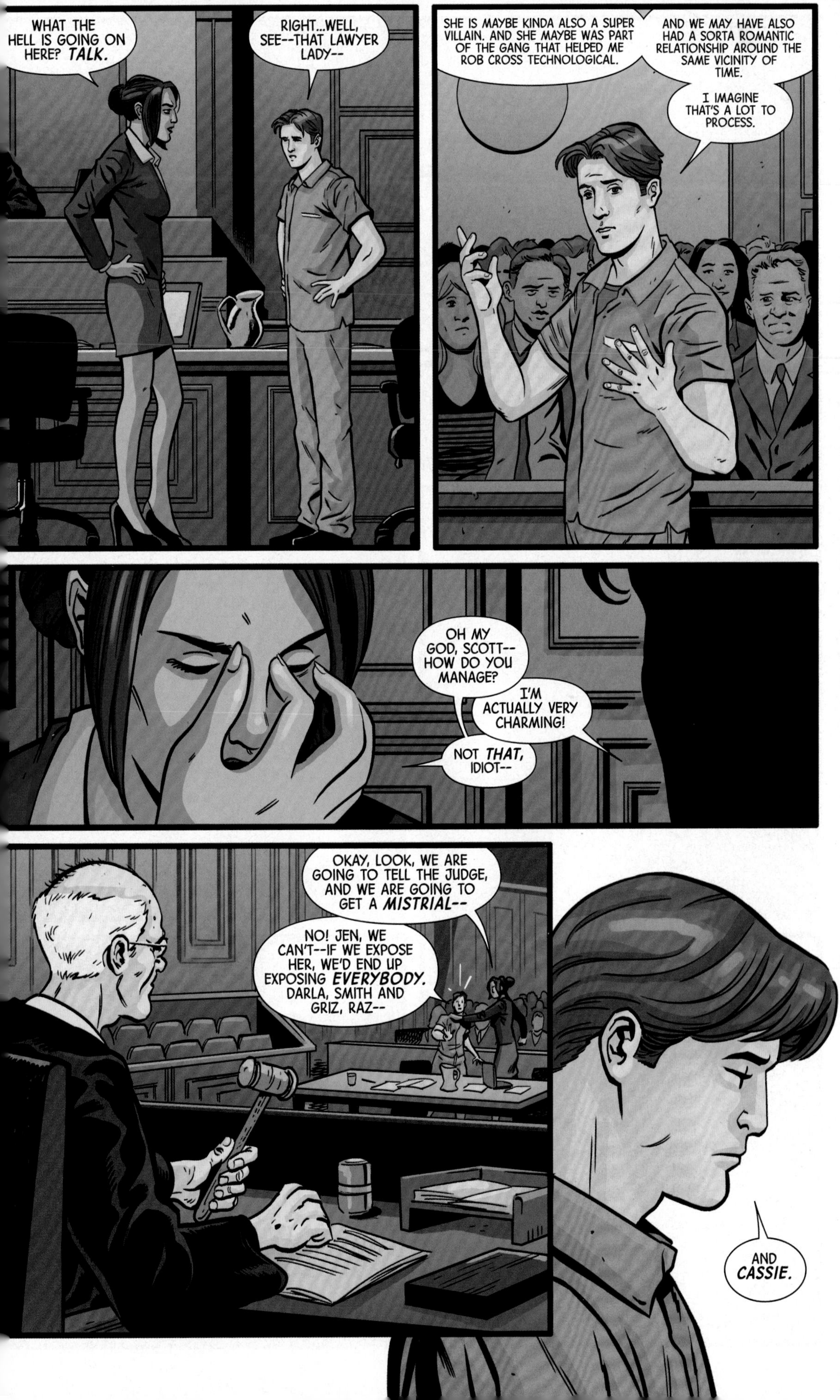
WHAT THE HELL IS GOING ON HERE? *TALK.*
RIGHT...WELL, SEE--THAT LAWYER LADY--
SHE IS MAYBE KINDA ALSO A SUPER VILLAIN. AND SHE MAYBE WAS PART OF THE GANG THAT HELPED ME ROB CROSS TECHNOLOGICAL.
AND WE MAY HAVE ALSO HAD A SORTA ROMANTIC RELATIONSHIP AROUND THE SAME VICINITY OF TIME.
I IMAGINE THAT'S A LOT TO PROCESS.
OH MY GOD, SCOTT-- HOW DO YOU MANAGE?
I'M ACTUALLY VERY CHARMING!
NOT *THAT,* IDIOT--
OKAY, LOOK, WE ARE GOING TO TELL THE JUDGE, AND WE ARE GOING TO GET A *MISTRIAL--*
NO! JEN, WE CAN'T--IF WE EXPOSE HER, WE'D END UP EXPOSING *EVERYBODY.* DARLA, SMITH AND GRIZ, RAZ--
AND *CASSIE.*

KNOCK KNOCK

LIVE FROM THE TRIAL OF SCOTT LANG, ALSO KNOWN AS ANT-MAN, WHERE OPENING ARGUMENTS ARE ABOUT TO BEGIN--

CASSIE?

YOU'RE SUPPOSED TO BE DOING HOMEWORK. WHAT ARE YOU--

OH, NO. TURN THAT OFF.

MOM, IT'S OKAY, I JUST--

THE HECK IT IS, YOUNG LADY. I DON'T WANT YOU PAYING ANY ATTENTION TO THAT TRIAL, YOU HEAR ME?

THAT MAN HAS HURT YOU ENOUGH--

BUT, MOM--

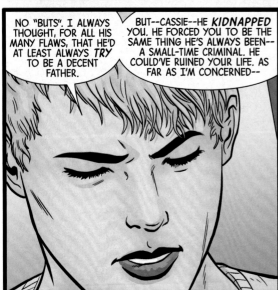

NO "BUTS". I ALWAYS THOUGHT, FOR ALL HIS MANY FLAWS, THAT HE'D AT LEAST ALWAYS TRY TO BE A DECENT FATHER.

BUT--CASSIE--HE KIDNAPPED YOU. HE FORCED YOU TO BE THE SAME THING HE'S ALWAYS BEEN-- A SMALL-TIME CRIMINAL. HE COULD'VE RUINED YOUR LIFE. AS FAR AS I'M CONCERNED--

--PRISON IS TOO GOOD FOR HIM.

DON'T SAY THAT...

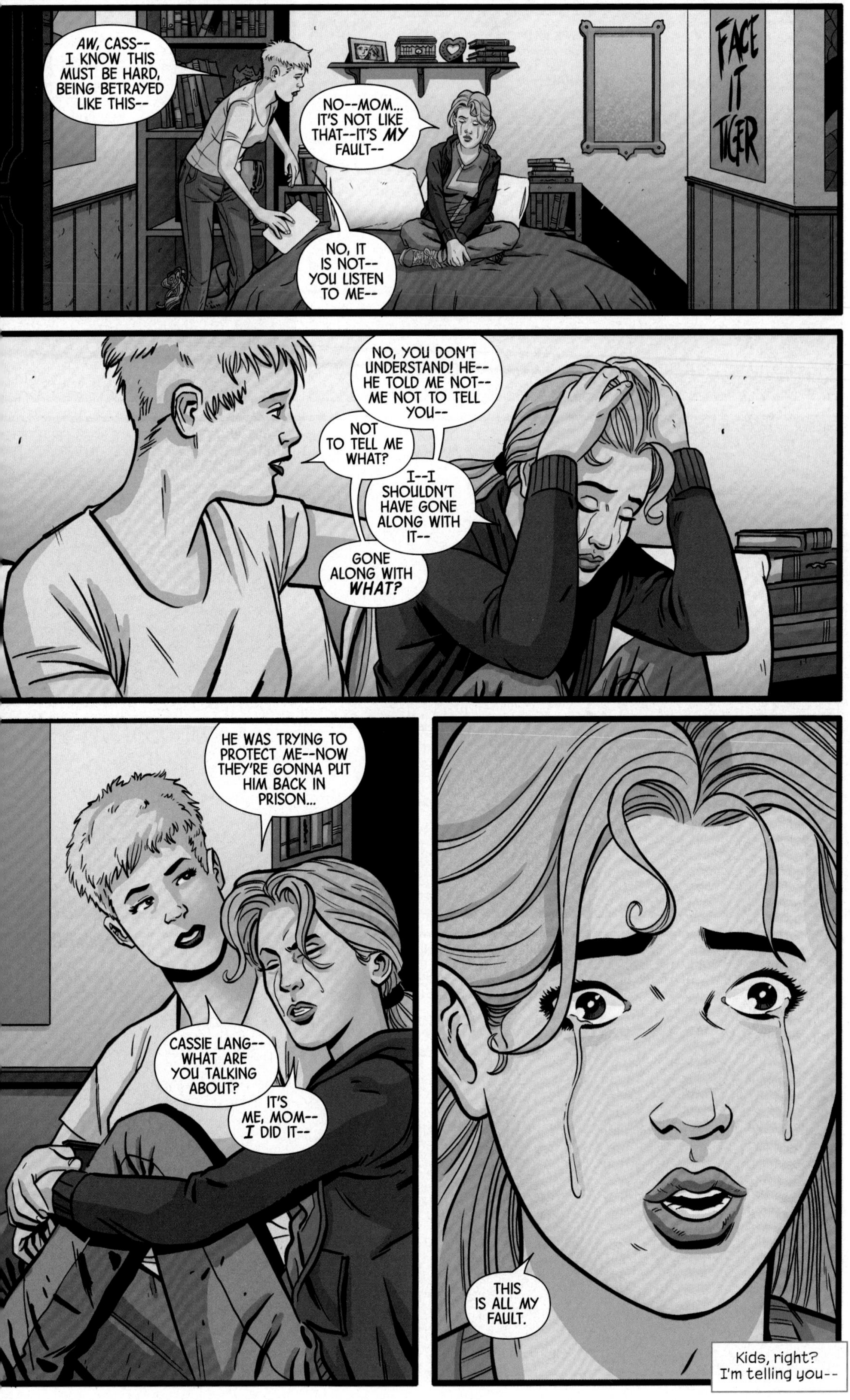
AW, CASS-- I KNOW THIS MUST BE HARD, BEING BETRAYED LIKE THIS--
NO--MOM... IT'S NOT LIKE THAT--IT'S *MY* FAULT--
NO, IT IS NOT-- YOU LISTEN TO ME--
FACE IT TIGER
NO, YOU DON'T UNDERSTAND! HE-- HE TOLD ME NOT-- ME NOT TO TELL YOU--
NOT TO TELL ME WHAT?
I--I SHOULDN'T HAVE GONE ALONG WITH IT--
GONE ALONG WITH ***WHAT?***
HE WAS TRYING TO PROTECT ME--NOW THEY'RE GONNA PUT HIM BACK IN PRISON...
CASSIE LANG-- WHAT ARE YOU TALKING ABOUT?
IT'S ME, MOM-- *I* DID IT--
THIS IS ALL MY FAULT.
Kids, right? I'm telling you--

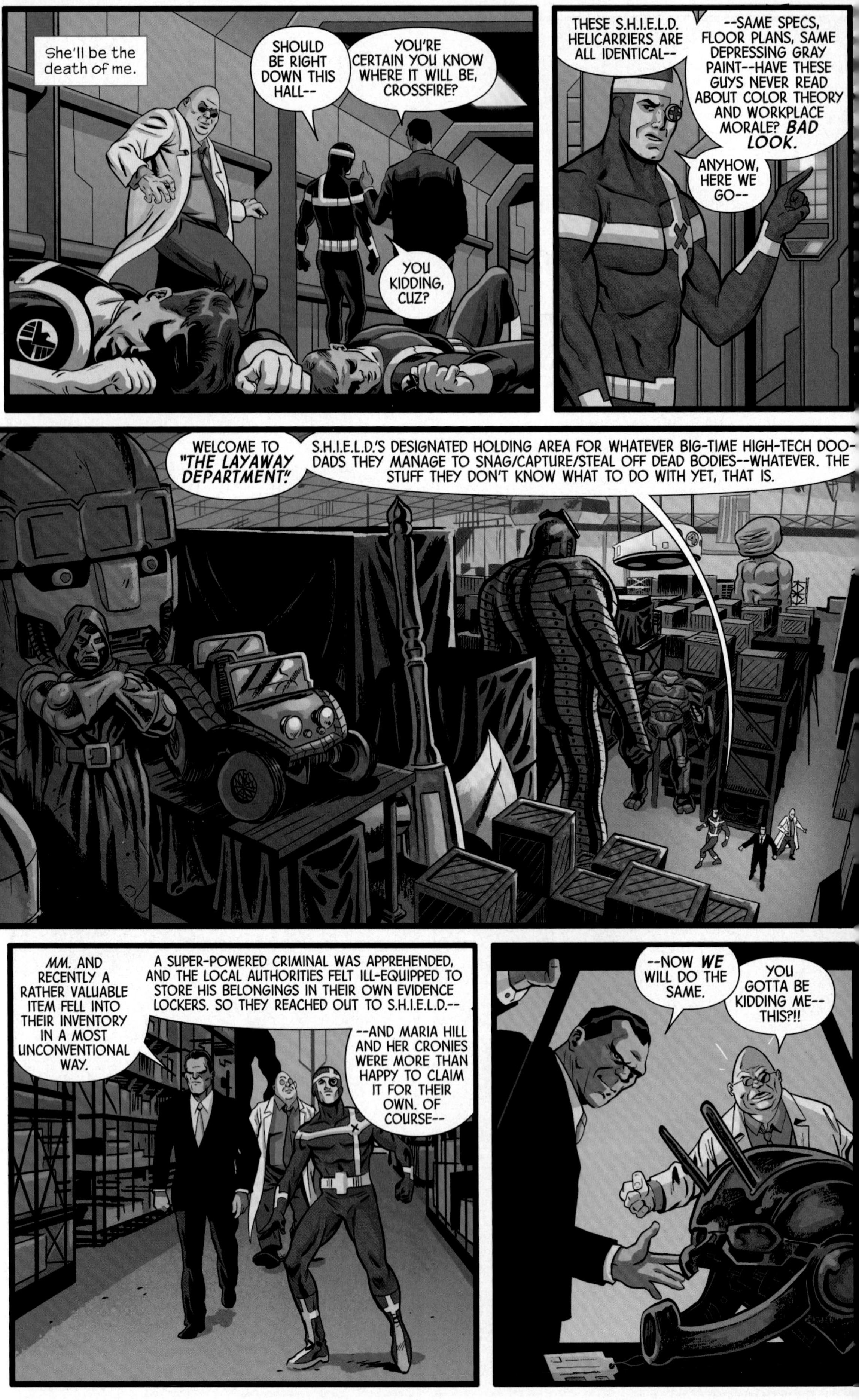
She'll be the death of me.
SHOULD BE RIGHT DOWN THIS HALL--
YOU'RE CERTAIN YOU KNOW WHERE IT WILL BE, CROSSFIRE?
YOU KIDDING, CUZ?
THESE S.H.I.E.L.D. HELICARRIERS ARE ALL IDENTICAL--
--SAME SPECS, FLOOR PLANS, SAME DEPRESSING GRAY PAINT--HAVE THESE GUYS NEVER READ ABOUT COLOR THEORY AND WORKPLACE MORALE? BAD LOOK.
ANYHOW, HERE WE GO--
WELCOME TO "THE LAYAWAY DEPARTMENT."
S.H.I.E.L.D.'S DESIGNATED HOLDING AREA FOR WHATEVER BIG-TIME HIGH-TECH DOODADS THEY MANAGE TO SNAG/CAPTURE/STEAL OFF DEAD BODIES--WHATEVER. THE STUFF THEY DON'T KNOW WHAT TO DO WITH YET, THAT IS.
MM. AND RECENTLY A RATHER VALUABLE ITEM FELL INTO THEIR INVENTORY IN A MOST UNCONVENTIONAL WAY.
A SUPER-POWERED CRIMINAL WAS APPREHENDED, AND THE LOCAL AUTHORITIES FELT ILL-EQUIPPED TO STORE HIS BELONGINGS IN THEIR OWN EVIDENCE LOCKERS. SO THEY REACHED OUT TO S.H.I.E.L.D.--
--AND MARIA HILL AND HER CRONIES WERE MORE THAN HAPPY TO CLAIM IT FOR THEIR OWN. OF COURSE--
--NOW WE WILL DO THE SAME.
YOU GOTTA BE KIDDING ME--THIS?!!

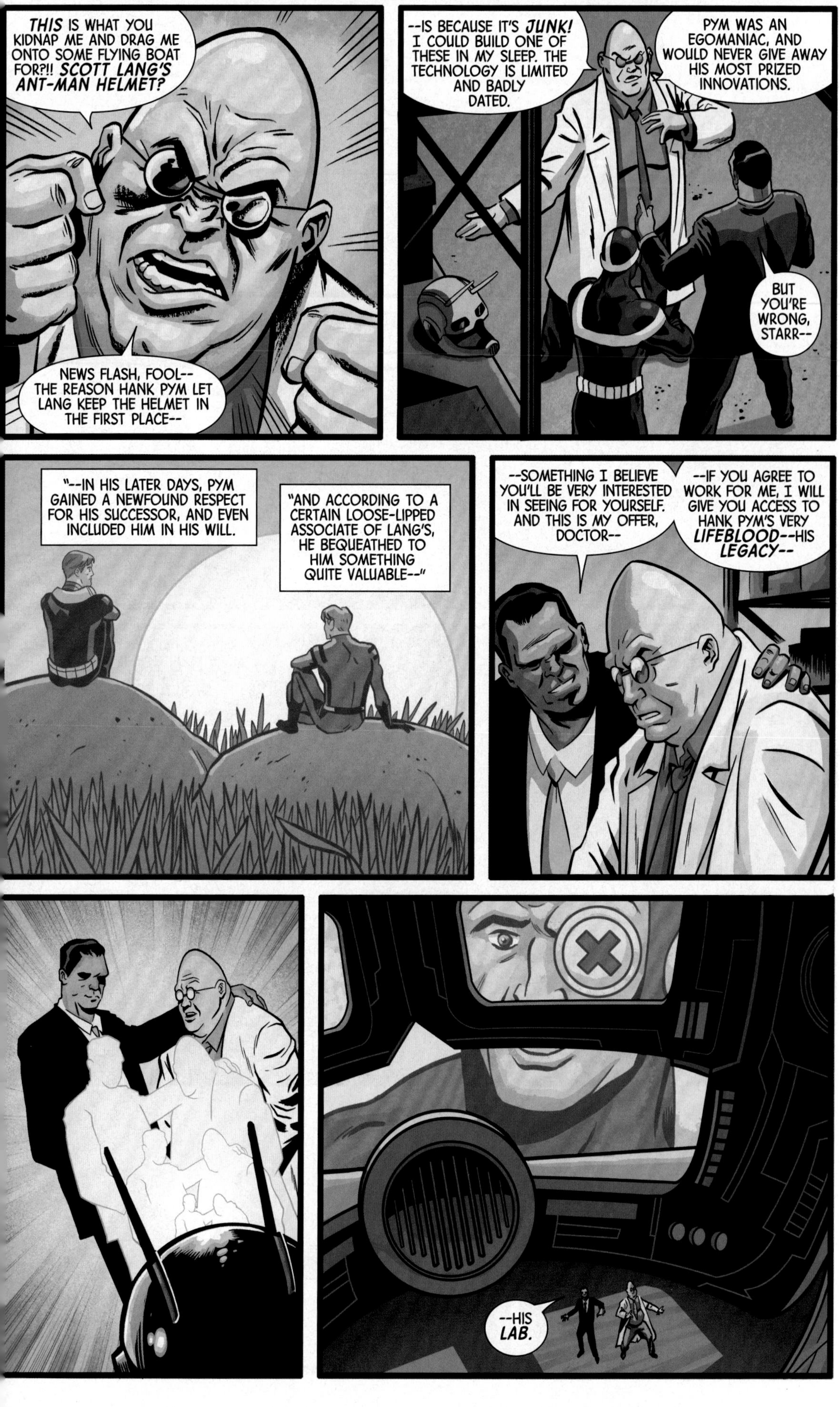
THIS IS WHAT YOU KIDNAP ME AND DRAG ME ONTO SOME FLYING BOAT FOR?!! SCOTT LANG'S ANT-MAN HELMET?
NEWS FLASH, FOOL-- THE REASON HANK PYM LET LANG KEEP THE HELMET IN THE FIRST PLACE--
--IS BECAUSE IT'S JUNK! I COULD BUILD ONE OF THESE IN MY SLEEP. THE TECHNOLOGY IS LIMITED AND BADLY DATED.
PYM WAS AN EGOMANIAC, AND WOULD NEVER GIVE AWAY HIS MOST PRIZED INNOVATIONS.
BUT YOU'RE WRONG, STARR--
"--IN HIS LATER DAYS, PYM GAINED A NEWFOUND RESPECT FOR HIS SUCCESSOR, AND EVEN INCLUDED HIM IN HIS WILL.
"AND ACCORDING TO A CERTAIN LOOSE-LIPPED ASSOCIATE OF LANG'S, HE BEQUEATHED TO HIM SOMETHING QUITE VALUABLE--"
--SOMETHING I BELIEVE YOU'LL BE VERY INTERESTED IN SEEING FOR YOURSELF. AND THIS IS MY OFFER, DOCTOR--
--IF YOU AGREE TO WORK FOR ME, I WILL GIVE YOU ACCESS TO HANK PYM'S VERY LIFEBLOOD--HIS LEGACY--
--HIS LAB.

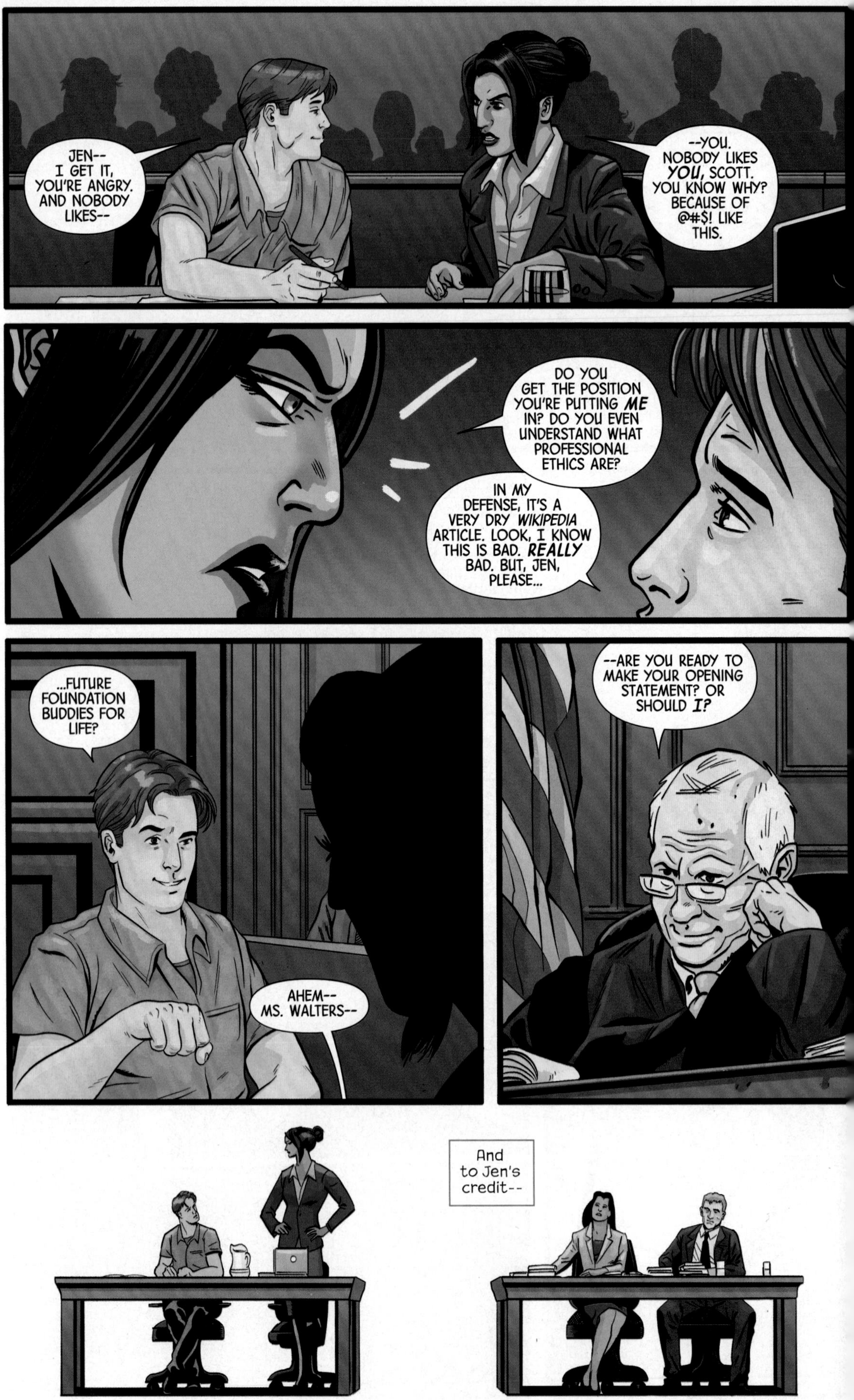
JEN-- I GET IT, YOU'RE ANGRY. AND NOBODY LIKES--
--YOU. NOBODY LIKES YOU, SCOTT. YOU KNOW WHY? BECAUSE OF @#$! LIKE THIS.
DO YOU GET THE POSITION YOU'RE PUTTING ME IN? DO YOU EVEN UNDERSTAND WHAT PROFESSIONAL ETHICS ARE?
IN MY DEFENSE, IT'S A VERY DRY WIKIPEDIA ARTICLE. LOOK, I KNOW THIS IS BAD. REALLY BAD. BUT, JEN, PLEASE...
...FUTURE FOUNDATION BUDDIES FOR LIFE?
AHEM-- MS. WALTERS--
--ARE YOU READY TO MAKE YOUR OPENING STATEMENT? OR SHOULD I?
And to Jen's credit--

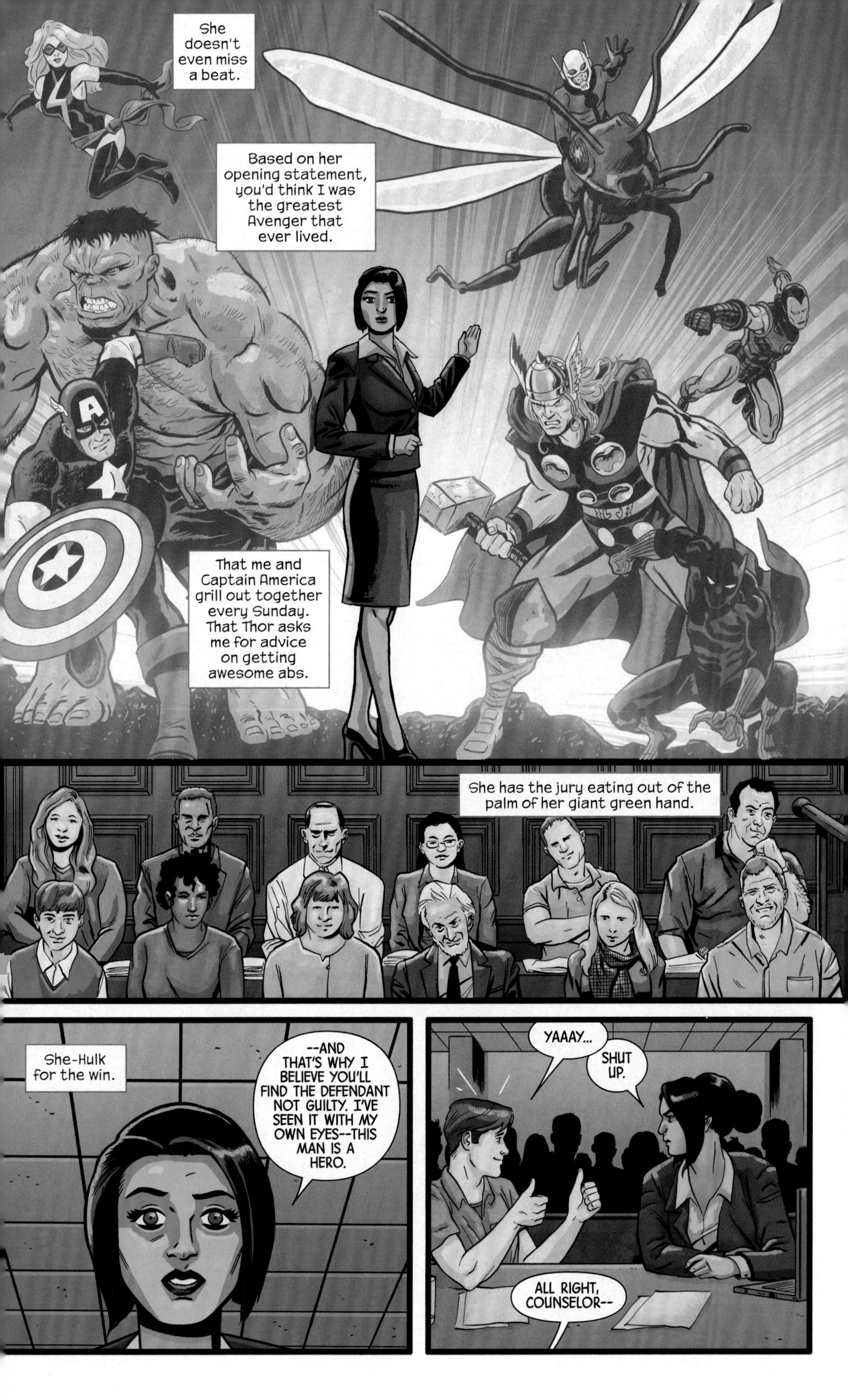
She doesn't even miss a beat.
Based on her opening statement, you'd think I was the greatest Avenger that ever lived.
That me and Captain America grill out together every Sunday. That Thor asks me for advice on getting awesome abs.
She has the jury eating out of the palm of her giant green hand.
She-Hulk for the win.
--AND THAT'S WHY I BELIEVE YOU'LL FIND THE DEFENDANT NOT GUILTY. I'VE SEEN IT WITH MY OWN EYES--THIS MAN IS A HERO.
YAAAY...
SHUT UP.
ALL RIGHT, COUNSELOR--

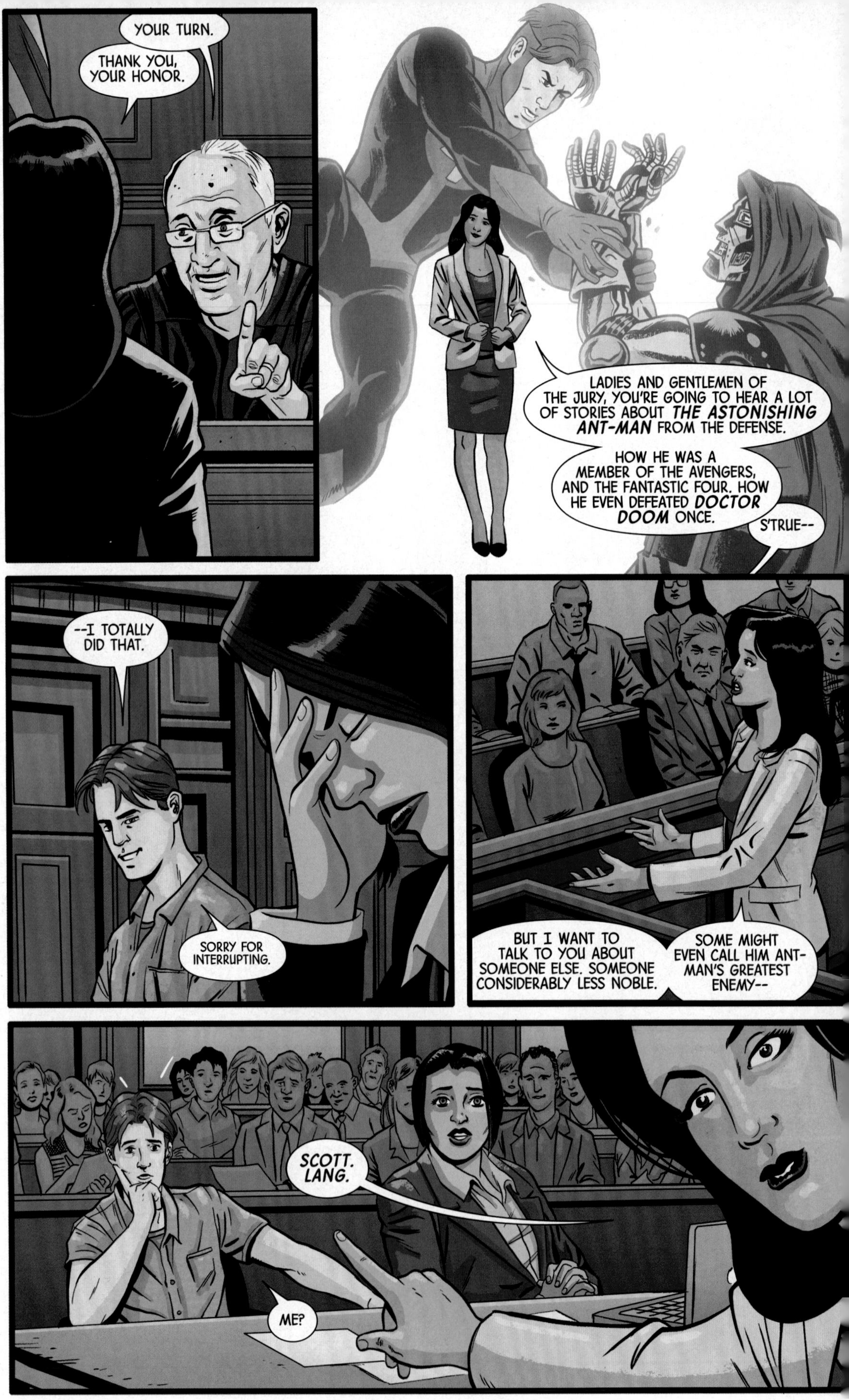
YOUR TURN.
THANK YOU, YOUR HONOR.
LADIES AND GENTLEMEN OF THE JURY, YOU'RE GOING TO HEAR A LOT OF STORIES ABOUT *THE ASTONISHING ANT-MAN* FROM THE DEFENSE.
HOW HE WAS A MEMBER OF THE AVENGERS, AND THE FANTASTIC FOUR. HOW HE EVEN DEFEATED *DOCTOR DOOM* ONCE.
S'TRUE--
--I TOTALLY DID THAT.
SORRY FOR INTERRUPTING.
BUT I WANT TO TALK TO YOU ABOUT SOMEONE ELSE. SOMEONE CONSIDERABLY LESS NOBLE.
SOME MIGHT EVEN CALL HIM ANT-MAN'S GREATEST ENEMY--
SCOTT. LANG.
ME?

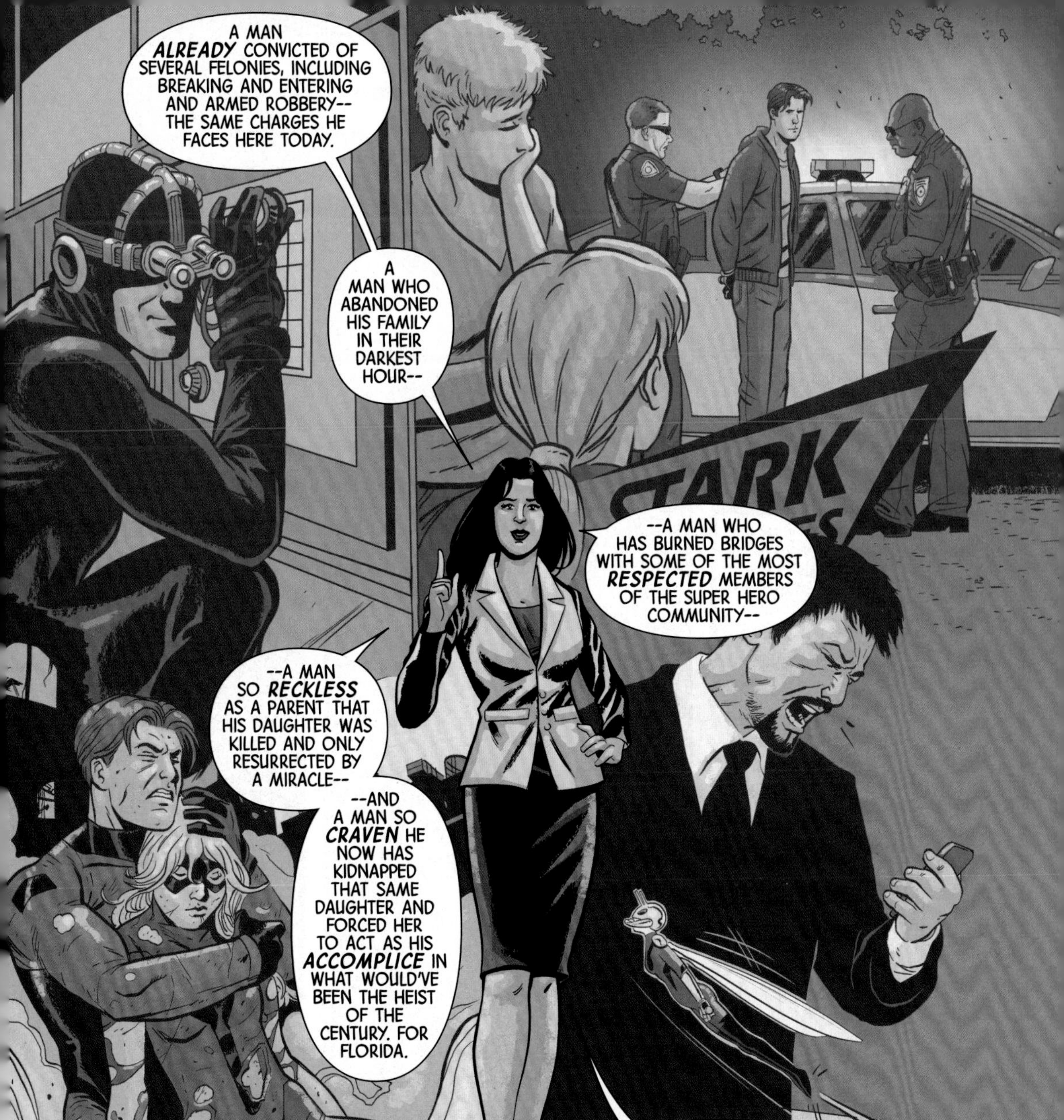
A MAN *ALREADY* CONVICTED OF SEVERAL FELONIES, INCLUDING BREAKING AND ENTERING AND ARMED ROBBERY-- THE SAME CHARGES HE FACES HERE TODAY.
A MAN WHO ABANDONED HIS FAMILY IN THEIR DARKEST HOUR--
--A MAN WHO HAS BURNED BRIDGES WITH SOME OF THE MOST *RESPECTED* MEMBERS OF THE SUPER HERO COMMUNITY--
--A MAN SO *RECKLESS* AS A PARENT THAT HIS DAUGHTER WAS KILLED AND ONLY RESURRECTED BY A MIRACLE--
--AND A MAN SO *CRAVEN* HE NOW HAS KIDNAPPED THAT SAME DAUGHTER AND FORCED HER TO ACT AS HIS *ACCOMPLICE* IN WHAT WOULD'VE BEEN THE HEIST OF THE CENTURY. FOR FLORIDA.
NOT ONLY THAT, BUT I AM ALSO GOING TO SHOW YOU IN PAINSTAKING DETAIL EXACTLY HOW HE CARRIED OUT THIS CRIME, BEYOND **ANY** REASONABLE DOUBT.

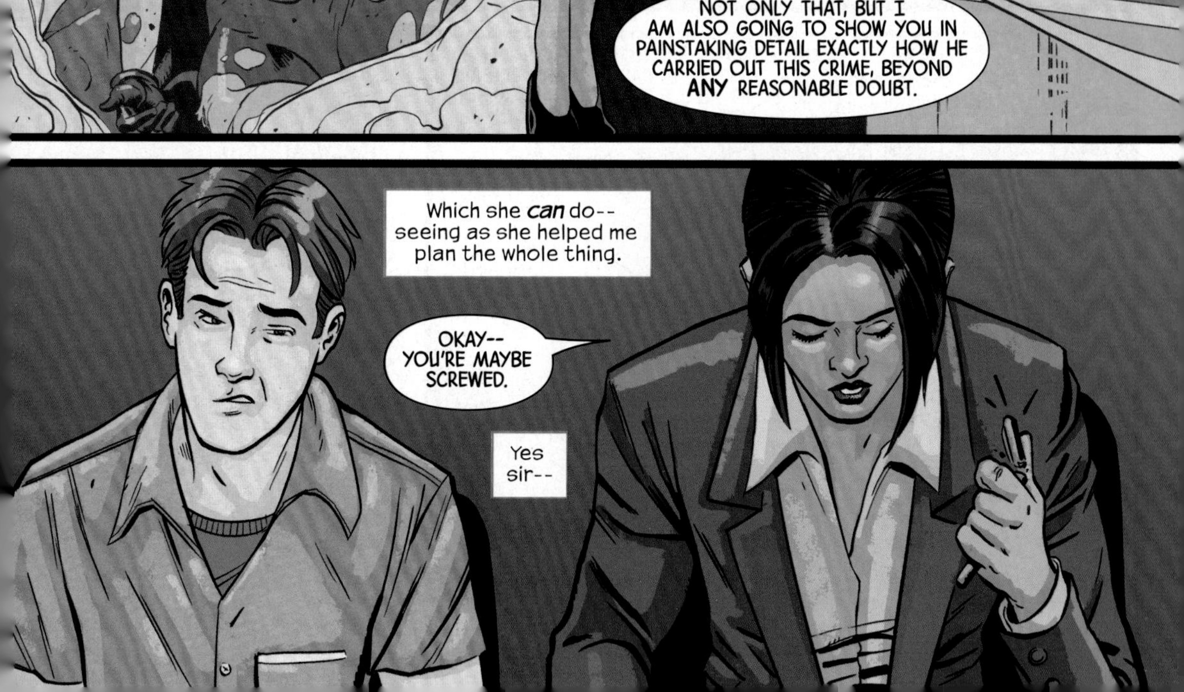
Which she *can* do-- seeing as she helped me plan the whole thing.
OKAY-- YOU'RE MAYBE SCREWED.
Yes sir--

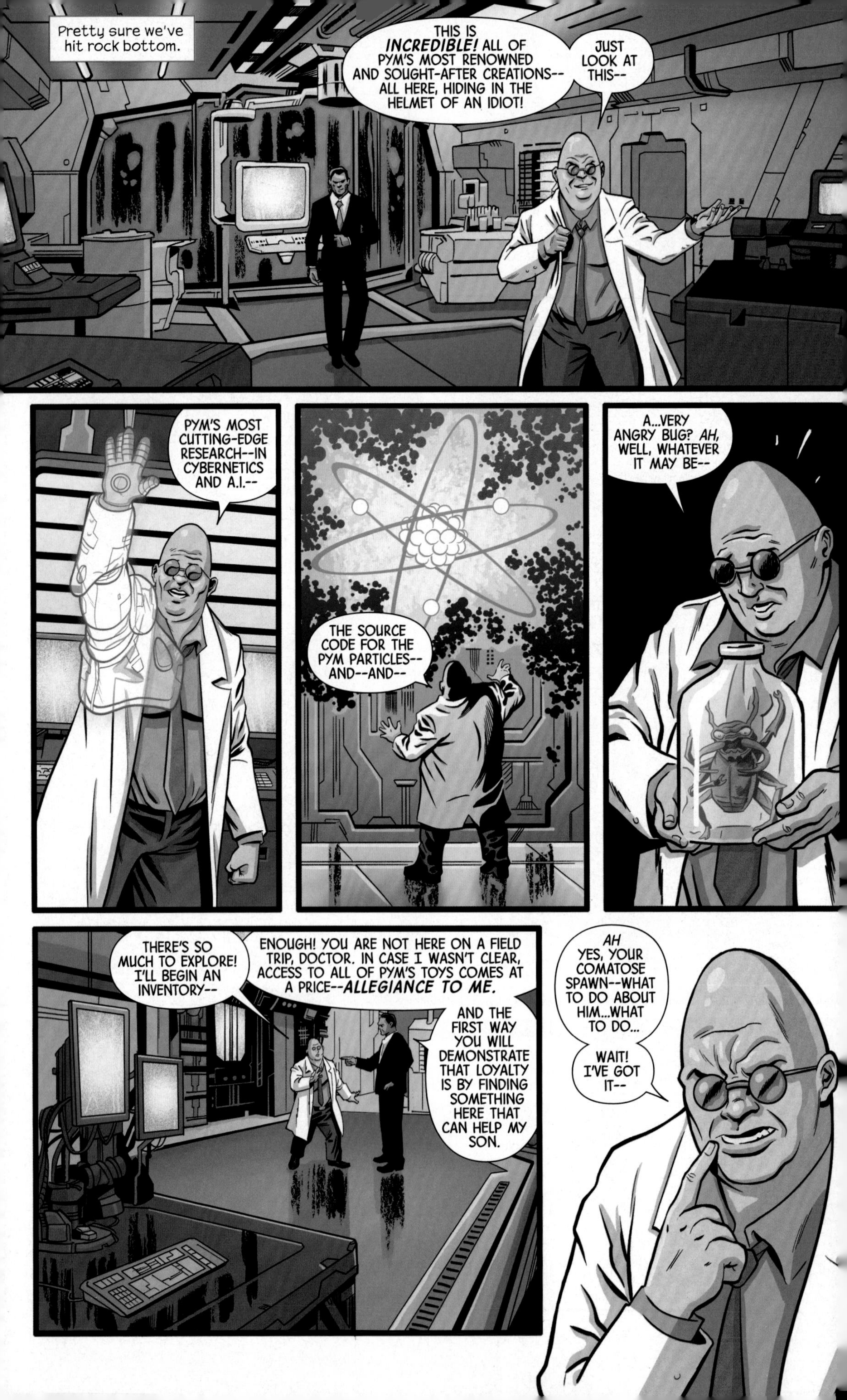

Pretty sure we've hit rock bottom.
THIS IS INCREDIBLE! ALL OF PYM'S MOST RENOWNED AND SOUGHT-AFTER CREATIONS-- ALL HERE, HIDING IN THE HELMET OF AN IDIOT!
JUST LOOK AT THIS--
PYM'S MOST CUTTING-EDGE RESEARCH--IN CYBERNETICS AND A.I.--
THE SOURCE CODE FOR THE PYM PARTICLES-- AND--AND--
A...VERY ANGRY BUG? AH, WELL, WHATEVER IT MAY BE--
THERE'S SO MUCH TO EXPLORE! I'LL BEGIN AN INVENTORY--
ENOUGH! YOU ARE NOT HERE ON A FIELD TRIP, DOCTOR. IN CASE I WASN'T CLEAR, ACCESS TO ALL OF PYM'S TOYS COMES AT A PRICE--ALLEGIANCE TO ME.
AND THE FIRST WAY YOU WILL DEMONSTRATE THAT LOYALTY IS BY FINDING SOMETHING HERE THAT CAN HELP MY SON.
AH YES, YOUR COMATOSE SPAWN--WHAT TO DO ABOUT HIM...WHAT TO DO...
WAIT! I'VE GOT IT--

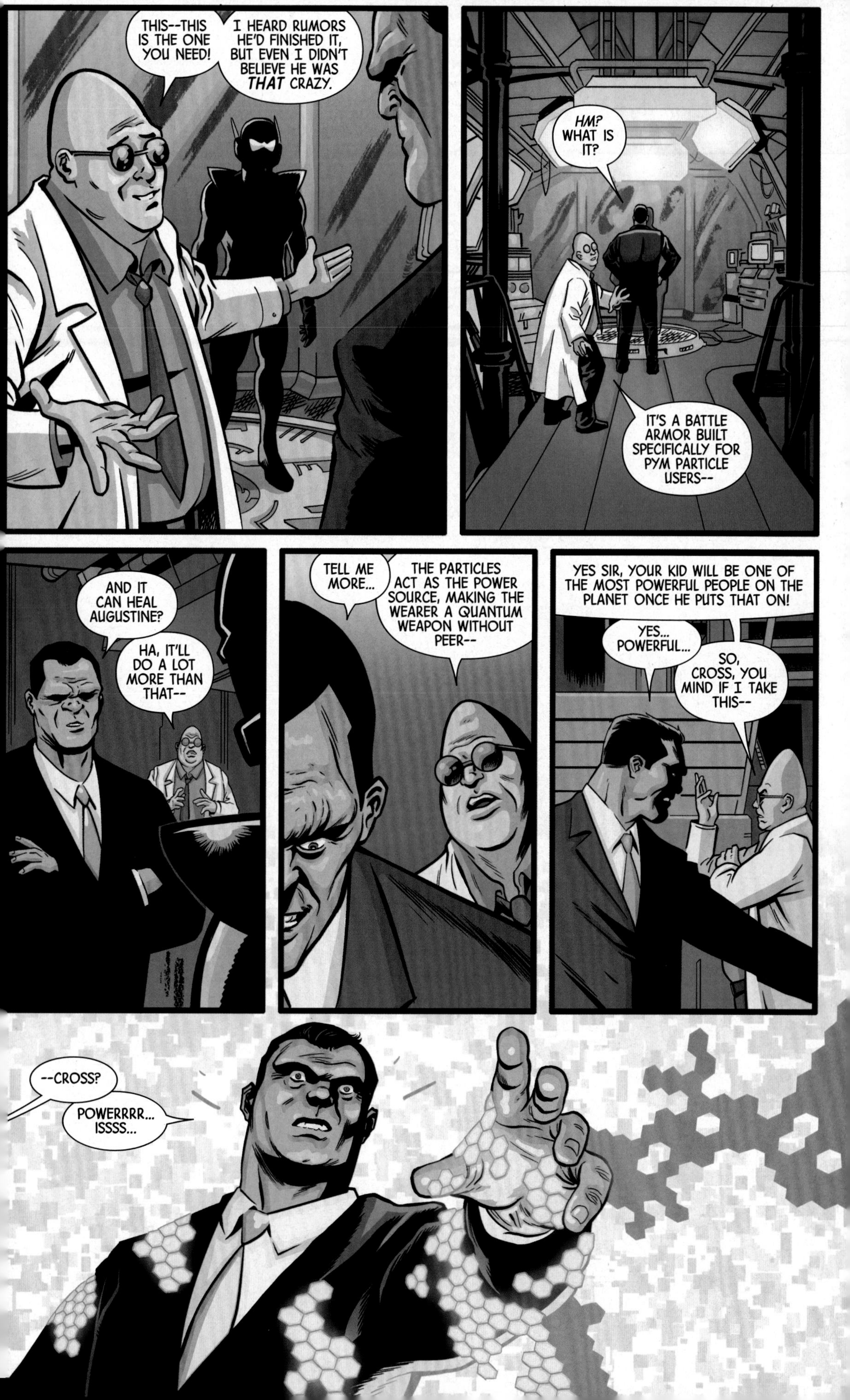
THIS--THIS IS THE ONE YOU NEED!
I HEARD RUMORS HE'D FINISHED IT, BUT EVEN I DIDN'T BELIEVE HE WAS *THAT* CRAZY.
HM? WHAT IS IT?
IT'S A BATTLE ARMOR BUILT SPECIFICALLY FOR PYM PARTICLE USERS--
AND IT CAN HEAL AUGUSTINE?
HA, IT'LL DO A LOT MORE THAN THAT--
TELL ME MORE...
THE PARTICLES ACT AS THE POWER SOURCE, MAKING THE WEARER A QUANTUM WEAPON WITHOUT PEER--
YES SIR, YOUR KID WILL BE ONE OF THE MOST POWERFUL PEOPLE ON THE PLANET ONCE HE PUTS THAT ON!
YES... POWERFUL...
SO, CROSS, YOU MIND IF I TAKE THIS--
--CROSS?
POWERRRR... ISSSS...

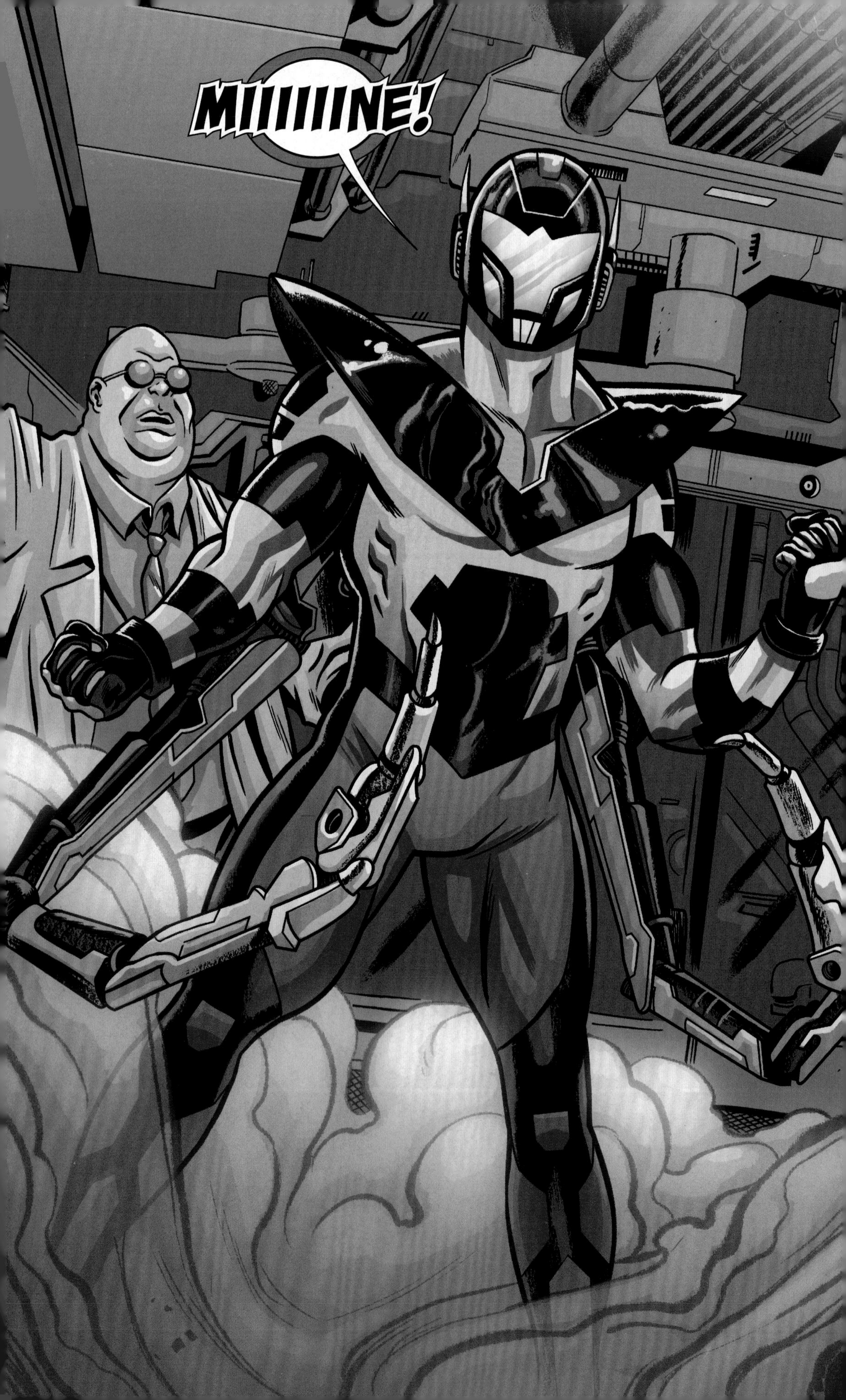
MIIIIIINE!

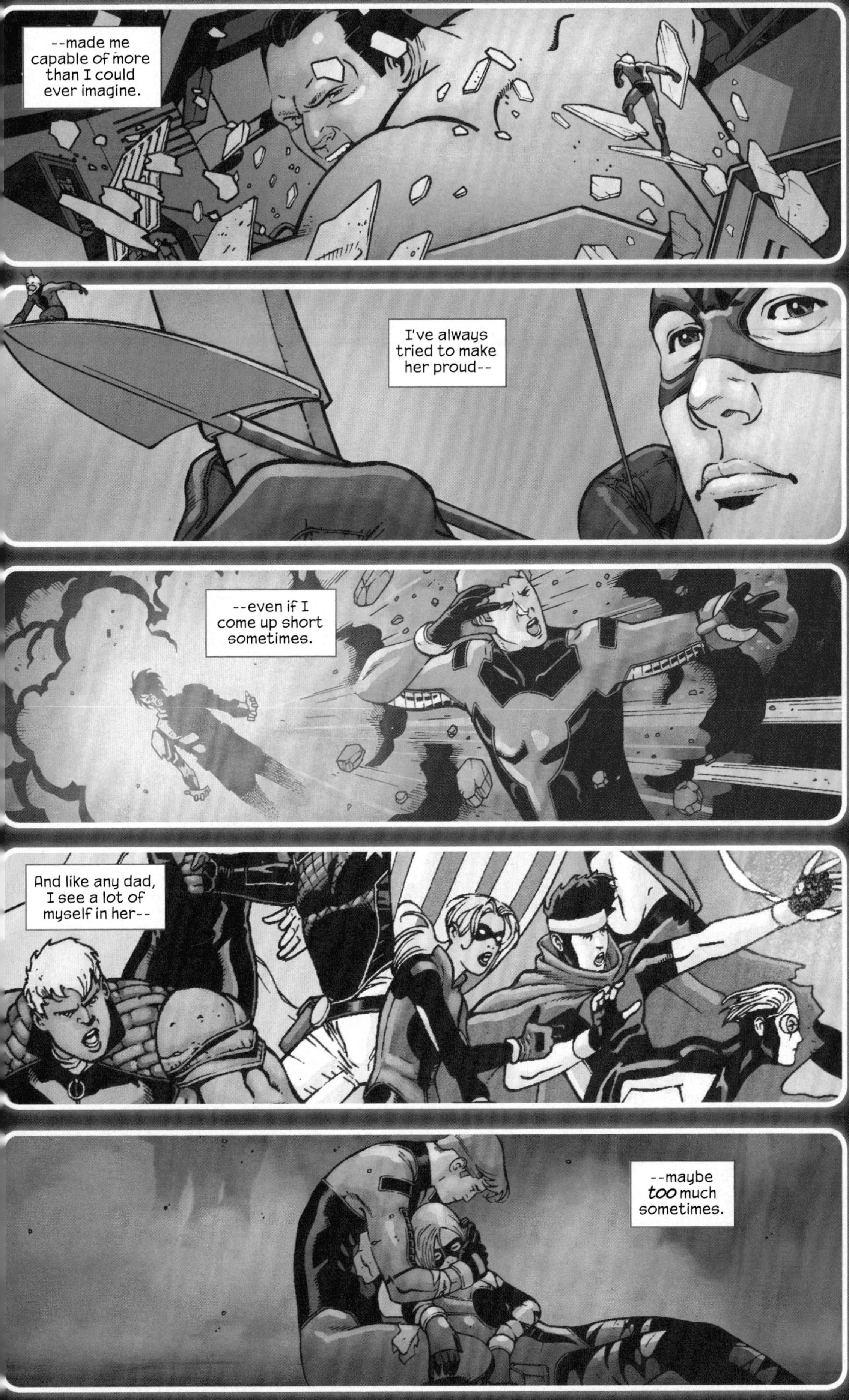
--made me capable of more than I could ever imagine.
I've always tried to make her proud--
--even if I come up short sometimes.
And like any dad, I see a lot of myself in her--
--maybe *too* much sometimes.

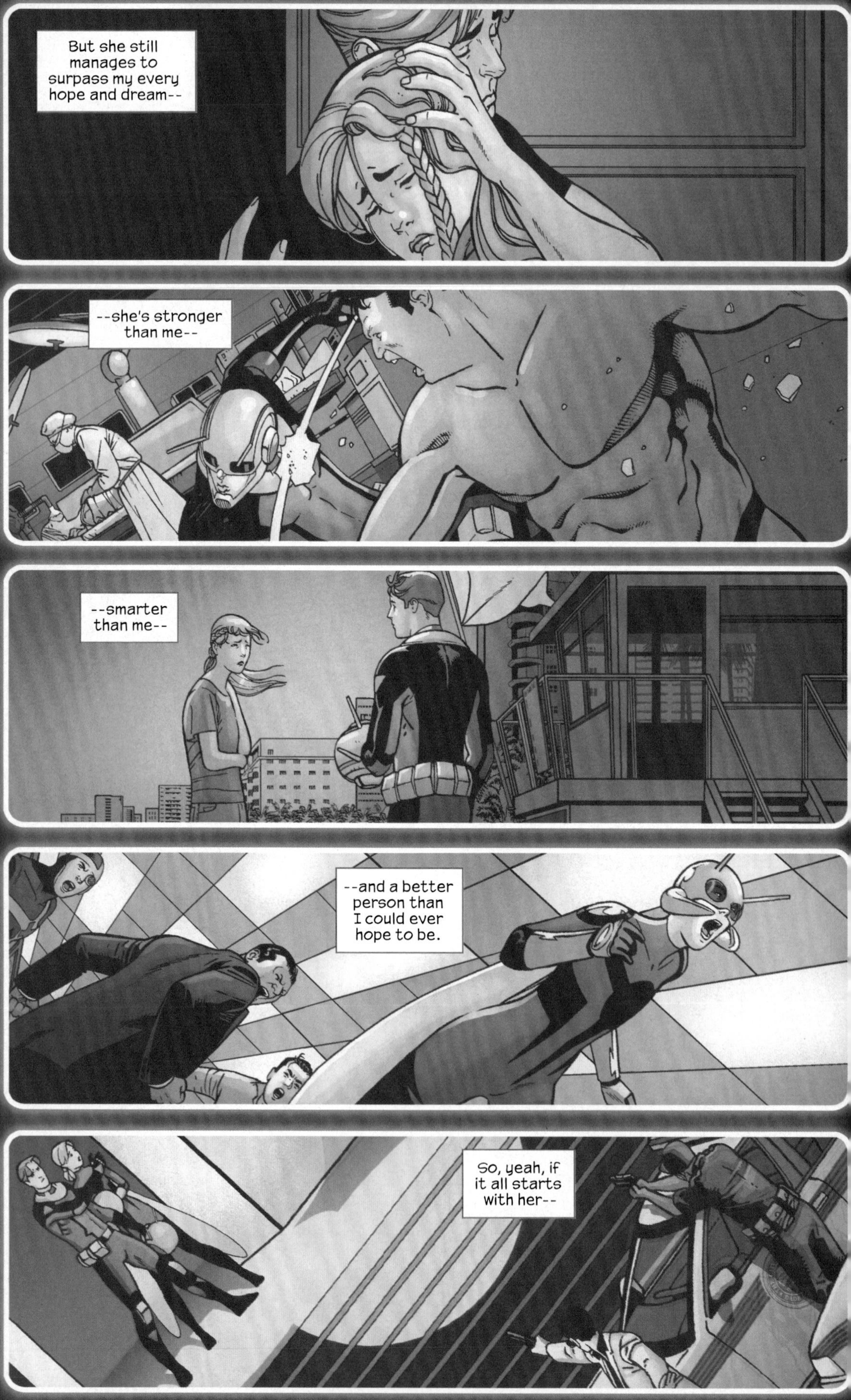
But she still manages to surpass my every hope and dream--
--she's stronger than me--
--smarter than me--
--and a better person than I could ever hope to be.
So, yeah, if it all starts with her--

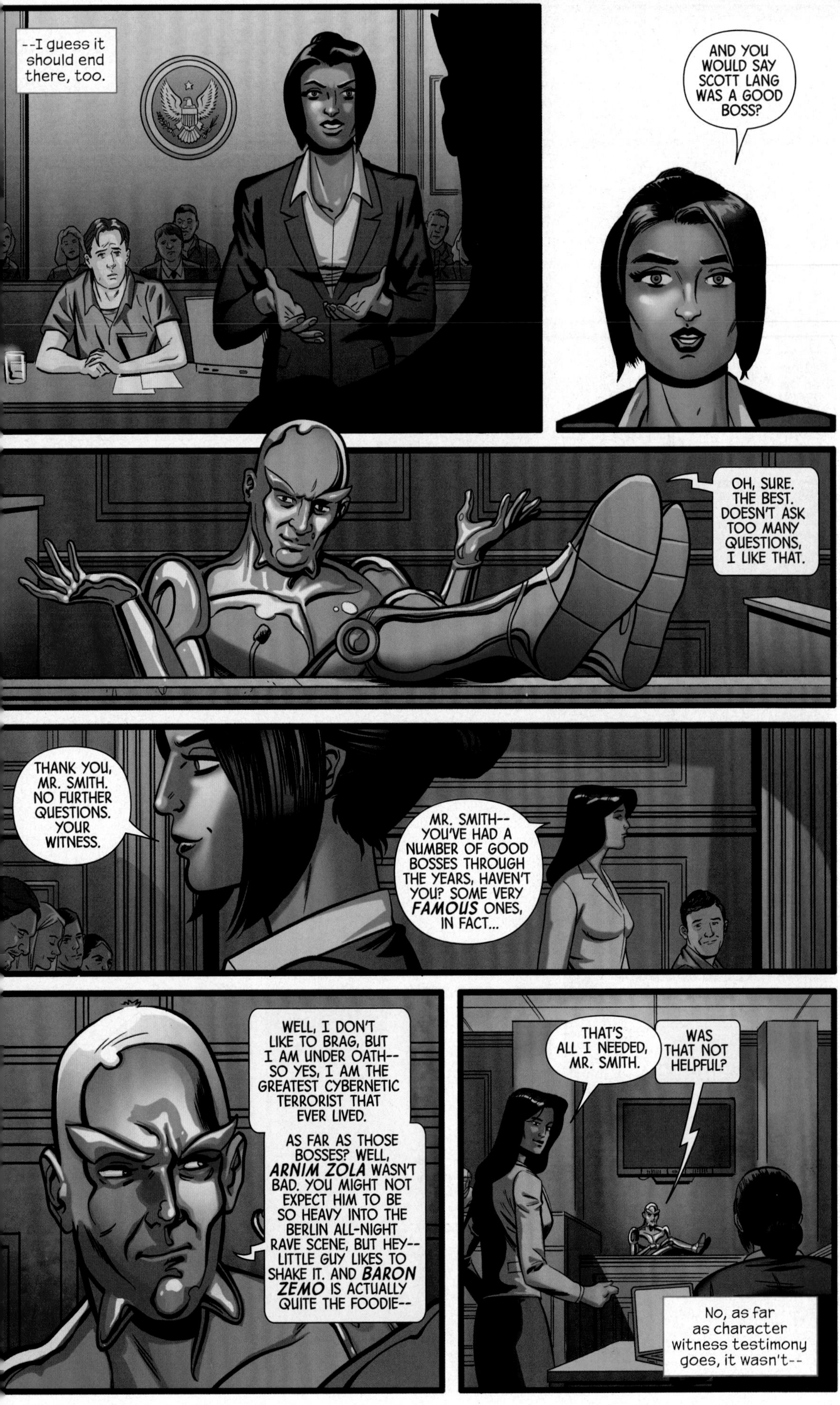
--I guess it should end there, too.
AND YOU WOULD SAY SCOTT LANG WAS A GOOD BOSS?
OH, SURE. THE BEST. DOESN'T ASK TOO MANY QUESTIONS, I LIKE THAT.
THANK YOU, MR. SMITH. NO FURTHER QUESTIONS. YOUR WITNESS.
MR. SMITH-- YOU'VE HAD A NUMBER OF GOOD BOSSES THROUGH THE YEARS, HAVEN'T YOU? SOME VERY FAMOUS ONES, IN FACT...
WELL, I DON'T LIKE TO BRAG, BUT I AM UNDER OATH-- SO YES, I AM THE GREATEST CYBERNETIC TERRORIST THAT EVER LIVED.
AS FAR AS THOSE BOSSES? WELL, ARNIM ZOLA WASN'T BAD. YOU MIGHT NOT EXPECT HIM TO BE SO HEAVY INTO THE BERLIN ALL-NIGHT RAVE SCENE, BUT HEY-- LITTLE GUY LIKES TO SHAKE IT. AND BARON ZEMO IS ACTUALLY QUITE THE FOODIE--
THAT'S ALL I NEEDED, MR. SMITH.
WAS THAT NOT HELPFUL?
No, as far as character witness testimony goes, it wasn't--

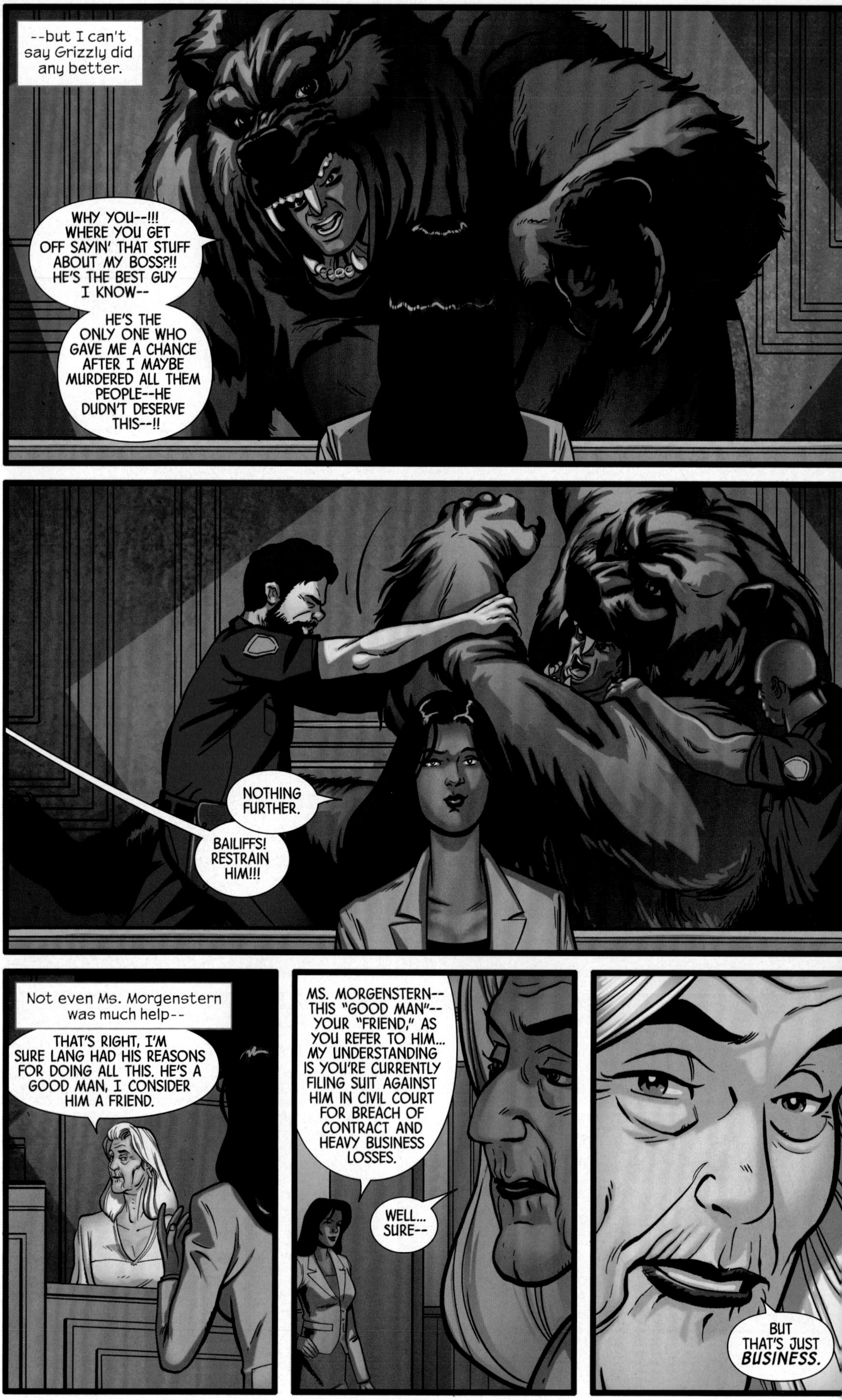
--but I can't say Grizzly did any better.
WHY YOU--!!! WHERE YOU GET OFF SAYIN' THAT STUFF ABOUT MY BOSS?!! HE'S THE BEST GUY I KNOW--
HE'S THE ONLY ONE WHO GAVE ME A CHANCE AFTER I MAYBE MURDERED ALL THEM PEOPLE--HE DIDN'T DESERVE THIS--!!
NOTHING FURTHER.
BAILIFFS! RESTRAIN HIM!!!
Not even Ms. Morgenstern was much help--
THAT'S RIGHT, I'M SURE LANG HAD HIS REASONS FOR DOING ALL THIS. HE'S A GOOD MAN, I CONSIDER HIM A FRIEND.
MS. MORGENSTERN--THIS "GOOD MAN"--YOUR "FRIEND," AS YOU REFER TO HIM... MY UNDERSTANDING IS YOU'RE CURRENTLY FILING SUIT AGAINST HIM IN CIVIL COURT FOR BREACH OF CONTRACT AND HEAVY BUSINESS LOSSES.
WELL... SURE--
BUT THAT'S JUST BUSINESS.

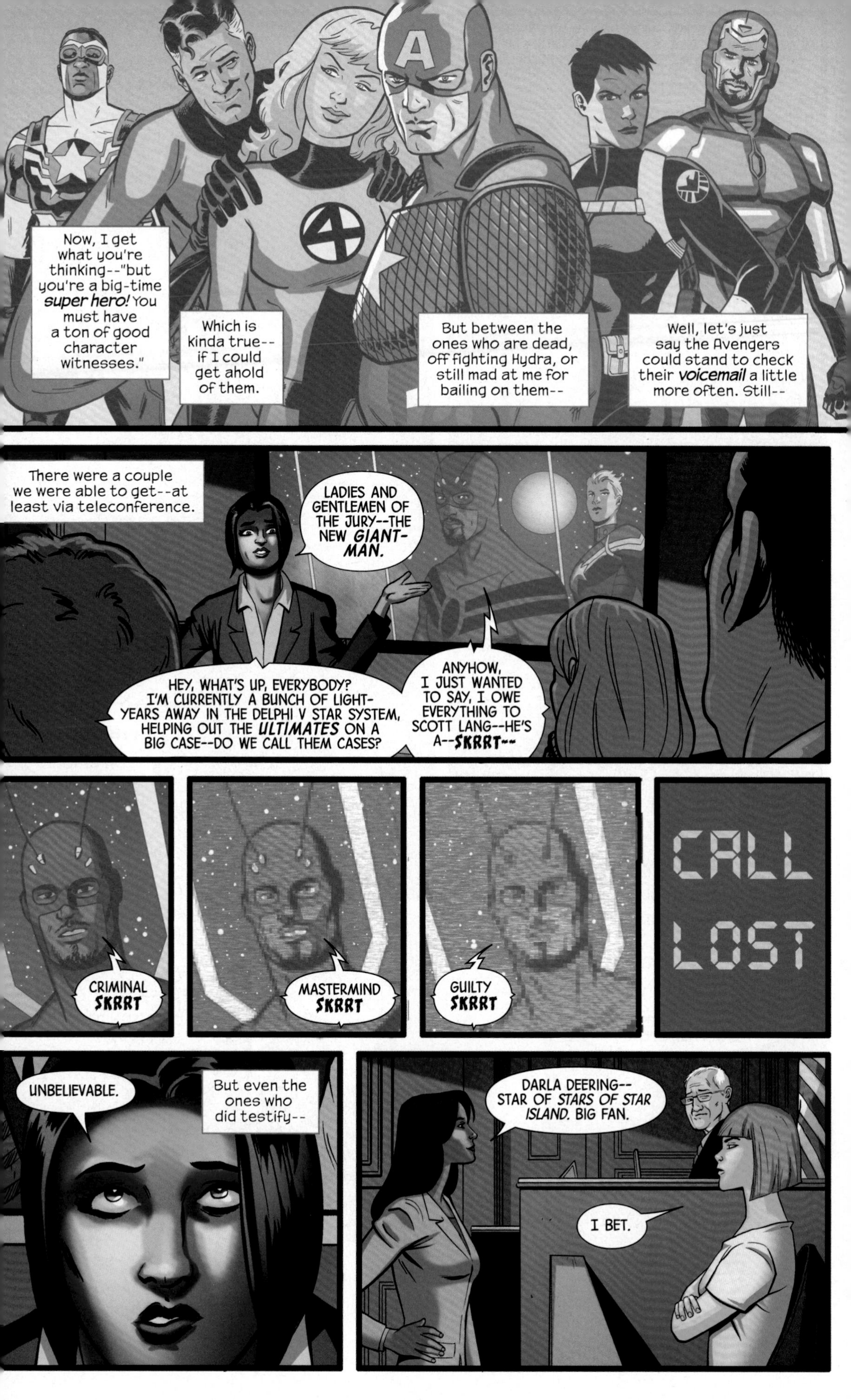

Now, I get what you're thinking--"but you're a big-time *super hero!* You must have a ton of good character witnesses."
Which is kinda true--if I could get ahold of them.
But between the ones who are dead, off fighting Hydra, or still mad at me for bailing on them--
Well, let's just say the Avengers could stand to check their *voicemail* a little more often. Still--
There were a couple we were able to get--at least via teleconference.
LADIES AND GENTLEMEN OF THE JURY--THE NEW *GIANT-MAN.*
HEY, WHAT'S UP, EVERYBODY? I'M CURRENTLY A BUNCH OF LIGHT-YEARS AWAY IN THE DELPHI V STAR SYSTEM, HELPING OUT THE *ULTIMATES* ON A BIG CASE--DO WE CALL THEM CASES?
ANYHOW, I JUST WANTED TO SAY, I OWE EVERYTHING TO SCOTT LANG--HE'S A--**SKRRT**--
CRIMINAL **SKRRT**
MASTERMIND **SKRRT**
GUILTY **SKRRT**
CALL LOST
UNBELIEVABLE.
But even the ones who did testify--
DARLA DEERING--STAR OF *STARS OF STAR ISLAND.* BIG FAN.
I BET.

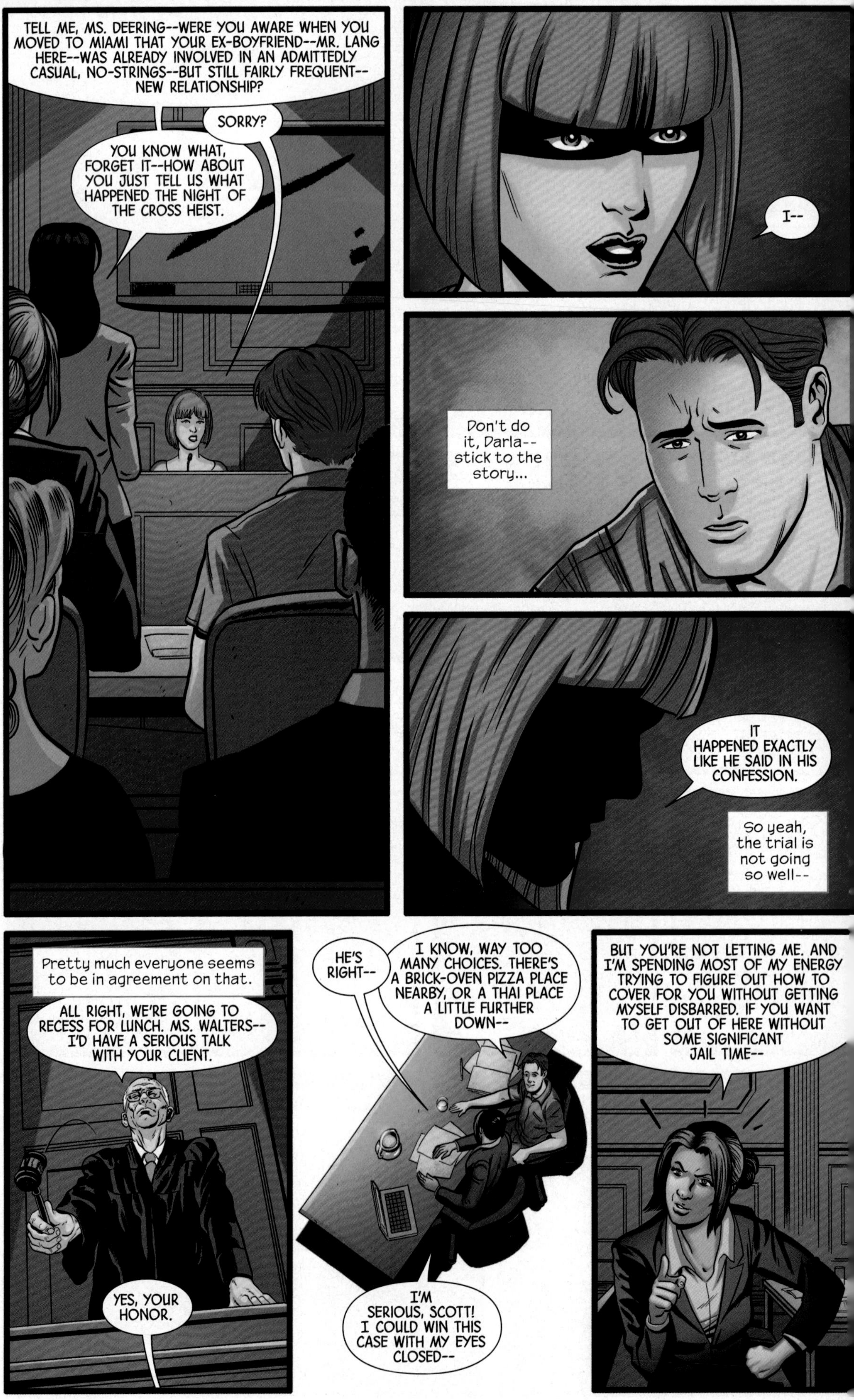

TELL ME, MS. DEERING--WERE YOU AWARE WHEN YOU MOVED TO MIAMI THAT YOUR EX-BOYFRIEND--MR. LANG HERE--WAS ALREADY INVOLVED IN AN ADMITTEDLY CASUAL, NO-STRINGS--BUT STILL FAIRLY FREQUENT--NEW RELATIONSHIP?
SORRY?
YOU KNOW WHAT, FORGET IT--HOW ABOUT YOU JUST TELL US WHAT HAPPENED THE NIGHT OF THE CROSS HEIST.
I--
Don't do it, Darla--stick to the story...
IT HAPPENED EXACTLY LIKE HE SAID IN HIS CONFESSION.
So yeah, the trial is not going so well--
Pretty much everyone seems to be in agreement on that.
ALL RIGHT, WE'RE GOING TO RECESS FOR LUNCH. MS. WALTERS--I'D HAVE A SERIOUS TALK WITH YOUR CLIENT.
YES, YOUR HONOR.
HE'S RIGHT--
I KNOW, WAY TOO MANY CHOICES. THERE'S A BRICK-OVEN PIZZA PLACE NEARBY, OR A THAI PLACE A LITTLE FURTHER DOWN--
I'M SERIOUS, SCOTT! I COULD WIN THIS CASE WITH MY EYES CLOSED--
BUT YOU'RE NOT LETTING ME. AND I'M SPENDING MOST OF MY ENERGY TRYING TO FIGURE OUT HOW TO COVER FOR YOU WITHOUT GETTING MYSELF DISBARRED. IF YOU WANT TO GET OUT OF HERE WITHOUT SOME SIGNIFICANT JAIL TIME--

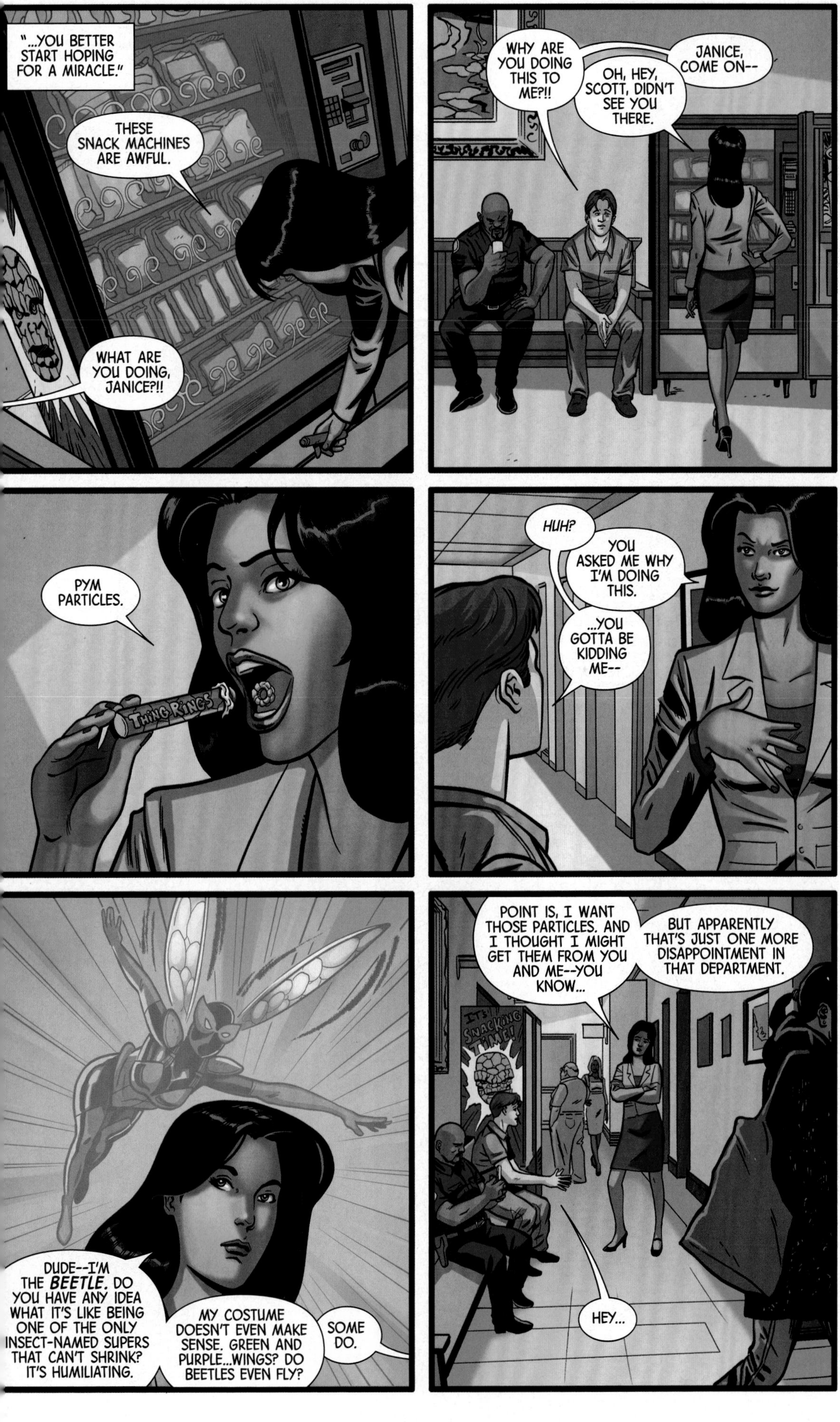
"...YOU BETTER START HOPING FOR A MIRACLE."
THESE SNACK MACHINES ARE AWFUL.
WHAT ARE YOU DOING, JANICE?!!
WHY ARE YOU DOING THIS TO ME?!!
JANICE, COME ON--
OH, HEY, SCOTT, DIDN'T SEE YOU THERE.
PYM PARTICLES.
THING RINGS
HUH?
YOU ASKED ME WHY I'M DOING THIS.
...YOU GOTTA BE KIDDING ME--
DUDE--I'M THE BEETLE. DO YOU HAVE ANY IDEA WHAT IT'S LIKE BEING ONE OF THE ONLY INSECT-NAMED SUPERS THAT CAN'T SHRINK? IT'S HUMILIATING.
MY COSTUME DOESN'T EVEN MAKE SENSE. GREEN AND PURPLE...WINGS? DO BEETLES EVEN FLY?
SOME DO.
POINT IS, I WANT THOSE PARTICLES. AND I THOUGHT I MIGHT GET THEM FROM YOU AND ME--YOU KNOW...
BUT APPARENTLY THAT'S JUST ONE MORE DISAPPOINTMENT IN THAT DEPARTMENT.
IT'S SNACKING TIME!
HEY...

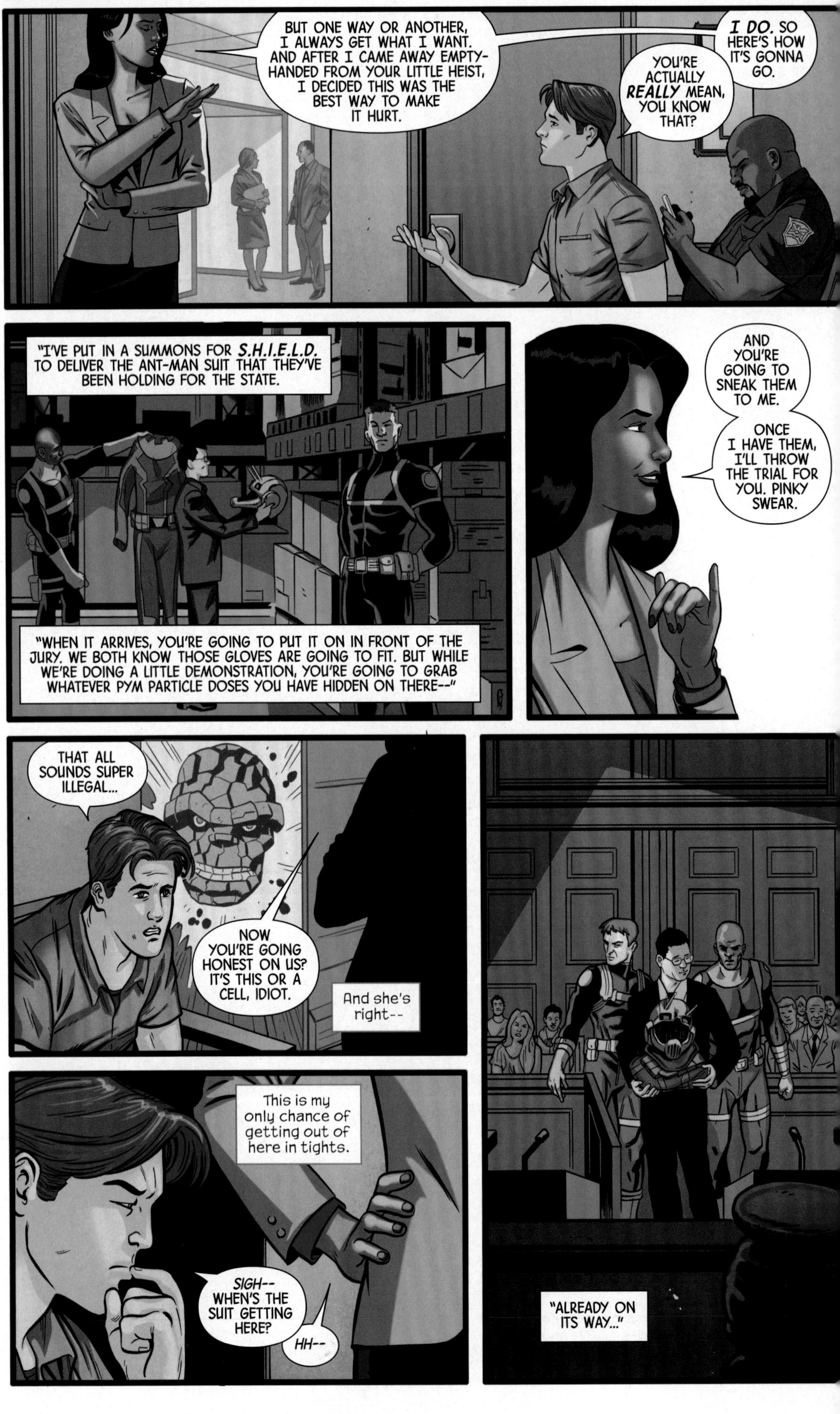

BUT ONE WAY OR ANOTHER, I ALWAYS GET WHAT I WANT. AND AFTER I CAME AWAY EMPTY-HANDED FROM YOUR LITTLE HEIST, I DECIDED THIS WAS THE BEST WAY TO MAKE IT HURT.
YOU'RE ACTUALLY REALLY MEAN, YOU KNOW THAT?
I DO. SO HERE'S HOW IT'S GONNA GO.
"I'VE PUT IN A SUMMONS FOR S.H.I.E.L.D. TO DELIVER THE ANT-MAN SUIT THAT THEY'VE BEEN HOLDING FOR THE STATE.
"WHEN IT ARRIVES, YOU'RE GOING TO PUT IT ON IN FRONT OF THE JURY. WE BOTH KNOW THOSE GLOVES ARE GOING TO FIT. BUT WHILE WE'RE DOING A LITTLE DEMONSTRATION, YOU'RE GOING TO GRAB WHATEVER PYM PARTICLE DOSES YOU HAVE HIDDEN ON THERE--"
AND YOU'RE GOING TO SNEAK THEM TO ME.
ONCE I HAVE THEM, I'LL THROW THE TRIAL FOR YOU. PINKY SWEAR.
THAT ALL SOUNDS SUPER ILLEGAL...
NOW YOU'RE GOING HONEST ON US? IT'S THIS OR A CELL, IDIOT.
And she's right--
This is my only chance of getting out of here in tights.
SIGH-- WHEN'S THE SUIT GETTING HERE?
HH--
"ALREADY ON ITS WAY..."

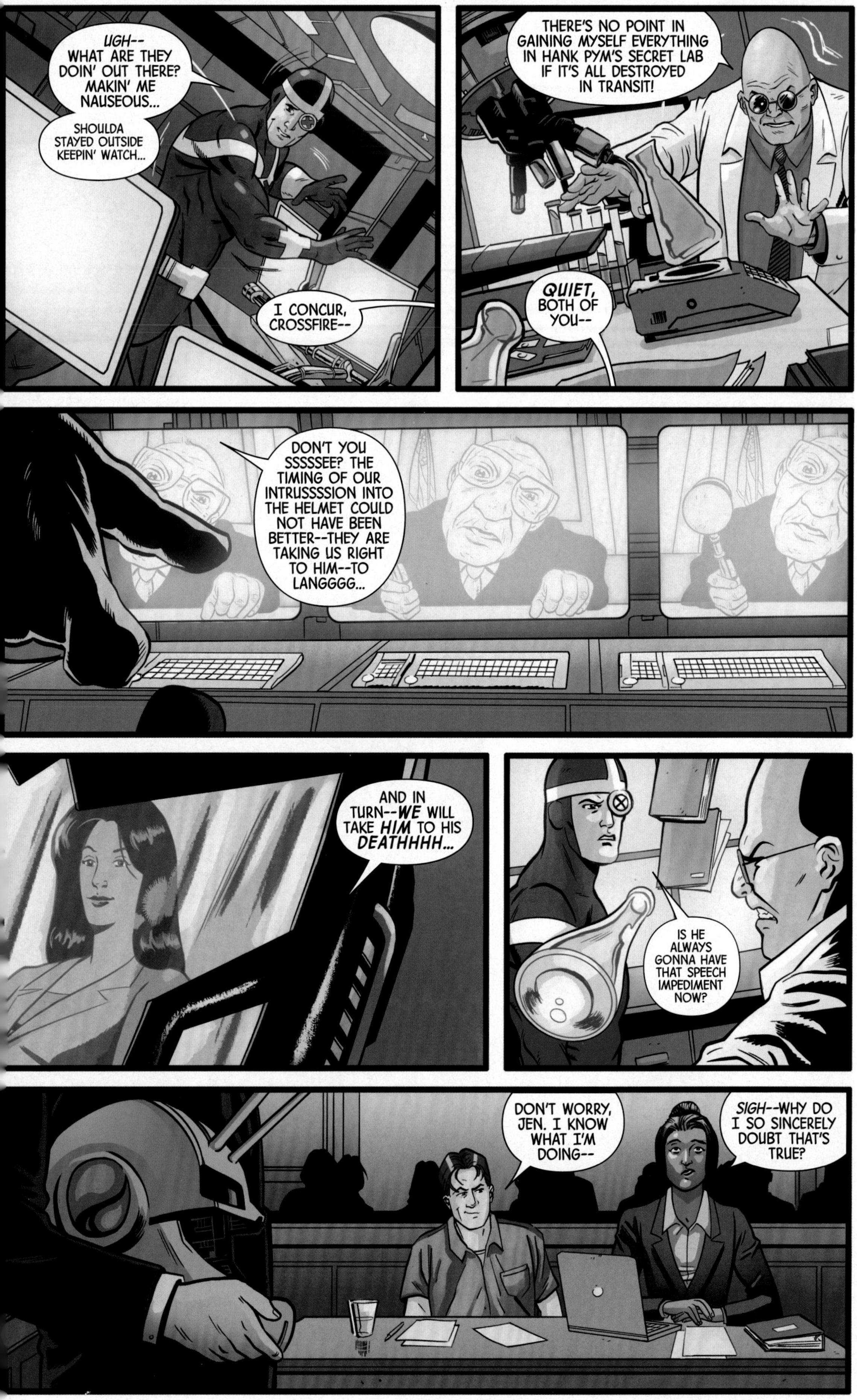
UGH--
WHAT ARE THEY DOIN' OUT THERE? MAKIN' ME NAUSEOUS...
SHOULDA STAYED OUTSIDE KEEPIN' WATCH...
I CONCUR, CROSSFIRE--
THERE'S NO POINT IN GAINING MYSELF EVERYTHING IN HANK PYM'S SECRET LAB IF IT'S ALL DESTROYED IN TRANSIT!
QUIET, BOTH OF YOU--
DON'T YOU SSSSSEE? THE TIMING OF OUR INTRUSSSSION INTO THE HELMET COULD NOT HAVE BEEN BETTER--THEY ARE TAKING US RIGHT TO HIM--TO LANGGGG...
AND IN TURN--WE WILL TAKE HIM TO HIS DEATHHHH...
IS HE ALWAYS GONNA HAVE THAT SPEECH IMPEDIMENT NOW?
DON'T WORRY, JEN. I KNOW WHAT I'M DOING--
SIGH--WHY DO I SO SINCERELY DOUBT THAT'S TRUE?

AND NOW, LADIES AND GENTLEMEN, WE ARE GOING TO WALK YOU THROUGH, STEP BY STEP, THE HEINOUS CRIME THAT WAS COMMITTED HERE--AT THE CROSS TECHNOLOGIES MIAMI CAMPUS.

TO DO SO, MR. LANG WILL BE ASKED TO DEMONSTRATE HOW HE SHRINKS DOWN IN SIZE. BUT I ASSURE YOU, THERE IS NOTHING TO FEAR--

--AS S.H.I.E.L.D.'S PYMBUSTER AGENTS ARE ON HAND IN CASE THE DEFENDANT TRIES TO ESCAPE OR RESORTS TO VIOLENCE.

SHALL WE, MR. LANG?

UH, SURE...

DON'T NORMALLY WEAR THIS MANY LAYERS, BUT--

STILL WORKS.

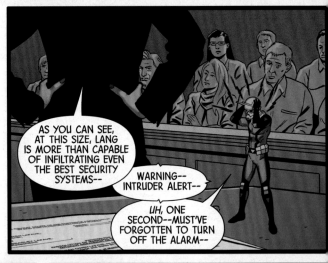

AS YOU CAN SEE, AT THIS SIZE, LANG IS MORE THAN CAPABLE OF INFILTRATING EVEN THE BEST SECURITY SYSTEMS--

WARNING-- INTRUDER ALERT--

UH, ONE SECOND--MUST'VE FORGOTTEN TO TURN OFF THE ALARM--

HELMET LAB COMPROMISED--

HOLD ON-- SOMETHING'S NOT RIGHT--

THAT'S GOOD-- DISTRACT THEM.

NO, REALLY--

EVERYBODY GET OUT OF THE COURTROOM!!!

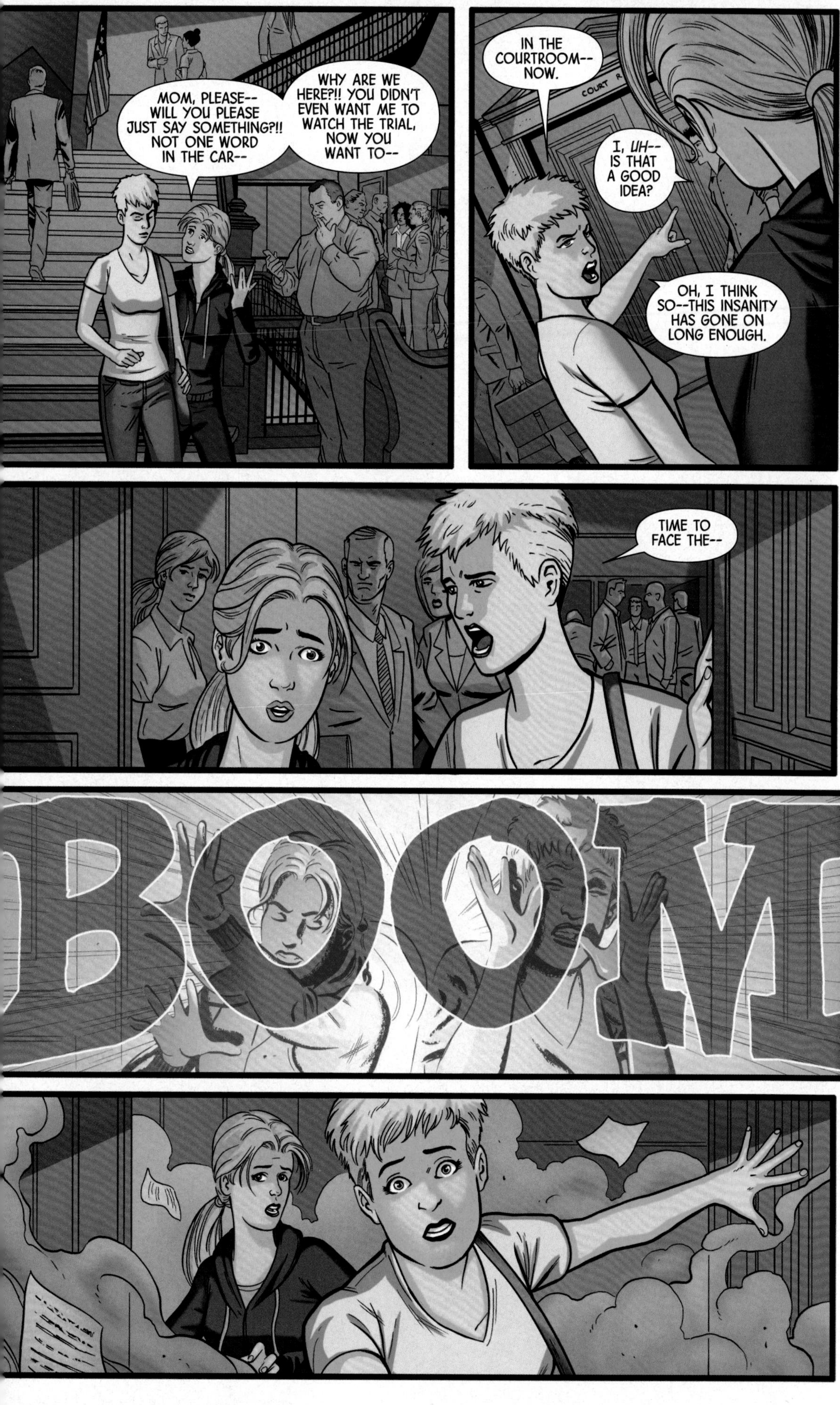
MOM, PLEASE--
WILL YOU PLEASE
JUST SAY SOMETHING?!!
NOT ONE WORD
IN THE CAR--
WHY ARE WE HERE?!! YOU DIDN'T EVEN WANT ME TO WATCH THE TRIAL, NOW YOU WANT TO--
IN THE COURTROOM--NOW.
COURT R
I, *UH*--IS THAT A GOOD IDEA?
OH, I THINK SO--THIS INSANITY HAS GONE ON LONG ENOUGH.
TIME TO FACE THE--
BOOM

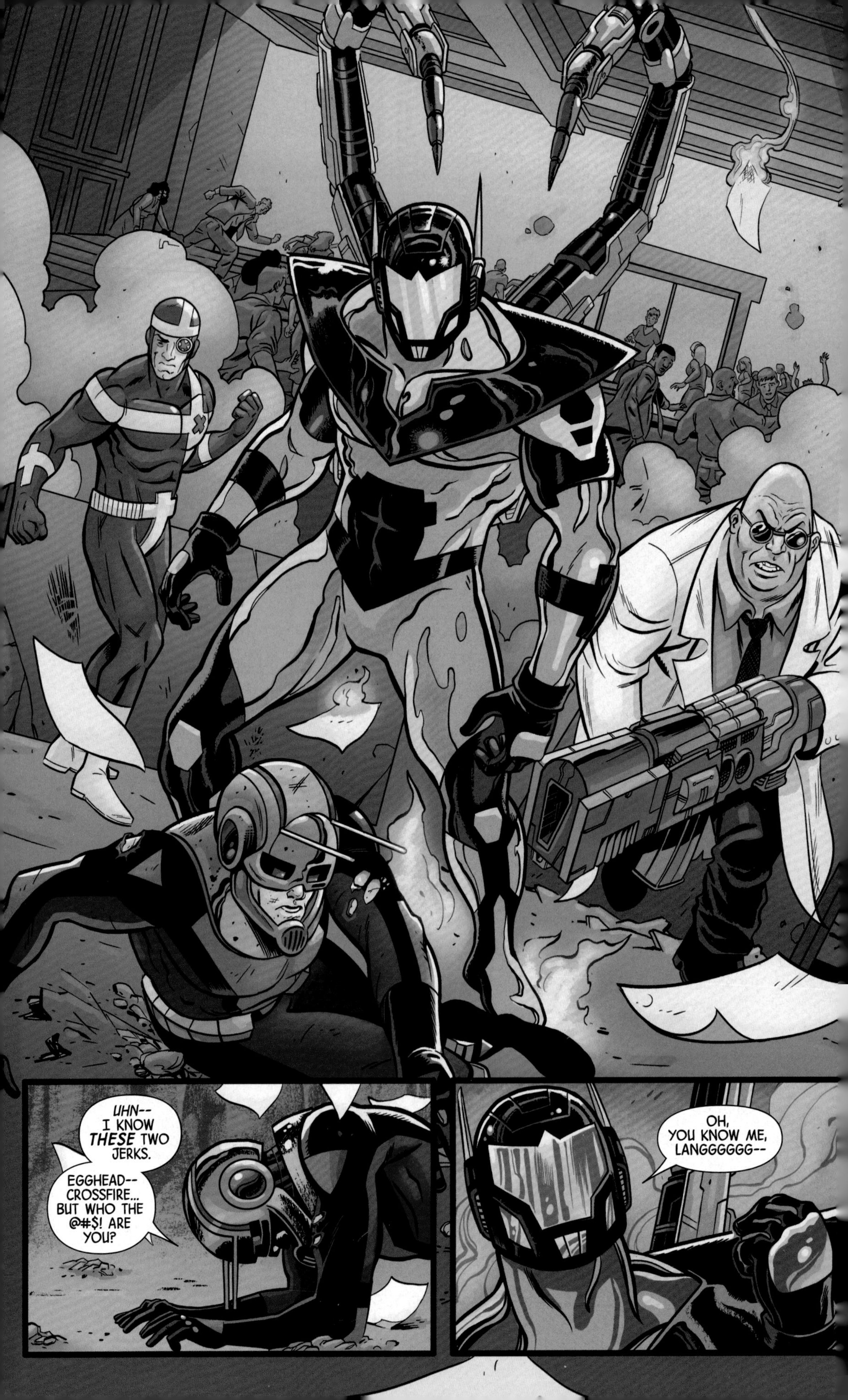
UHN-- I KNOW THESE TWO JERKS.
EGGHEAD-- CROSSFIRE... BUT WHO THE @#$! ARE YOU?
OH, YOU KNOW ME, LANGGGGGG--

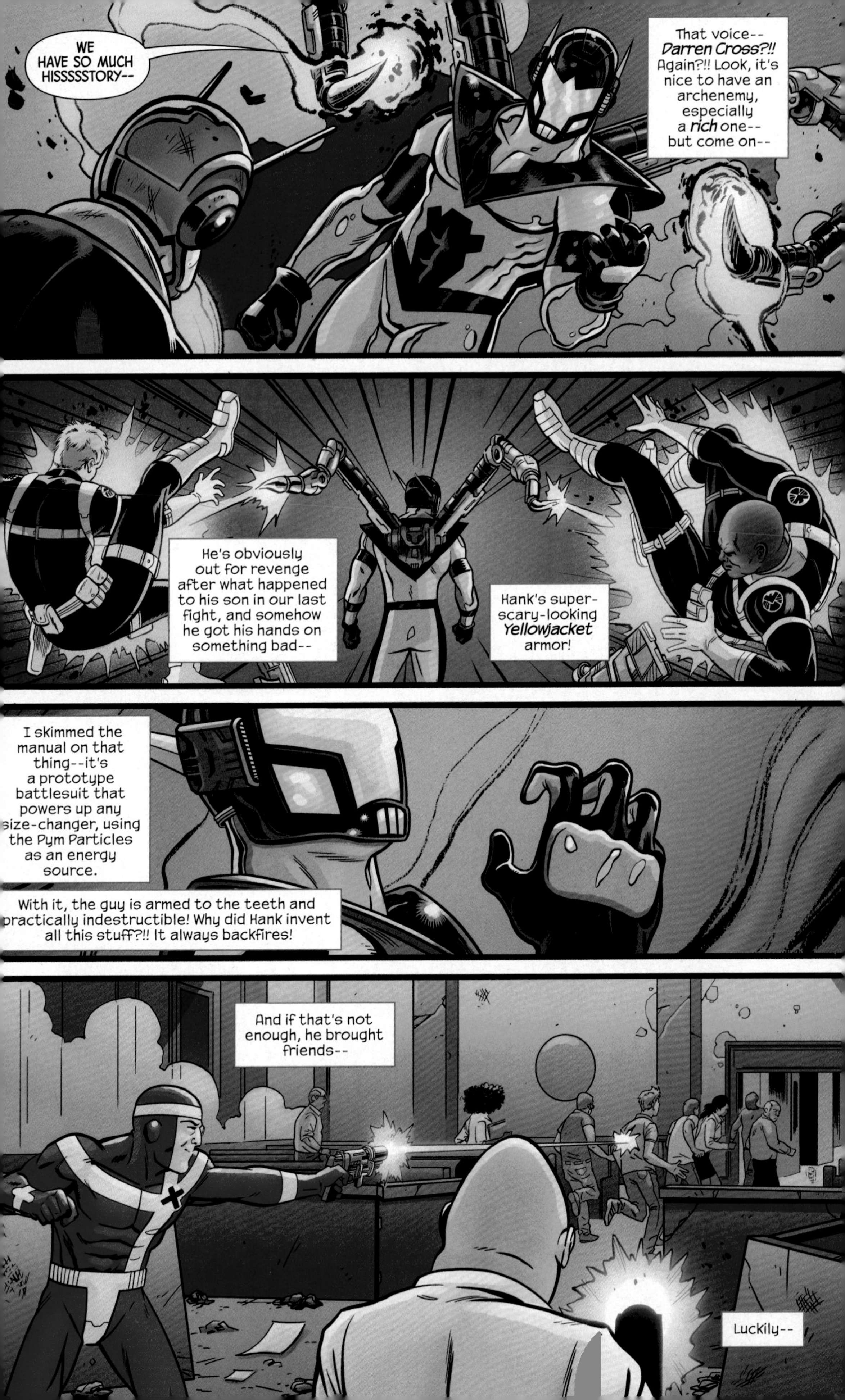

WE HAVE SO MUCH HISSSSSTORY--
That voice-- Darren Cross?!! Again?!! Look, it's nice to have an archenemy, especially a rich one-- but come on--
He's obviously out for revenge after what happened to his son in our last fight, and somehow he got his hands on something bad--
Hank's super-scary-looking Yellowjacket armor!
I skimmed the manual on that thing--it's a prototype battlesuit that powers up any size-changer, using the Pym Particles as an energy source.
With it, the guy is armed to the teeth and practically indestructible! Why did Hank invent all this stuff?!! It always backfires!
And if that's not enough, he brought friends--
Luckily--

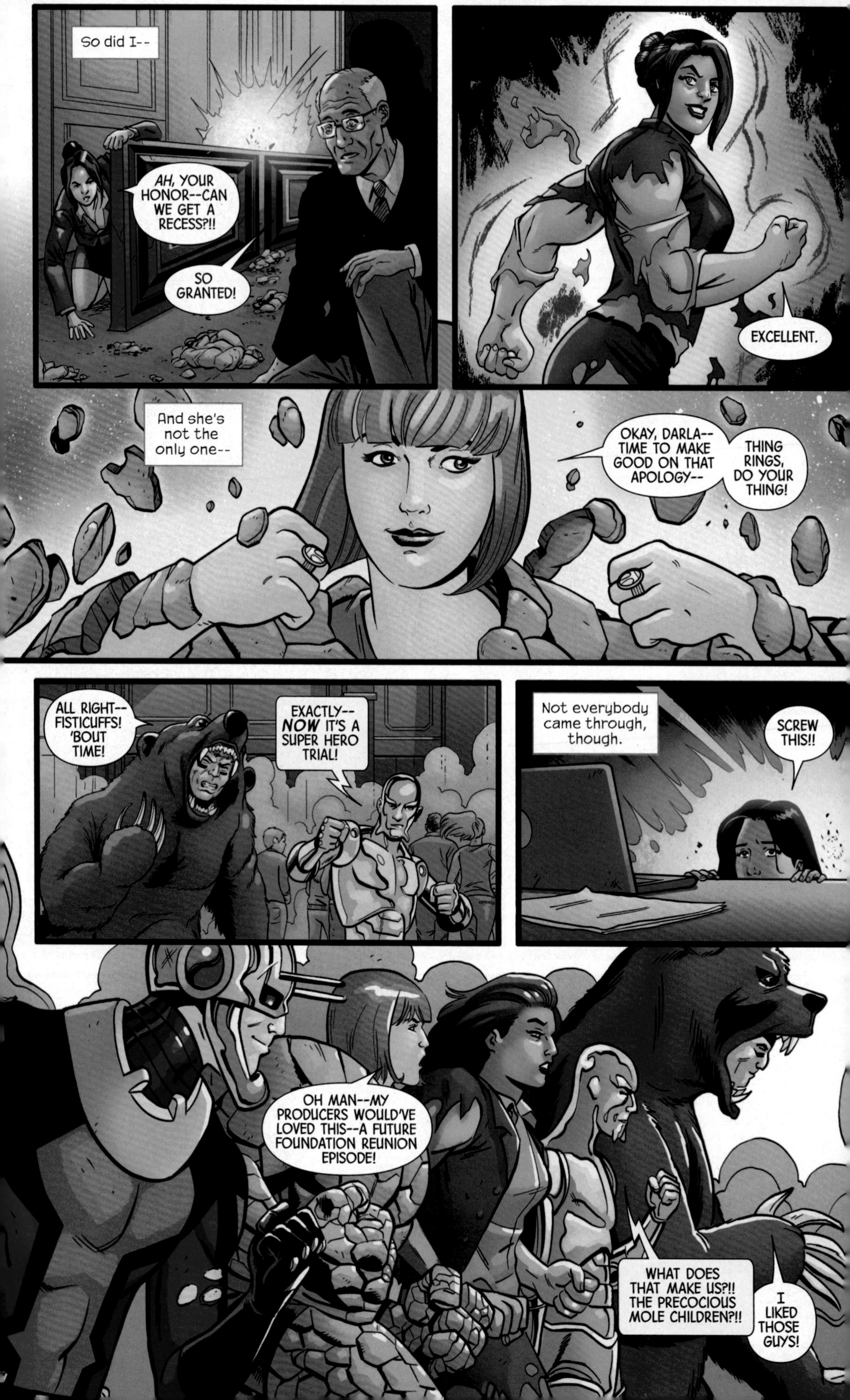
So did I--
AH, YOUR HONOR--CAN WE GET A RECESS?!!
SO GRANTED!
EXCELLENT.
And she's not the only one--
OKAY, DARLA--TIME TO MAKE GOOD ON THAT APOLOGY--
THING RINGS, DO YOUR THING!
ALL RIGHT--FISTICUFFS! 'BOUT TIME!
EXACTLY--NOW IT'S A SUPER HERO TRIAL!
Not everybody came through, though.
SCREW THIS!!
OH MAN--MY PRODUCERS WOULD'VE LOVED THIS--A FUTURE FOUNDATION REUNION EPISODE!
WHAT DOES THAT MAKE US?!! THE PRECOCIOUS MOLE CHILDREN?!!
I LIKED THOSE GUYS!

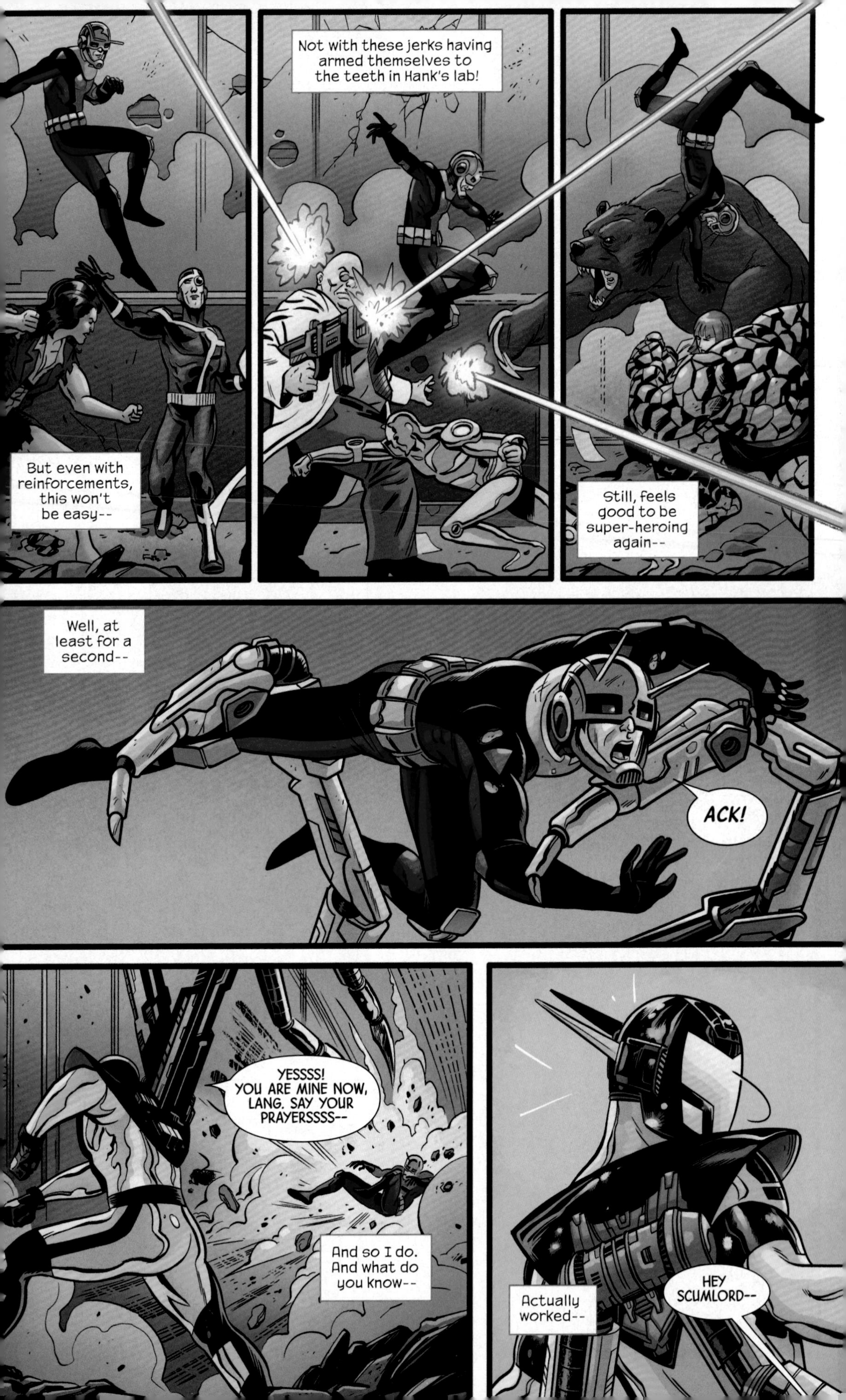

But even with reinforcements, this won't be easy--
Not with these jerks having armed themselves to the teeth in Hank's lab!
Still, feels good to be super-heroing again--
Well, at least for a second--
ACK!
YESSSS! YOU ARE MINE NOW, LANG. SAY YOUR PRAYERSSSS--
And so I do. And what do you know--
Actually worked--
HEY SCUMLORD--

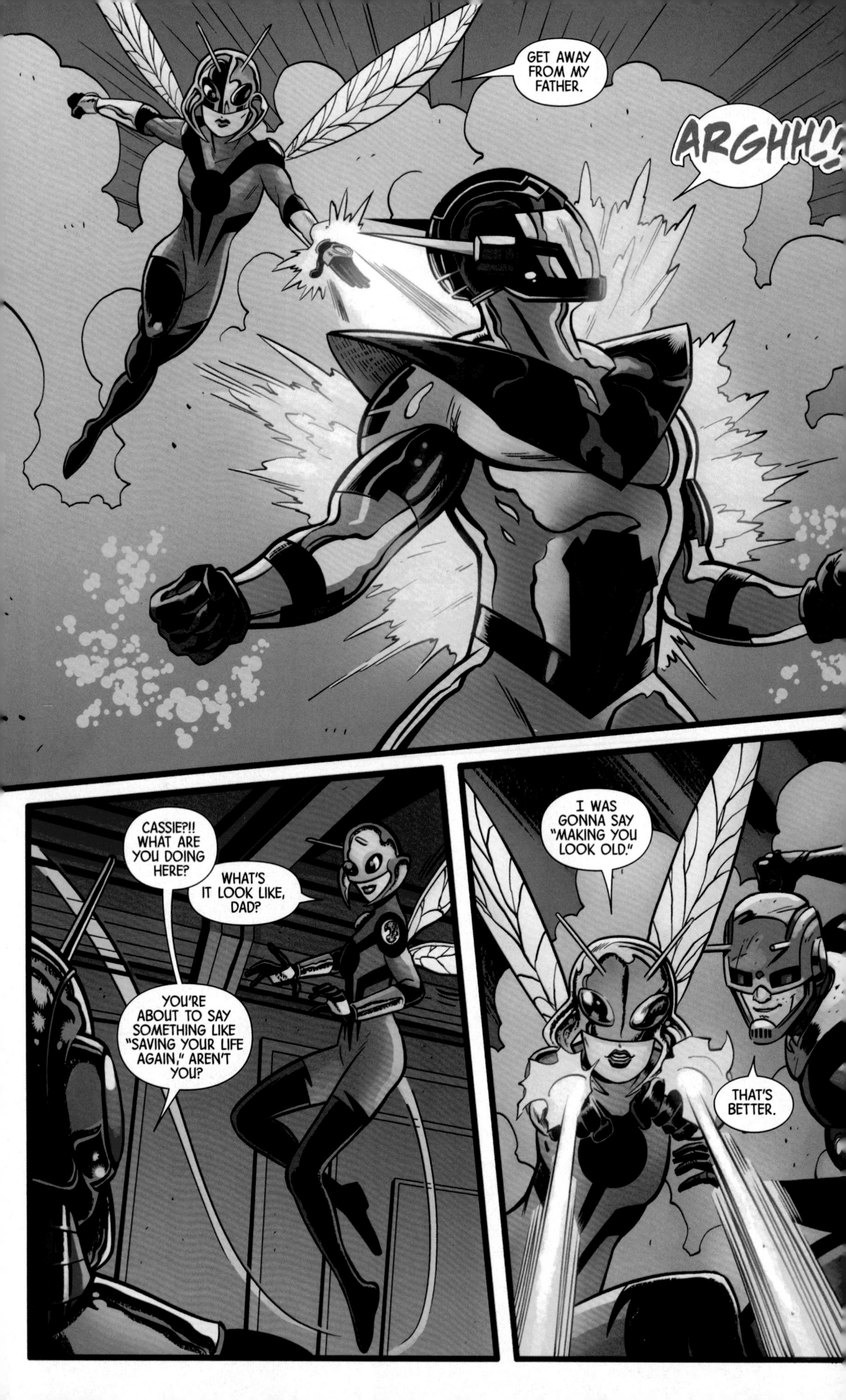
GET AWAY FROM MY FATHER.
ARGHH!!
CASSIE?!! WHAT ARE YOU DOING HERE?
WHAT'S IT LOOK LIKE, DAD?
YOU'RE ABOUT TO SAY SOMETHING LIKE "SAVING YOUR LIFE AGAIN," AREN'T YOU?
I WAS GONNA SAY "MAKING YOU LOOK OLD."
THAT'S BETTER.

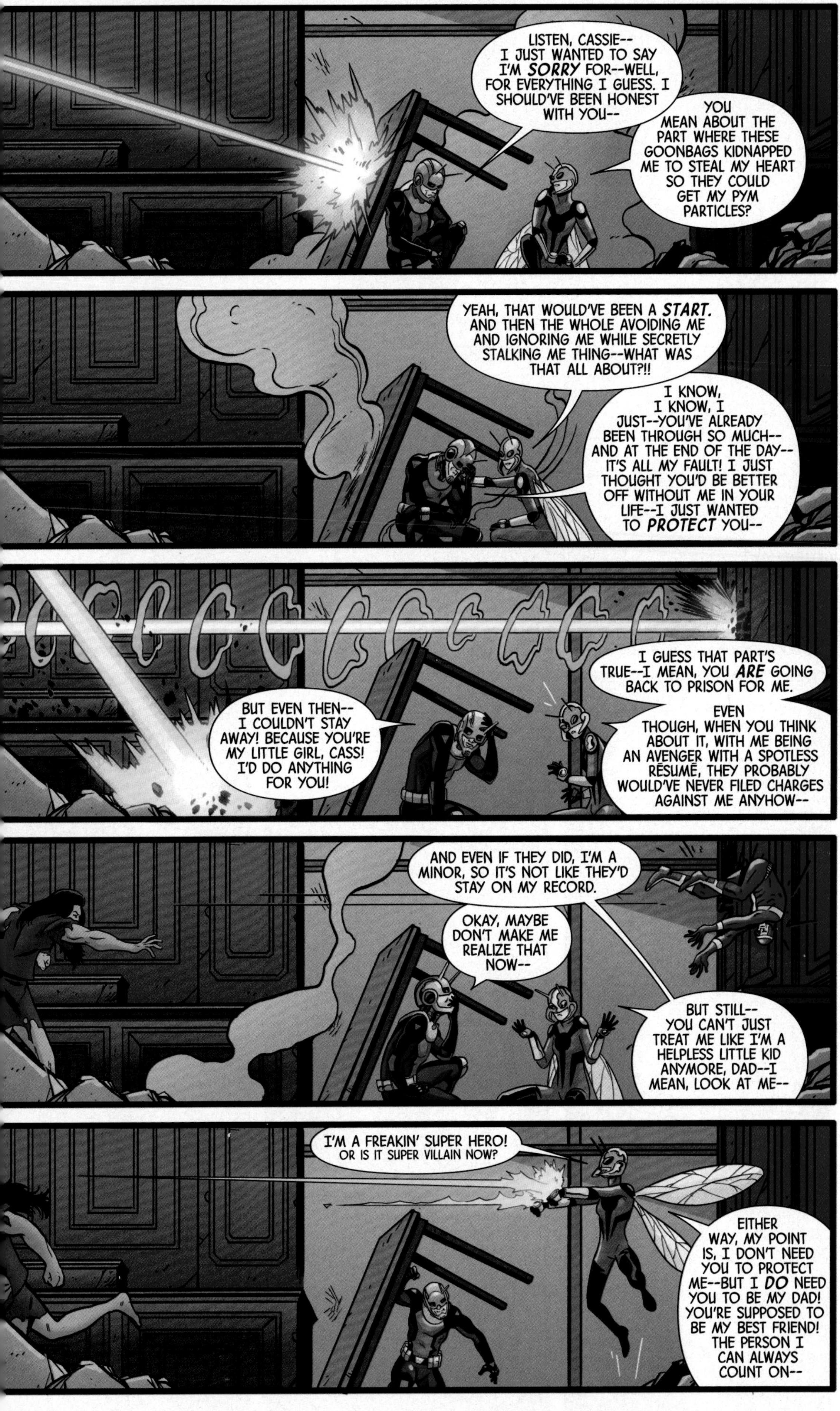
LISTEN, CASSIE-- I JUST WANTED TO SAY I'M SORRY FOR--WELL, FOR EVERYTHING I GUESS. I SHOULD'VE BEEN HONEST WITH YOU--
YOU MEAN ABOUT THE PART WHERE THESE GOONBAGS KIDNAPPED ME TO STEAL MY HEART SO THEY COULD GET MY PYM PARTICLES?
YEAH, THAT WOULD'VE BEEN A START. AND THEN THE WHOLE AVOIDING ME AND IGNORING ME WHILE SECRETLY STALKING ME THING--WHAT WAS THAT ALL ABOUT?!!
I KNOW, I KNOW, I JUST--YOU'VE ALREADY BEEN THROUGH SO MUCH-- AND AT THE END OF THE DAY-- IT'S ALL MY FAULT! I JUST THOUGHT YOU'D BE BETTER OFF WITHOUT ME IN YOUR LIFE--I JUST WANTED TO PROTECT YOU--
BUT EVEN THEN-- I COULDN'T STAY AWAY! BECAUSE YOU'RE MY LITTLE GIRL, CASS! I'D DO ANYTHING FOR YOU!
I GUESS THAT PART'S TRUE--I MEAN, YOU ARE GOING BACK TO PRISON FOR ME.
EVEN THOUGH, WHEN YOU THINK ABOUT IT, WITH ME BEING AN AVENGER WITH A SPOTLESS RÉSUMÉ, THEY PROBABLY WOULD'VE NEVER FILED CHARGES AGAINST ME ANYHOW--
AND EVEN IF THEY DID, I'M A MINOR, SO IT'S NOT LIKE THEY'D STAY ON MY RECORD.
OKAY, MAYBE DON'T MAKE ME REALIZE THAT NOW--
BUT STILL-- YOU CAN'T JUST TREAT ME LIKE I'M A HELPLESS LITTLE KID ANYMORE, DAD--I MEAN, LOOK AT ME--
I'M A FREAKIN' SUPER HERO! OR IS IT SUPER VILLAIN NOW?
EITHER WAY, MY POINT IS, I DON'T NEED YOU TO PROTECT ME--BUT I DO NEED YOU TO BE MY DAD! YOU'RE SUPPOSED TO BE MY BEST FRIEND! THE PERSON I CAN ALWAYS COUNT ON--

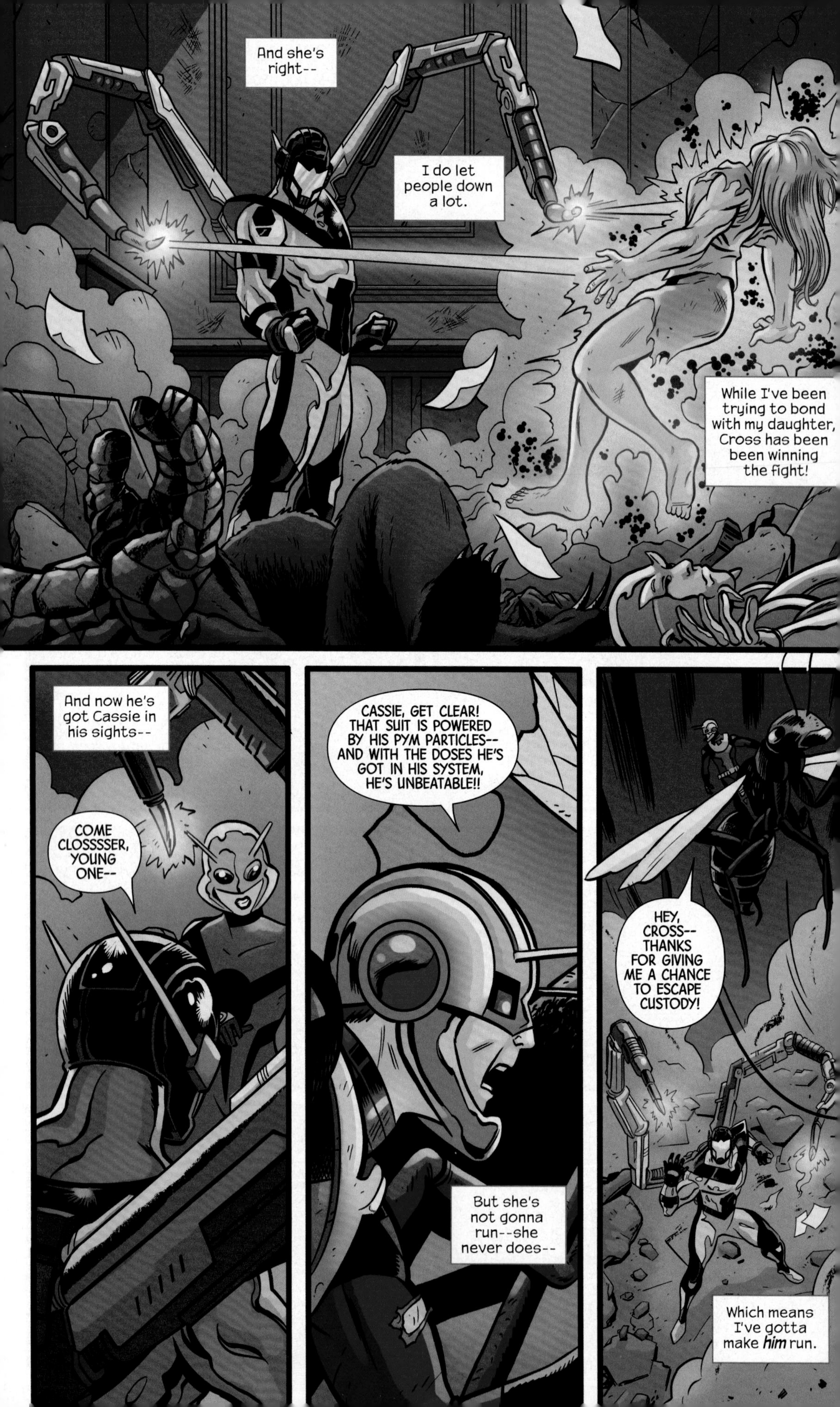
And she's right--
I do let people down a lot.
While I've been trying to bond with my daughter, Cross has been been winning the fight!
And now he's got Cassie in his sights--
COME CLOSSSSER, YOUNG ONE--
CASSIE, GET CLEAR! THAT SUIT IS POWERED BY HIS PYM PARTICLES-- AND WITH THE DOSES HE'S GOT IN HIS SYSTEM, HE'S UNBEATABLE!!
But she's not gonna run--she never does--
HEY, CROSS-- THANKS FOR GIVING ME A CHANCE TO ESCAPE CUSTODY!
Which means I've gotta make *him* run.

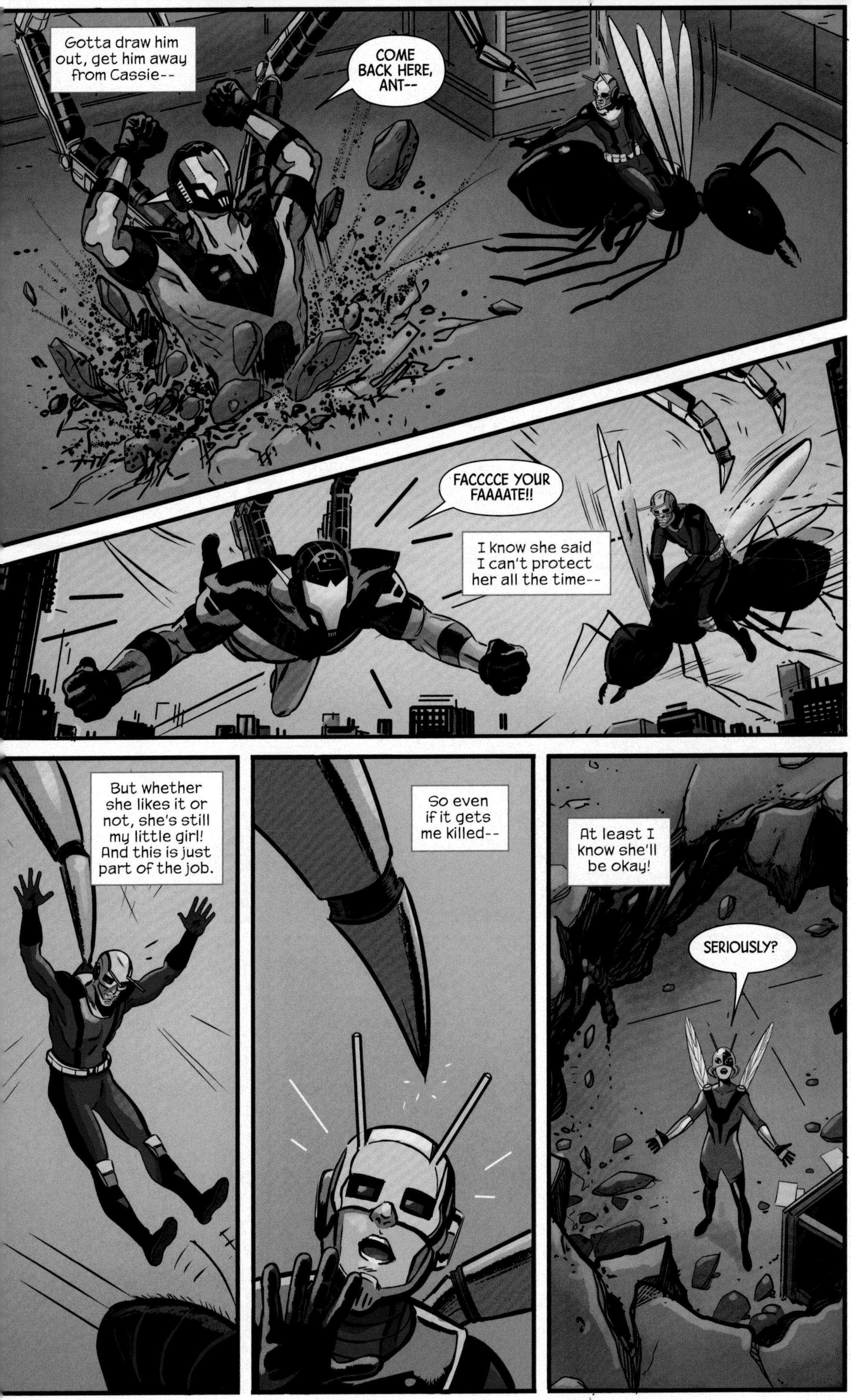

Gotta draw him out, get him away from Cassie--
COME BACK HERE, ANT--
FACCCCE YOUR FAAAATE!!
I know she said I can't protect her all the time--
But whether she likes it or not, she's still my little girl! And this is just part of the job.
So even if it gets me killed--
At least I know she'll be okay!
SERIOUSLY?

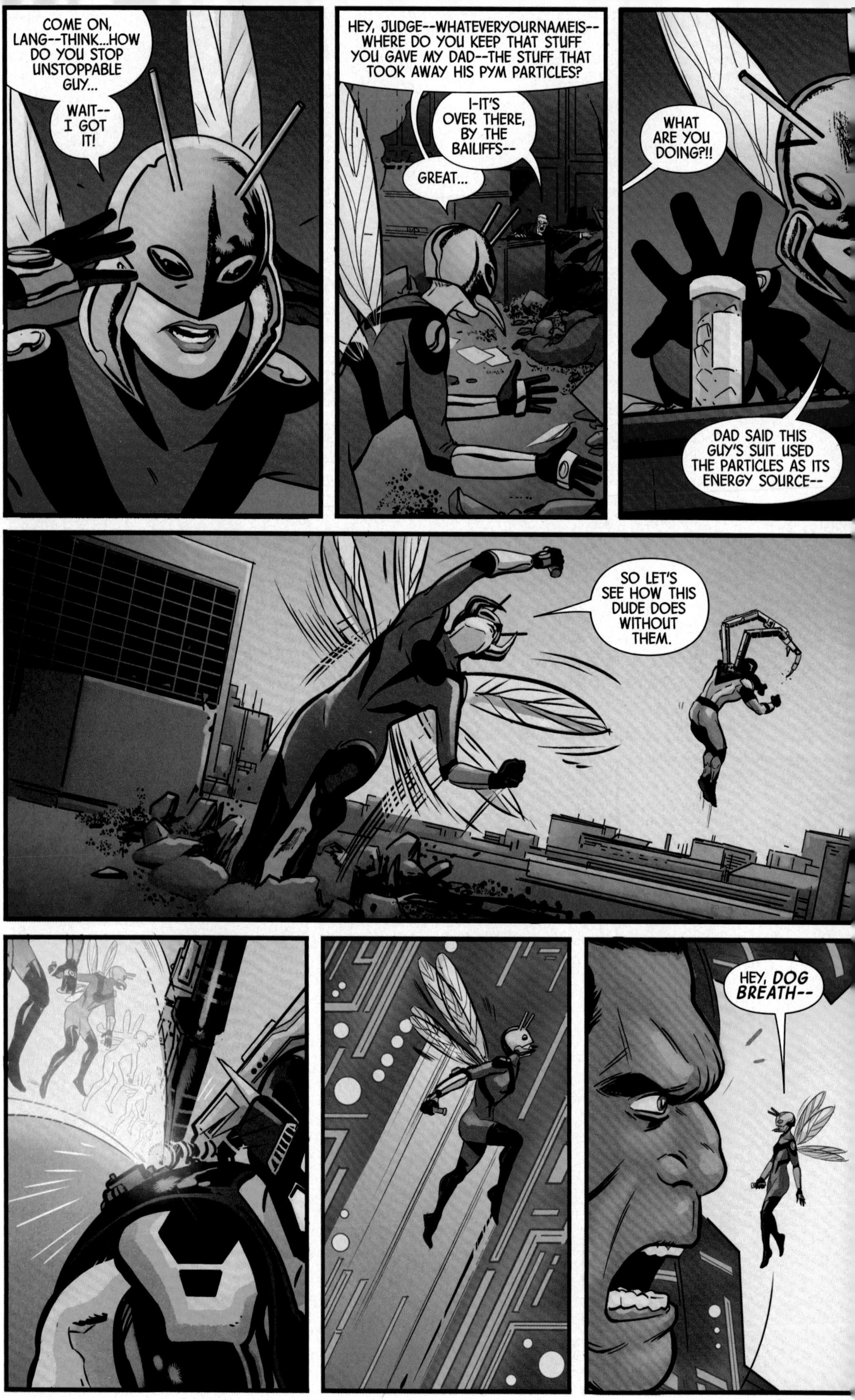
COME ON, LANG--THINK...HOW DO YOU STOP UNSTOPPABLE GUY...
WAIT-- I GOT IT!
HEY, JUDGE--WHATEVERYOURNAMEIS--WHERE DO YOU KEEP THAT STUFF YOU GAVE MY DAD--THE STUFF THAT TOOK AWAY HIS PYM PARTICLES?
I-IT'S OVER THERE, BY THE BAILIFFS--
GREAT...
WHAT ARE YOU DOING?!!
DAD SAID THIS GUY'S SUIT USED THE PARTICLES AS ITS ENERGY SOURCE--
SO LET'S SEE HOW THIS DUDE DOES WITHOUT THEM.
HEY, DOG BREATH--

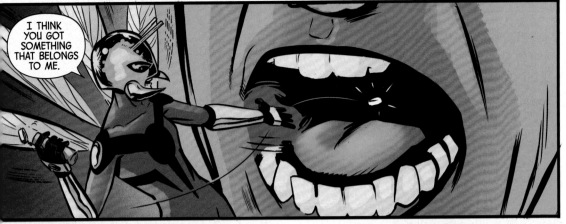

I THINK YOU GOT SOMETHING THAT BELONGS TO ME.

WARNING-- IMMEDIATE POWER LOSS. SYSTEM FAILURE--

NOOOO--

CRASH

NOW THIS IS ME SAVING YOUR LIFE AGAIN.

THAT'S FAIR.

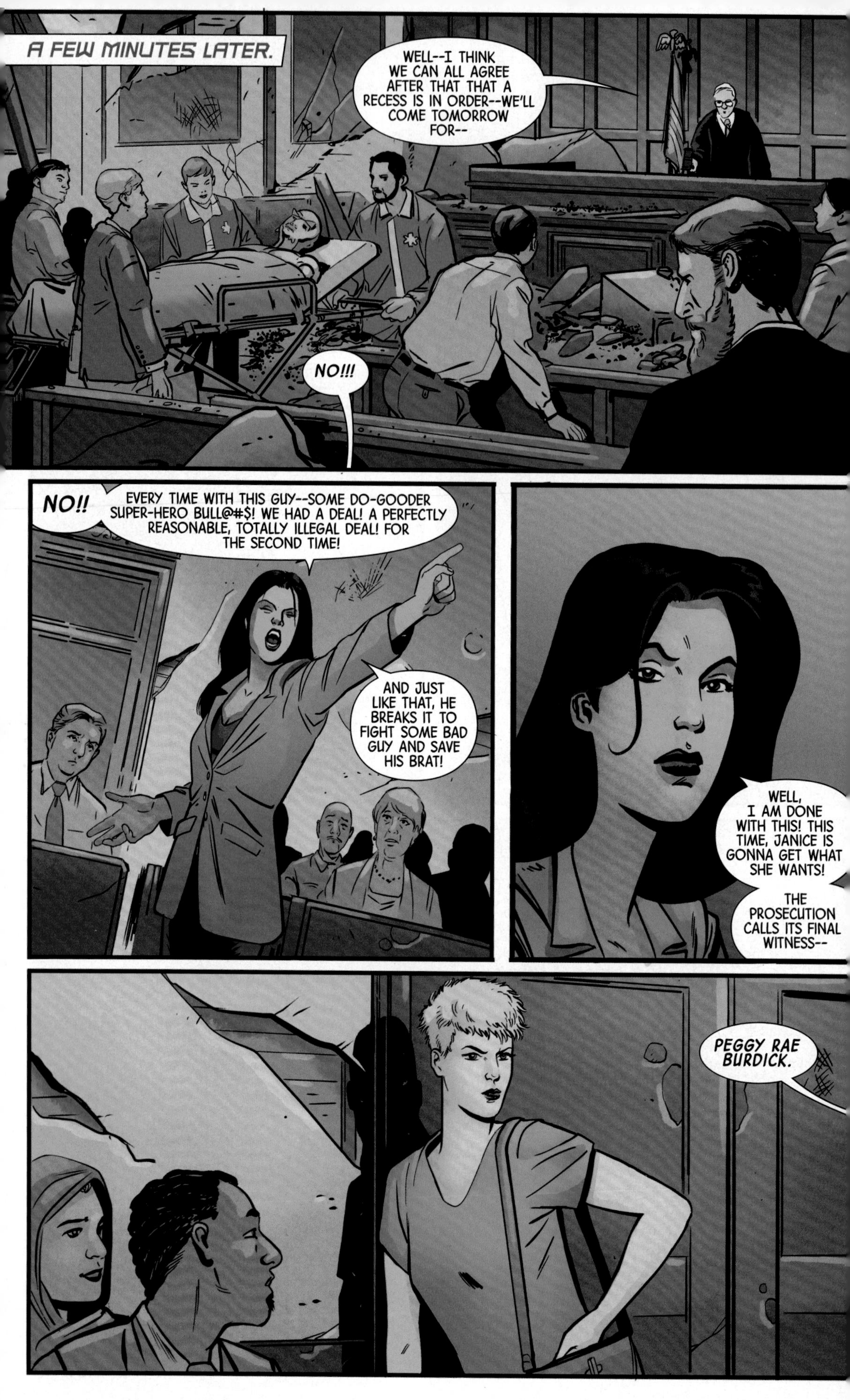
A FEW MINUTES LATER.
WELL--I THINK WE CAN ALL AGREE AFTER THAT THAT A RECESS IS IN ORDER--WE'LL COME TOMORROW FOR--
NO!!!
NO!!
EVERY TIME WITH THIS GUY--SOME DO-GOODER SUPER-HERO BULL@#$! WE HAD A DEAL! A PERFECTLY REASONABLE, TOTALLY ILLEGAL DEAL! FOR THE SECOND TIME!
AND JUST LIKE THAT, HE BREAKS IT TO FIGHT SOME BAD GUY AND SAVE HIS BRAT!
WELL, I AM DONE WITH THIS! THIS TIME, JANICE IS GONNA GET WHAT SHE WANTS!
THE PROSECUTION CALLS ITS FINAL WITNESS--
PEGGY RAE BURDICK.

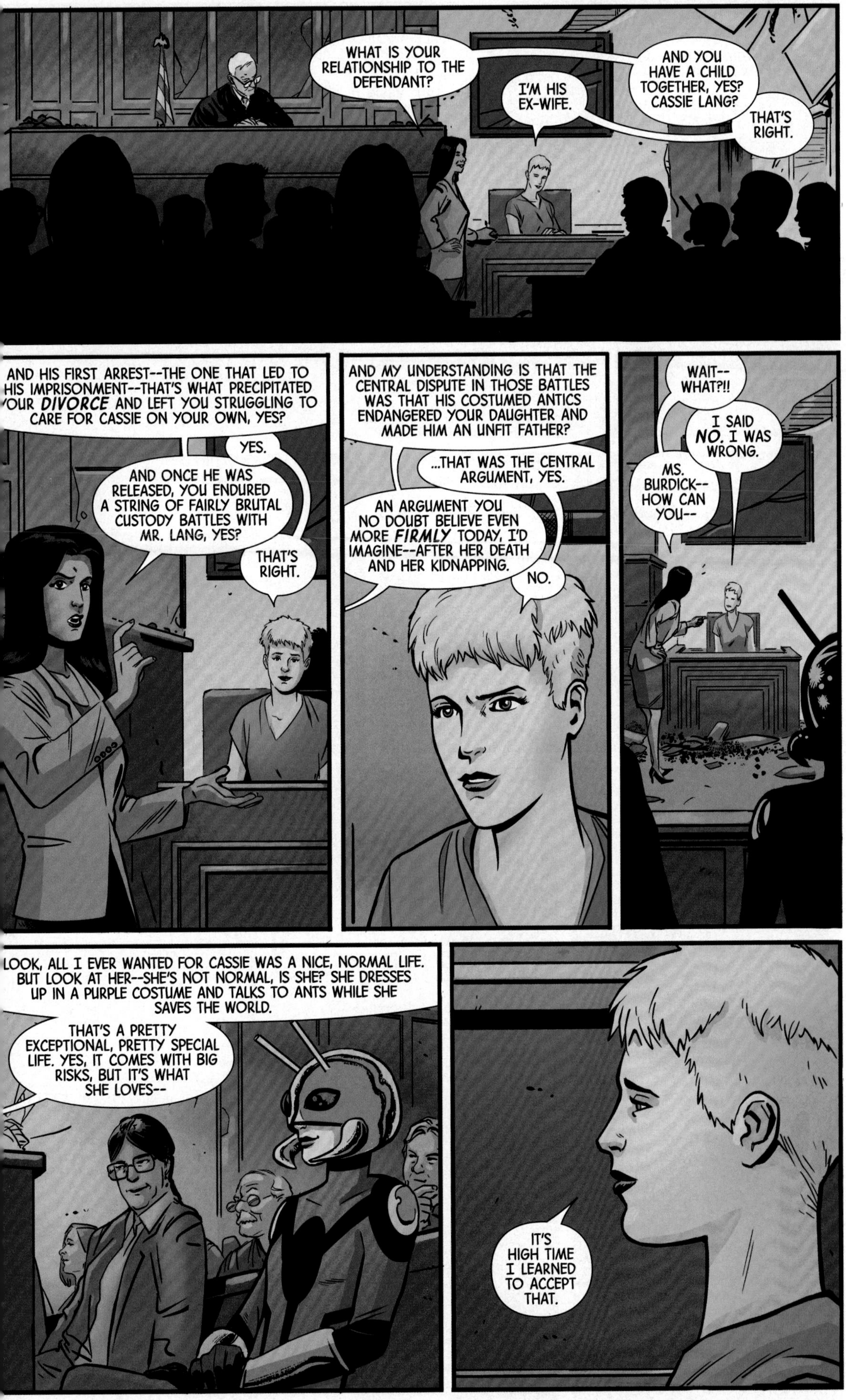
WHAT IS YOUR RELATIONSHIP TO THE DEFENDANT?
I'M HIS EX-WIFE.
AND YOU HAVE A CHILD TOGETHER, YES? CASSIE LANG?
THAT'S RIGHT.
AND HIS FIRST ARREST--THE ONE THAT LED TO HIS IMPRISONMENT--THAT'S WHAT PRECIPITATED YOUR DIVORCE AND LEFT YOU STRUGGLING TO CARE FOR CASSIE ON YOUR OWN, YES?
YES.
AND ONCE HE WAS RELEASED, YOU ENDURED A STRING OF FAIRLY BRUTAL CUSTODY BATTLES WITH MR. LANG, YES?
THAT'S RIGHT.
AND MY UNDERSTANDING IS THAT THE CENTRAL DISPUTE IN THOSE BATTLES WAS THAT HIS COSTUMED ANTICS ENDANGERED YOUR DAUGHTER AND MADE HIM AN UNFIT FATHER?
...THAT WAS THE CENTRAL ARGUMENT, YES.
AN ARGUMENT YOU NO DOUBT BELIEVE EVEN MORE FIRMLY TODAY, I'D IMAGINE--AFTER HER DEATH AND HER KIDNAPPING.
NO.
WAIT-- WHAT?!!
I SAID NO. I WAS WRONG.
MS. BURDICK-- HOW CAN YOU--
LOOK, ALL I EVER WANTED FOR CASSIE WAS A NICE, NORMAL LIFE. BUT LOOK AT HER--SHE'S NOT NORMAL, IS SHE? SHE DRESSES UP IN A PURPLE COSTUME AND TALKS TO ANTS WHILE SHE SAVES THE WORLD.
THAT'S A PRETTY EXCEPTIONAL, PRETTY SPECIAL LIFE. YES, IT COMES WITH BIG RISKS, BUT IT'S WHAT SHE LOVES--
IT'S HIGH TIME I LEARNED TO ACCEPT THAT.

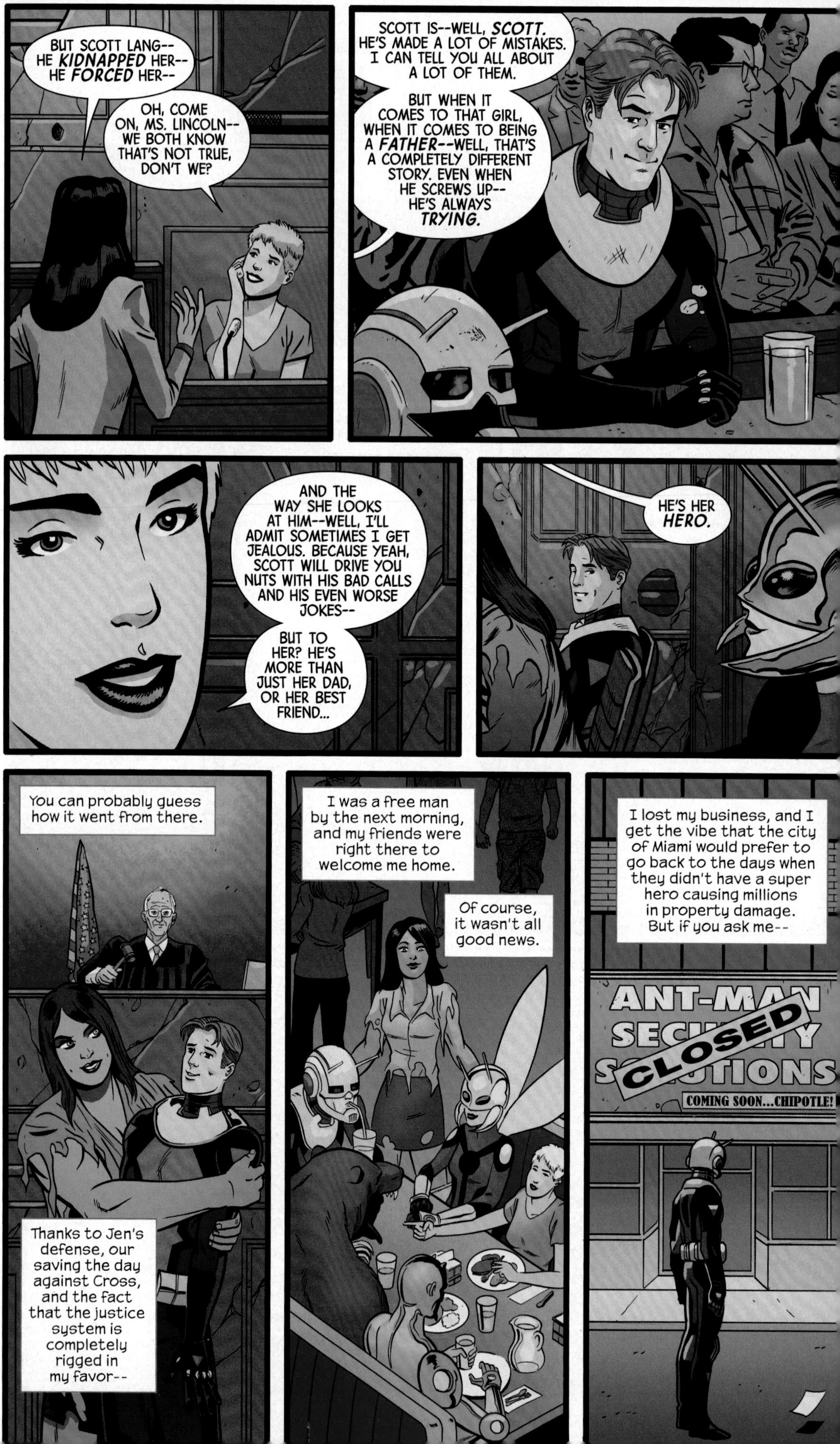

BUT SCOTT LANG--HE *KIDNAPPED* HER--HE *FORCED* HER--
OH, COME ON, MS. LINCOLN--WE BOTH KNOW THAT'S NOT TRUE, DON'T WE?
SCOTT IS--WELL, *SCOTT.* HE'S MADE A LOT OF MISTAKES. I CAN TELL YOU ALL ABOUT A LOT OF THEM.
BUT WHEN IT COMES TO THAT GIRL, WHEN IT COMES TO BEING A *FATHER*--WELL, THAT'S A COMPLETELY DIFFERENT STORY. EVEN WHEN HE SCREWS UP--HE'S ALWAYS *TRYING.*
AND THE WAY SHE LOOKS AT HIM--WELL, I'LL ADMIT SOMETIMES I GET JEALOUS. BECAUSE YEAH, SCOTT WILL DRIVE YOU NUTS WITH HIS BAD CALLS AND HIS EVEN WORSE JOKES--
BUT TO HER? HE'S MORE THAN JUST HER DAD, OR HER BEST FRIEND...
HE'S HER *HERO.*
You can probably guess how it went from there.
Thanks to Jen's defense, our saving the day against Cross, and the fact that the justice system is completely rigged in my favor--
I was a free man by the next morning, and my friends were right there to welcome me home.
Of course, it wasn't all good news.
I lost my business, and I get the vibe that the city of Miami would prefer to go back to the days when they didn't have a super hero causing millions in property damage. But if you ask me--
ANT-MAN SECURITY SOLUTIONS
CLOSED
COMING SOON...CHIPOTLE!

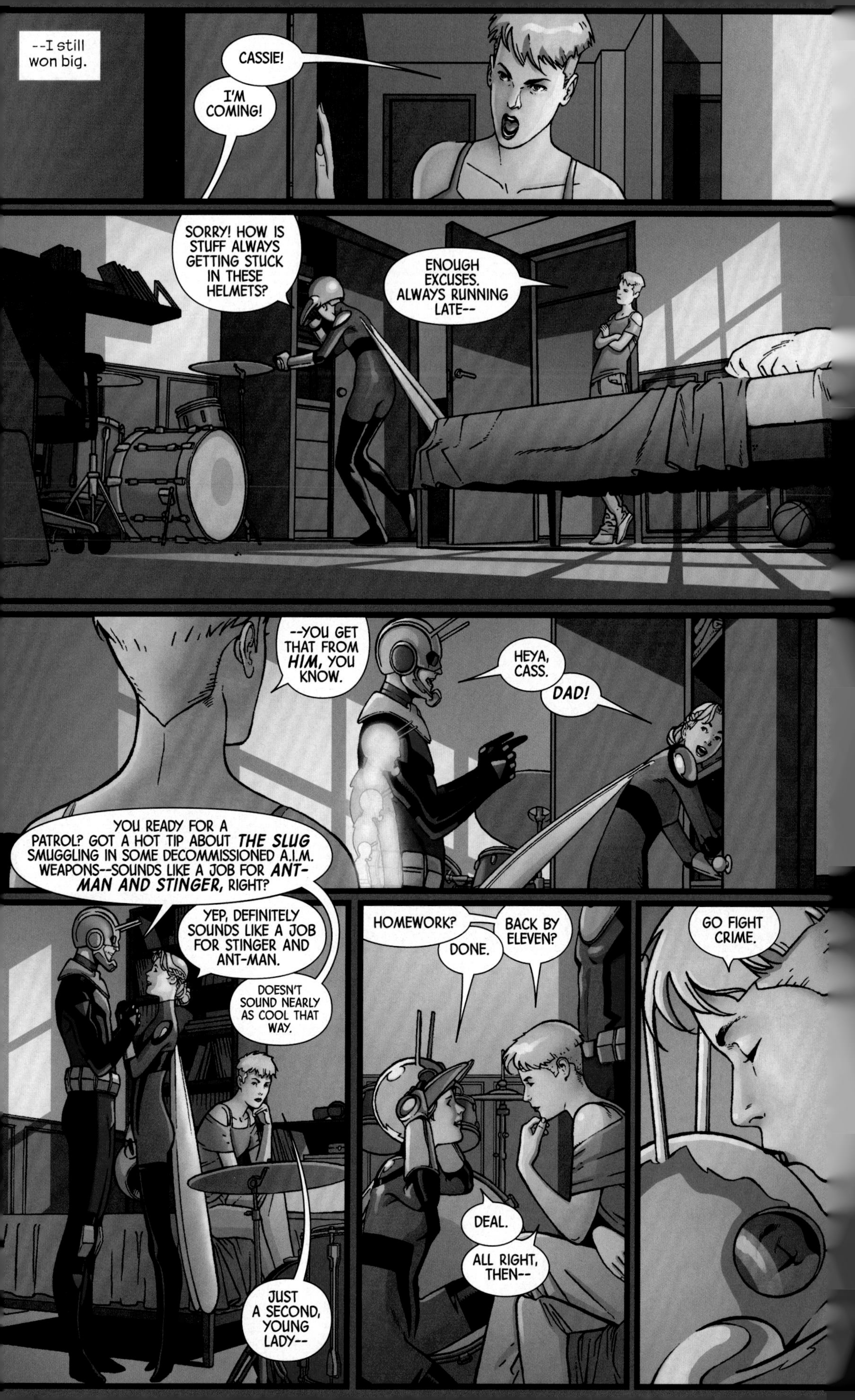
--I still won big.
CASSIE!
I'M COMING!
SORRY! HOW IS STUFF ALWAYS GETTING STUCK IN THESE HELMETS?
ENOUGH EXCUSES. ALWAYS RUNNING LATE--
--YOU GET THAT FROM HIM, YOU KNOW.
HEYA, CASS.
DAD!
YOU READY FOR A PATROL? GOT A HOT TIP ABOUT THE SLUG SMUGGLING IN SOME DECOMMISSIONED A.I.M. WEAPONS--SOUNDS LIKE A JOB FOR ANT-MAN AND STINGER, RIGHT?
YEP, DEFINITELY SOUNDS LIKE A JOB FOR STINGER AND ANT-MAN.
DOESN'T SOUND NEARLY AS COOL THAT WAY.
JUST A SECOND, YOUNG LADY--
HOMEWORK?
DONE.
BACK BY ELEVEN?
DEAL.
ALL RIGHT, THEN--
GO FIGHT CRIME.

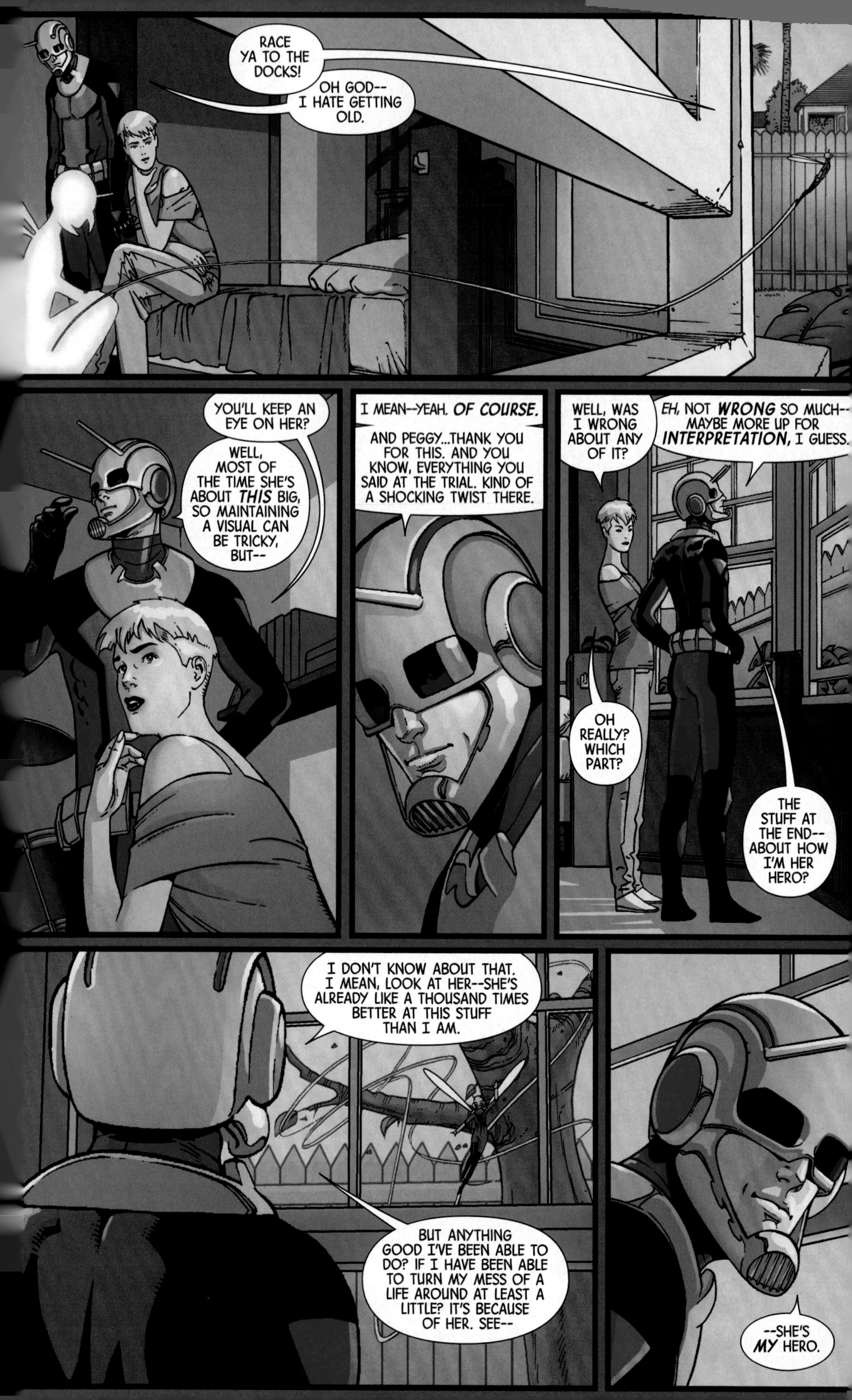
RACE YA TO THE DOCKS!
OH GOD-- I HATE GETTING OLD.
YOU'LL KEEP AN EYE ON HER?
WELL, MOST OF THE TIME SHE'S ABOUT *THIS* BIG, SO MAINTAINING A VISUAL CAN BE TRICKY, BUT--
I MEAN--YEAH. *OF COURSE.*
AND PEGGY...THANK YOU FOR THIS. AND YOU KNOW, EVERYTHING YOU SAID AT THE TRIAL. KIND OF A SHOCKING TWIST THERE.
WELL, WAS I WRONG ABOUT ANY OF IT?
EH, NOT *WRONG* SO MUCH-- MAYBE MORE UP FOR *INTERPRETATION,* I GUESS.
OH REALLY? WHICH PART?
THE STUFF AT THE END-- ABOUT HOW I'M HER HERO?
I DON'T KNOW ABOUT THAT. I MEAN, LOOK AT HER--SHE'S ALREADY LIKE A THOUSAND TIMES BETTER AT THIS STUFF THAN I AM.
BUT ANYTHING GOOD I'VE BEEN ABLE TO DO? IF I HAVE BEEN ABLE TO TURN MY MESS OF A LIFE AROUND AT LEAST A LITTLE? IT'S BECAUSE OF HER. SEE--
--SHE'S *MY* HERO.

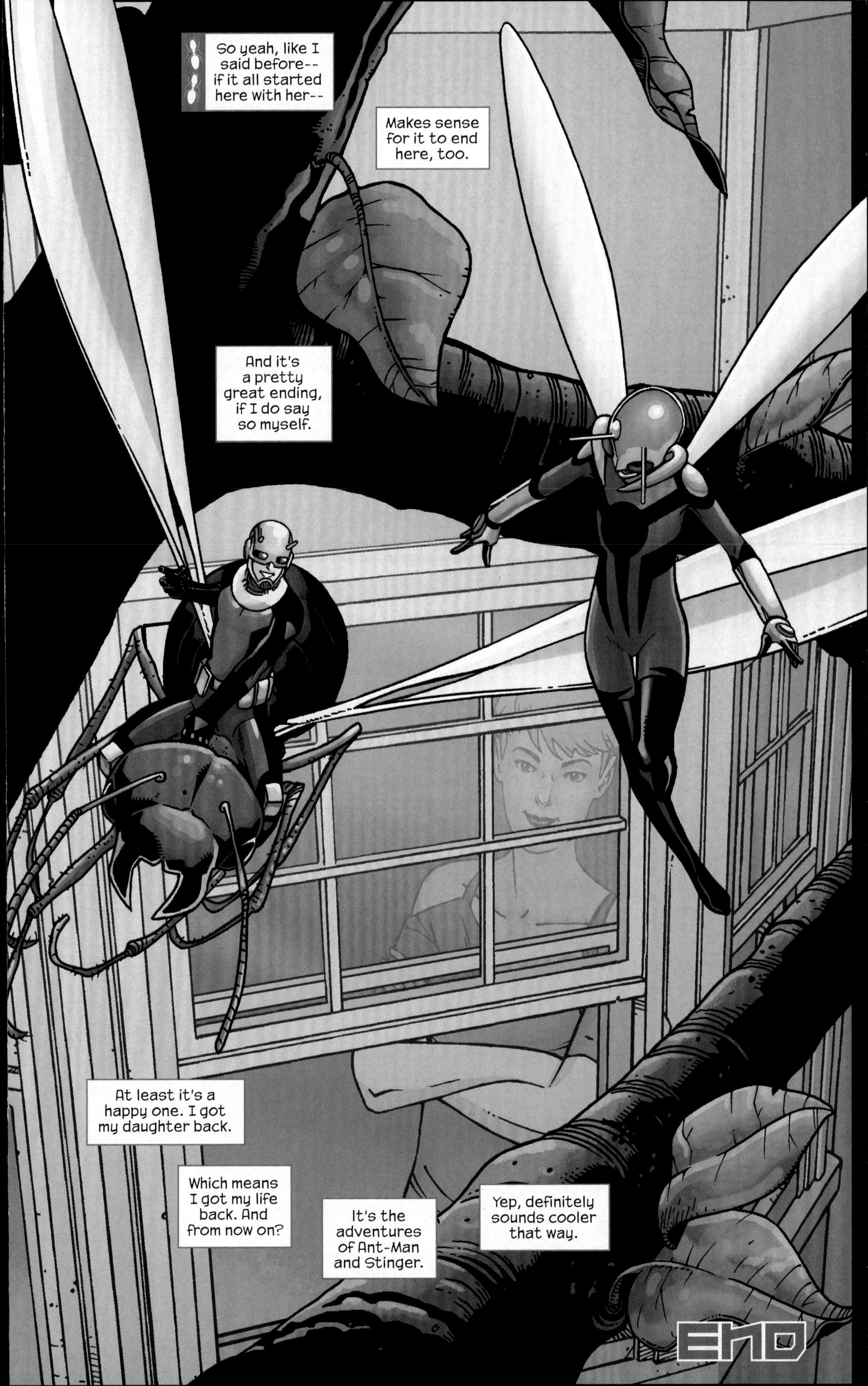
So yeah, like I said before--if it all started here with her--
Makes sense for it to end here, too.
And it's a pretty great ending, if I do say so myself.
At least it's a happy one. I got my daughter back.
Which means I got my life back. And from now on?
It's the adventures of Ant-Man and Stinger.
Yep, definitely sounds cooler that way.
END

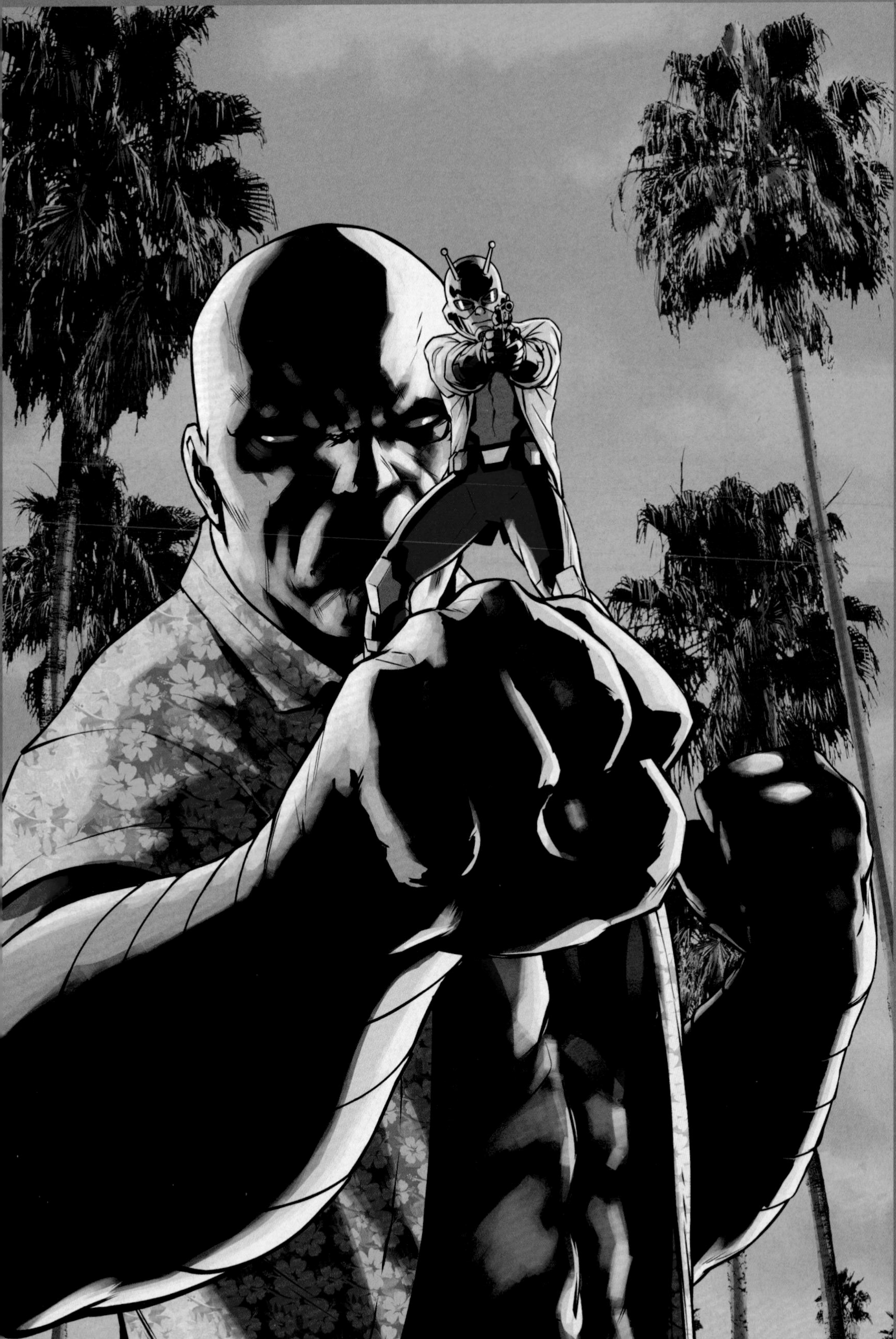

GUARDIANS TEAM-UP #7

THE ENTIRE GALAXY IS A MESS. WARRING EMPIRES AND COSMIC TERRORISTS PLAGUE EVERY CORNER. SOMEONE HAS TO RISE ABOVE IT ALL AND FIGHT FOR THOSE WHO HAVE NO ONE TO FIGHT FOR THEM.

THE GUARDIANS OF THE GALAXY ARE PETER QUILL A.K.A. STAR-LORD, GAMORA, THE MOST DANGEROUS WOMAN IN THE UNIVERSE, DRAX THE DESTROYER, THE MYSTERIOUS WARRIOR ANGELA, VENOM, CAPTAIN MARVEL, ROCKET RACCOON AND GROOT.

GUARDIANS OF THE GALAXY

DRAX THE DESTROYER. HE'S BIG. HE'S GREEN. HE'S STRONG. HE'S NOT THE HULK. HE HATES THANOS AND METAPHORS.

ANT-MAN. HE SHRINKS. HE TALKS TO ANTS. HE HAS A SORDID PAST. HE DIDN'T INVENT ULTRON. HE HATES MONDAYS.

DURING THE CHAOS OF ORIGINAL SIN, SOME OF THE ITEMS IN UATU THE WATCHER'S VAULT WENT MISSING. ONE SUCH ITEM WAS AN INCREDIBLY POWERFUL WEAPON CAPABLE OF ENDING THE UNIVERSE AS WE KNOW IT. THE EXACT WHEREABOUTS OF THE WEAPON IS UNKNOWN, HOWEVER THE GUARDIANS HAVE TRACKED DOWN ITS POTENTIAL BUYER, THE DEADLY DANNKO AND HIS CREW, TO A REMOTE PLANET. BUT YOU DON'T NEED SPIDEY SENSE TO KNOW SOMETHING IS WRONG.

STAR-LORD GAMORA DRAX ANGELA VENOM CAPTAIN MARVEL ROCKET RACCOON GROOT

NICK GIOVANNETTI & PAUL SCHEER
WRITERS

SHAWN CRYSTAL
ARTIST

MATTHEW WILSON
COLORIST

VC'S CORY PETIT
LETTERER

DAVID LOPEZ
COVER ARTIST

XANDER JAROWEY
ASSISTANT EDITOR

KATIE KUBERT
EDITOR

AXEL ALONSO EDITOR IN CHIEF **JOE QUESADA** CHIEF CREATIVE OFFICER
DAN BUCKLEY PUBLISHER **ALAN FINE** EXECUTIVE PRODUCER

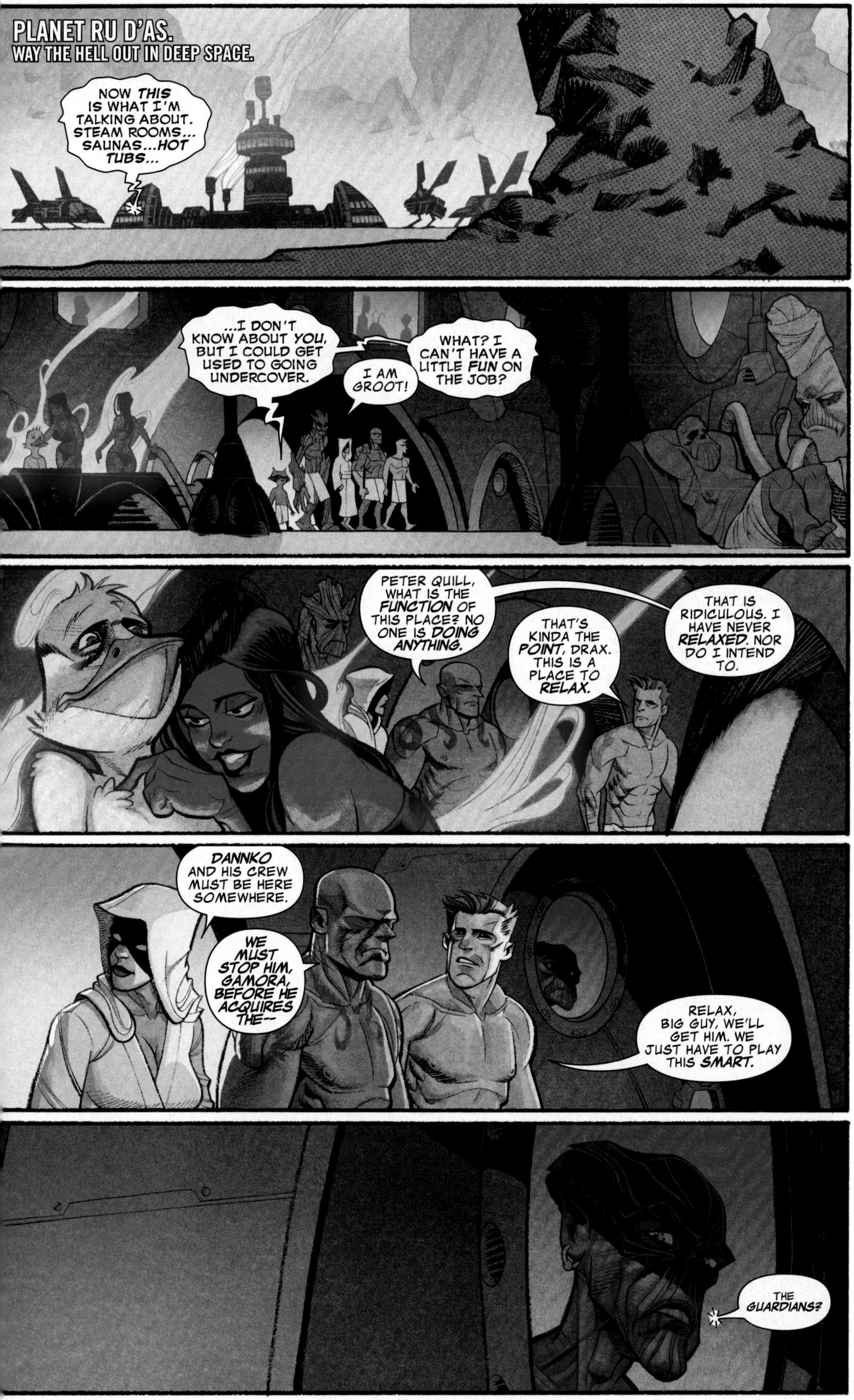
PLANET RU D'AS.
WAY THE HELL OUT IN DEEP SPACE.
NOW THIS IS WHAT I'M TALKING ABOUT. STEAM ROOMS... SAUNAS...HOT TUBS...
...I DON'T KNOW ABOUT YOU, BUT I COULD GET USED TO GOING UNDERCOVER.
I AM GROOT!
WHAT? I CAN'T HAVE A LITTLE FUN ON THE JOB?
PETER QUILL, WHAT IS THE FUNCTION OF THIS PLACE? NO ONE IS DOING ANYTHING.
THAT'S KINDA THE POINT, DRAX. THIS IS A PLACE TO RELAX.
THAT IS RIDICULOUS. I HAVE NEVER RELAXED. NOR DO I INTEND TO.
DANNKO AND HIS CREW MUST BE HERE SOMEWHERE.
WE MUST STOP HIM, GAMORA, BEFORE HE ACQUIRES THE--
RELAX, BIG GUY, WE'LL GET HIM. WE JUST HAVE TO PLAY THIS SMART.
THE GUARDIANS?

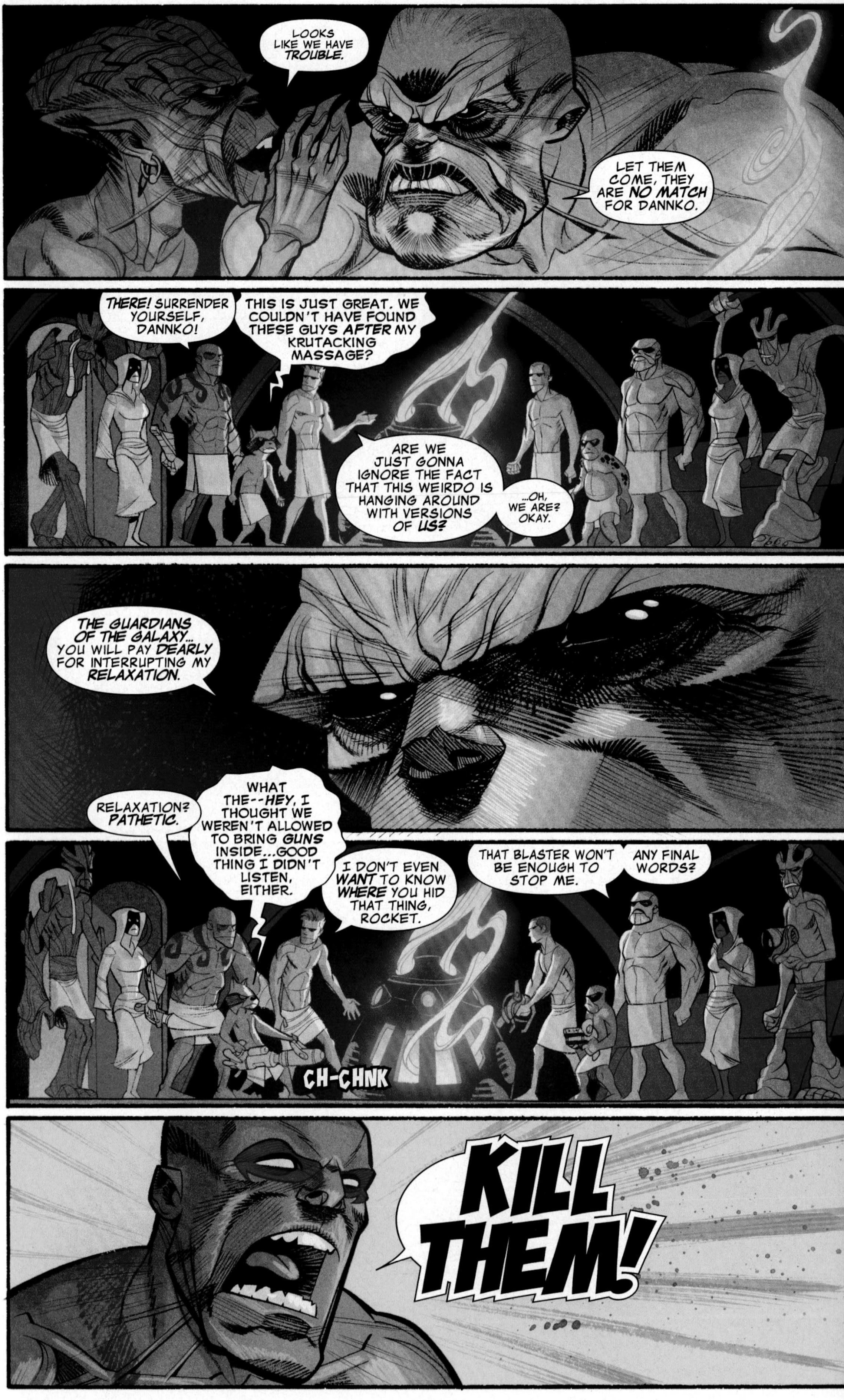
LOOKS LIKE WE HAVE TROUBLE.
LET THEM COME, THEY ARE NO MATCH FOR DANNKO.
THERE! SURRENDER YOURSELF, DANNKO!
THIS IS JUST GREAT. WE COULDN'T HAVE FOUND THESE GUYS AFTER MY KRUTACKING MASSAGE?
ARE WE JUST GONNA IGNORE THE FACT THAT THIS WEIRDO IS HANGING AROUND WITH VERSIONS OF US?
...OH, WE ARE? OKAY.
THE GUARDIANS OF THE GALAXY... YOU WILL PAY DEARLY FOR INTERRUPTING MY RELAXATION.
RELAXATION? PATHETIC.
WHAT THE--HEY, I THOUGHT WE WEREN'T ALLOWED TO BRING GUNS INSIDE...GOOD THING I DIDN'T LISTEN, EITHER.
I DON'T EVEN WANT TO KNOW WHERE YOU HID THAT THING, ROCKET.
THAT BLASTER WON'T BE ENOUGH TO STOP ME.
ANY FINAL WORDS?
CH-CHNK
KILL THEM!

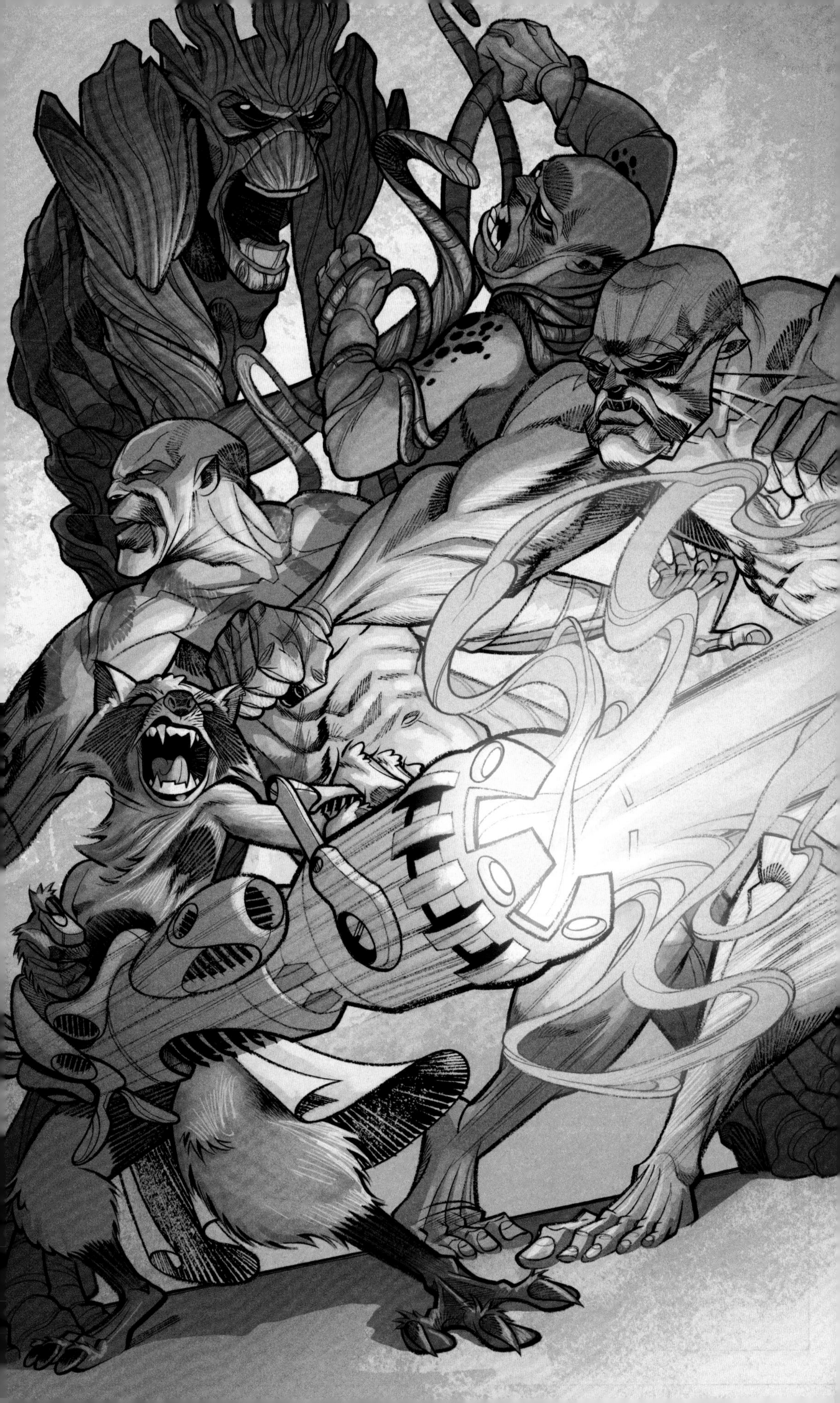

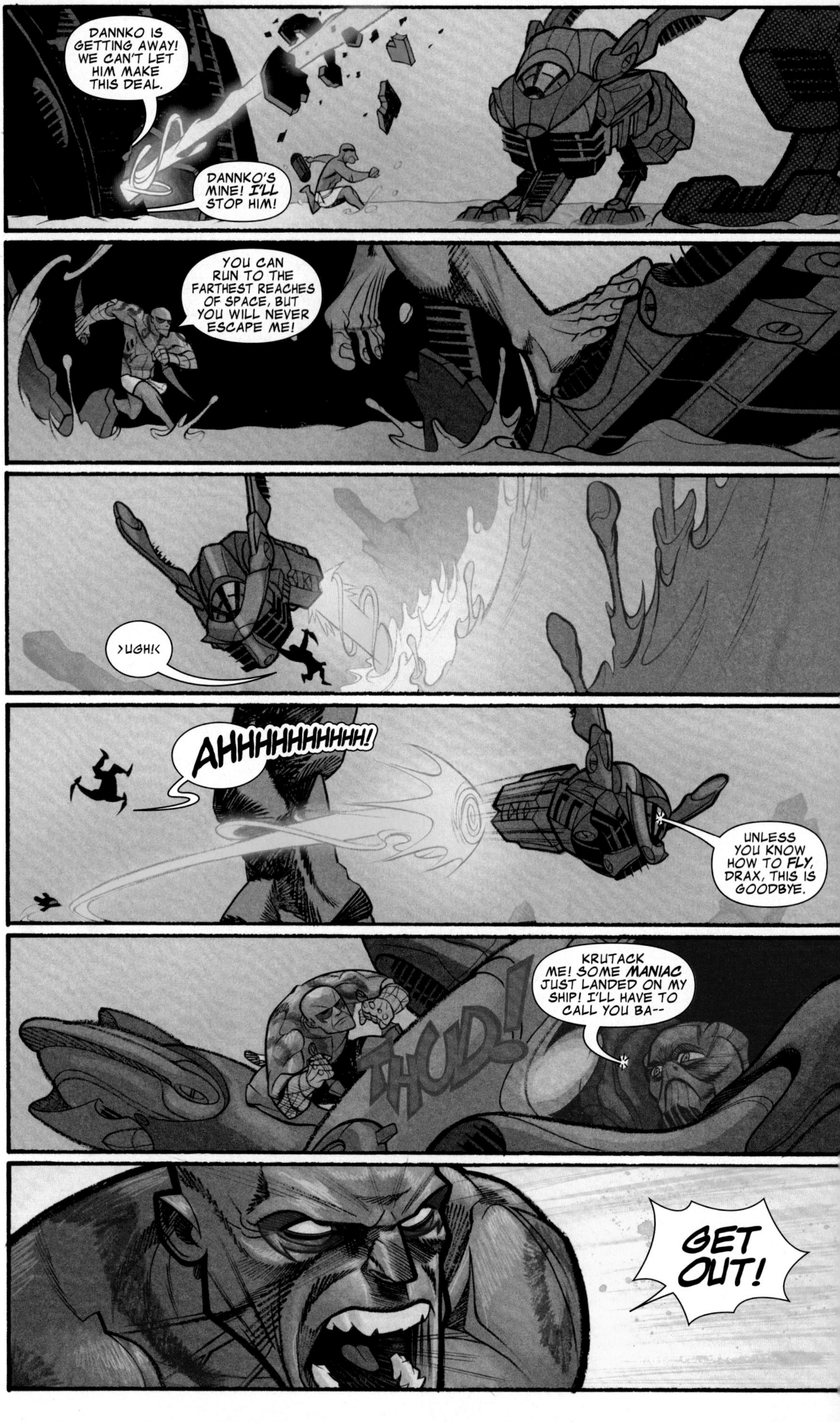
DANNKO IS GETTING AWAY! WE CAN'T LET HIM MAKE THIS DEAL.
DANNKO'S MINE! I'LL STOP HIM!
YOU CAN RUN TO THE FARTHEST REACHES OF SPACE, BUT YOU WILL NEVER ESCAPE ME!
>UGH!<
AHHHHHHHHH!
UNLESS YOU KNOW HOW TO FLY, DRAX, THIS IS GOODBYE.
KRUTACK ME! SOME MANIAC JUST LANDED ON MY SHIP! I'LL HAVE TO CALL YOU BA--
THUD!
GET OUT!

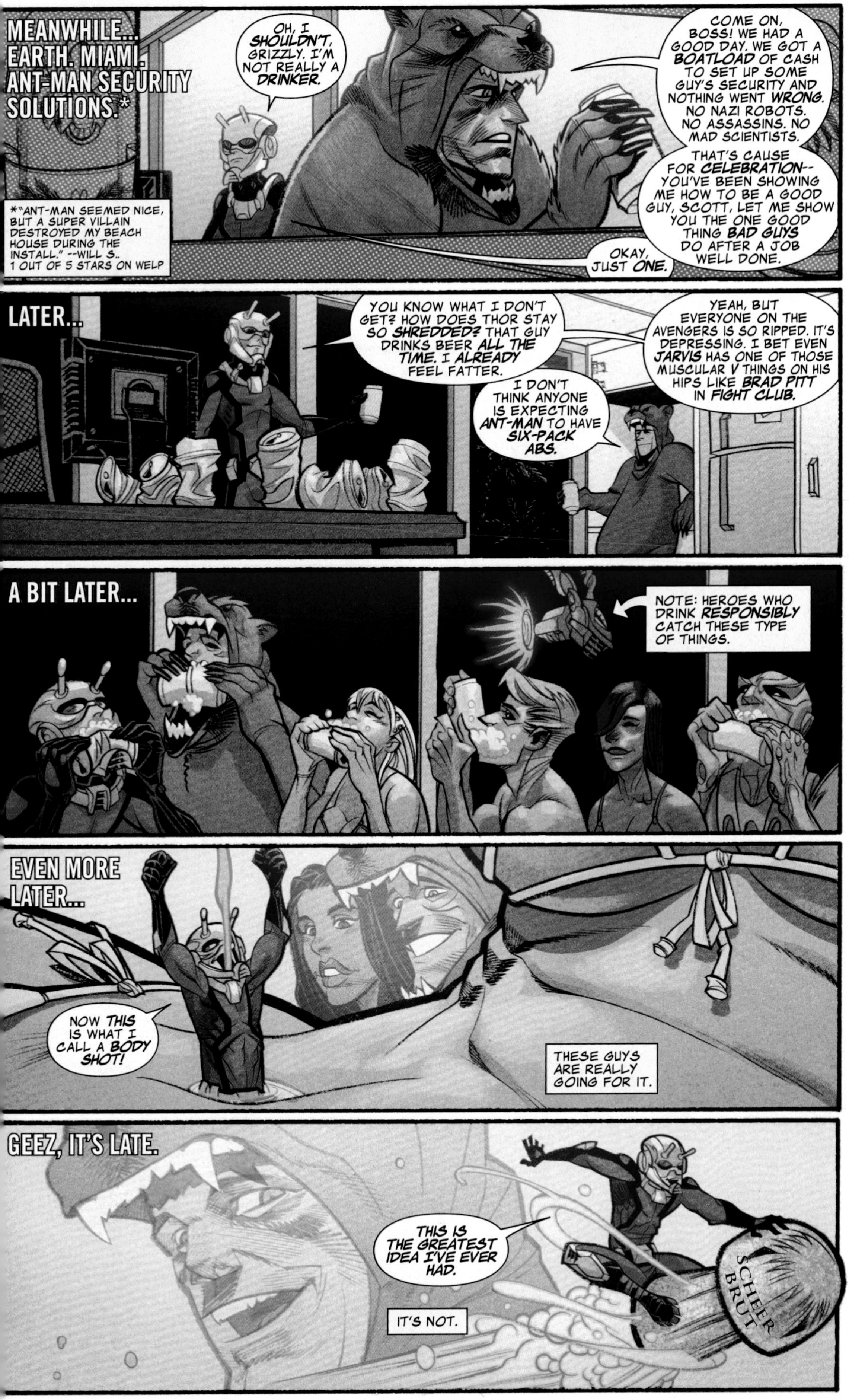

MEANWHILE... EARTH. MIAMI. ANT-MAN SECURITY SOLUTIONS.*
OH, I SHOULDN'T, GRIZZLY. I'M NOT REALLY A DRINKER.
COME ON, BOSS! WE HAD A GOOD DAY. WE GOT A BOATLOAD OF CASH TO SET UP SOME GUY'S SECURITY AND NOTHING WENT WRONG. NO NAZI ROBOTS. NO ASSASSINS. NO MAD SCIENTISTS.
THAT'S CAUSE FOR CELEBRATION-- YOU'VE BEEN SHOWING ME HOW TO BE A GOOD GUY, SCOTT, LET ME SHOW YOU THE ONE GOOD THING BAD GUYS DO AFTER A JOB WELL DONE.
OKAY, JUST ONE.
*"ANT-MAN SEEMED NICE, BUT A SUPER VILLAIN DESTROYED MY BEACH HOUSE DURING THE INSTALL." --WILL S.. 1 OUT OF 5 STARS ON WELP
LATER...
YOU KNOW WHAT I DON'T GET? HOW DOES THOR STAY SO SHREDDED? THAT GUY DRINKS BEER ALL THE TIME. I ALREADY FEEL FATTER.
I DON'T THINK ANYONE IS EXPECTING ANT-MAN TO HAVE SIX-PACK ABS.
YEAH, BUT EVERYONE ON THE AVENGERS IS SO RIPPED. IT'S DEPRESSING. I BET EVEN JARVIS HAS ONE OF THOSE MUSCULAR V THINGS ON HIS HIPS LIKE BRAD PITT IN FIGHT CLUB.
A BIT LATER...
NOTE: HEROES WHO DRINK RESPONSIBLY CATCH THESE TYPE OF THINGS.
EVEN MORE LATER...
NOW THIS IS WHAT I CALL A BODY SHOT!
THESE GUYS ARE REALLY GOING FOR IT.
GEEZ, IT'S LATE.
THIS IS THE GREATEST IDEA I'VE EVER HAD.
IT'S NOT.
SCHEER BRUT

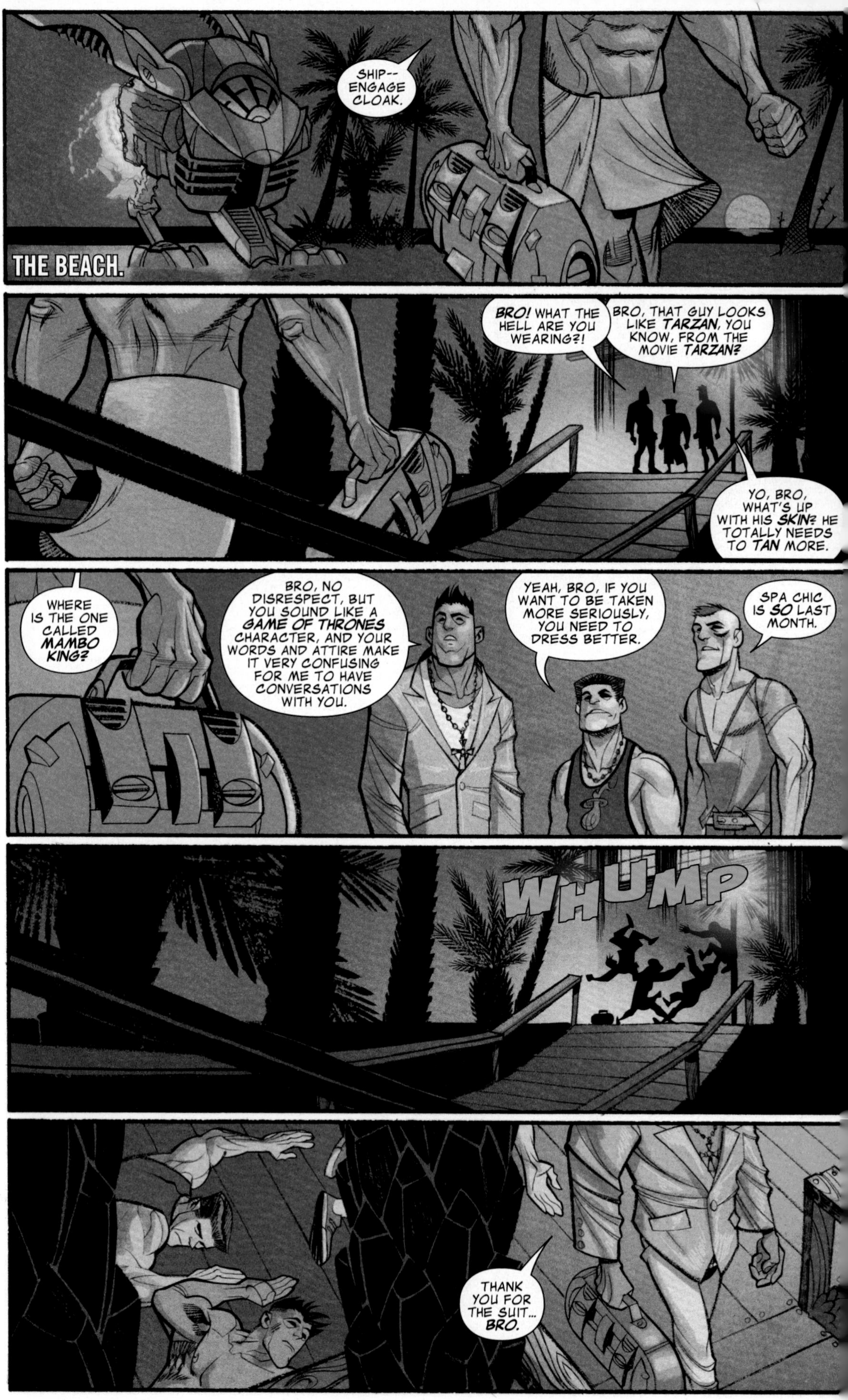
SHIP--
ENGAGE
CLOAK.
THE BEACH.
BRO! WHAT THE HELL ARE YOU WEARING?!
BRO, THAT GUY LOOKS LIKE TARZAN, YOU KNOW, FROM THE MOVIE TARZAN?
YO, BRO, WHAT'S UP WITH HIS SKIN? HE TOTALLY NEEDS TO TAN MORE.
WHERE IS THE ONE CALLED MAMBO KING?
BRO, NO DISRESPECT, BUT YOU SOUND LIKE A GAME OF THRONES CHARACTER, AND YOUR WORDS AND ATTIRE MAKE IT VERY CONFUSING FOR ME TO HAVE CONVERSATIONS WITH YOU.
YEAH, BRO, IF YOU WANT TO BE TAKEN MORE SERIOUSLY, YOU NEED TO DRESS BETTER.
SPA CHIC IS SO LAST MONTH.
WHUMP
THANK YOU FOR THE SUIT... BRO.

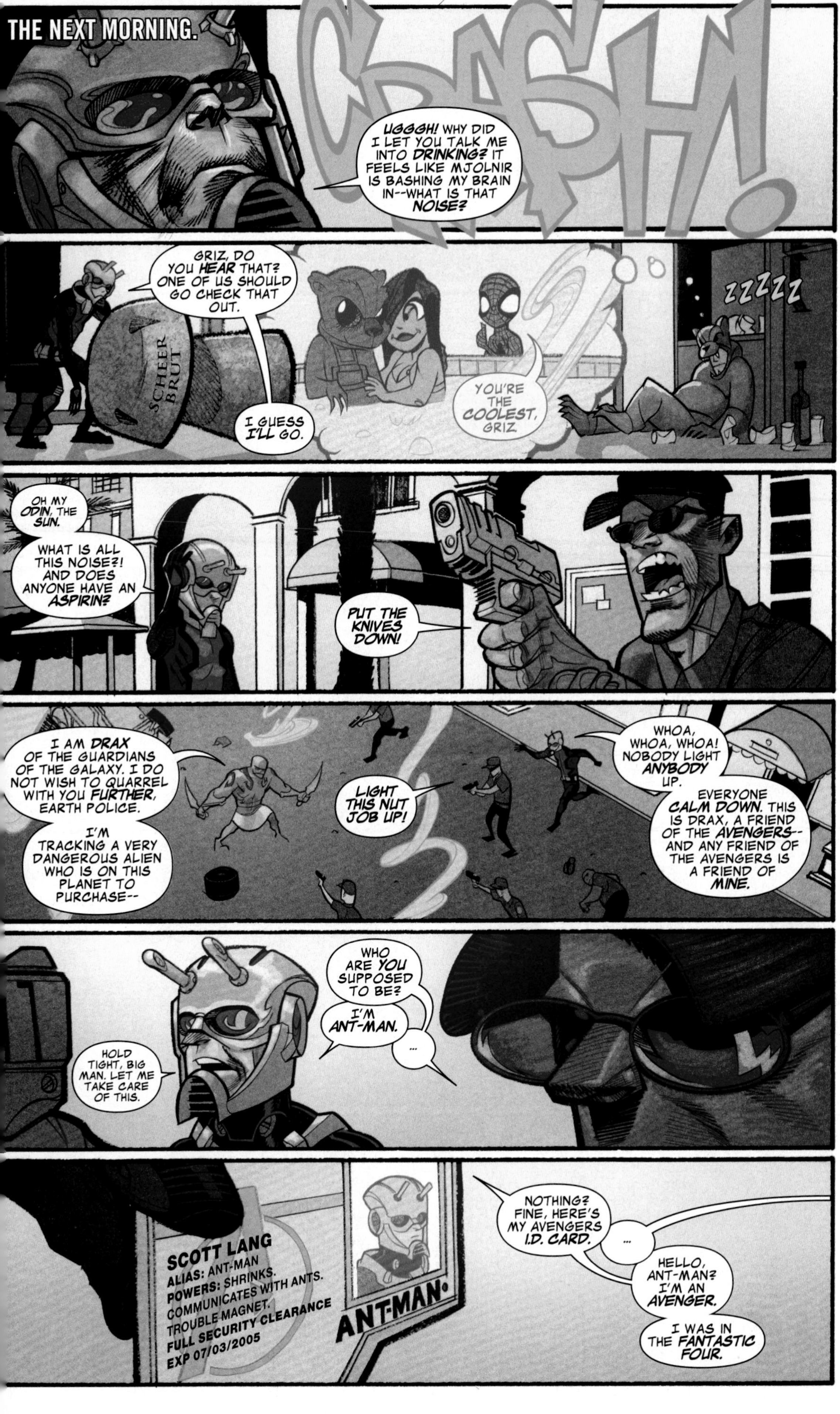
THE NEXT MORNING.
CRASH!
UGGGH! WHY DID I LET YOU TALK ME INTO DRINKING? IT FEELS LIKE MJOLNIR IS BASHING MY BRAIN IN--WHAT IS THAT NOISE?
GRIZ, DO YOU HEAR THAT? ONE OF US SHOULD GO CHECK THAT OUT.
SCHEER BRUT
YOU'RE THE COOLEST, GRIZ.
I GUESS I'LL GO.
ZZZZZ
OH MY ODIN, THE SUN.
WHAT IS ALL THIS NOISE?! AND DOES ANYONE HAVE AN ASPIRIN?
PUT THE KNIVES DOWN!
I AM DRAX OF THE GUARDIANS OF THE GALAXY. I DO NOT WISH TO QUARREL WITH YOU FURTHER, EARTH POLICE.
I'M TRACKING A VERY DANGEROUS ALIEN WHO IS ON THIS PLANET TO PURCHASE--
LIGHT THIS NUT JOB UP!
WHOA, WHOA, WHOA! NOBODY LIGHT ANYBODY UP.
EVERYONE CALM DOWN. THIS IS DRAX, A FRIEND OF THE AVENGERS-- AND ANY FRIEND OF THE AVENGERS IS A FRIEND OF MINE.
HOLD TIGHT, BIG MAN. LET ME TAKE CARE OF THIS.
WHO ARE YOU SUPPOSED TO BE?
I'M ANT-MAN.
...
SCOTT LANG
ALIAS: ANT-MAN
POWERS: SHRINKS. COMMUNICATES WITH ANTS. TROUBLE MAGNET.
FULL SECURITY CLEARANCE
EXP 07/03/2005
ANT-MAN
NOTHING? FINE, HERE'S MY AVENGERS I.D. CARD.
...
HELLO, ANT-MAN? I'M AN AVENGER.
I WAS IN THE FANTASTIC FOUR.

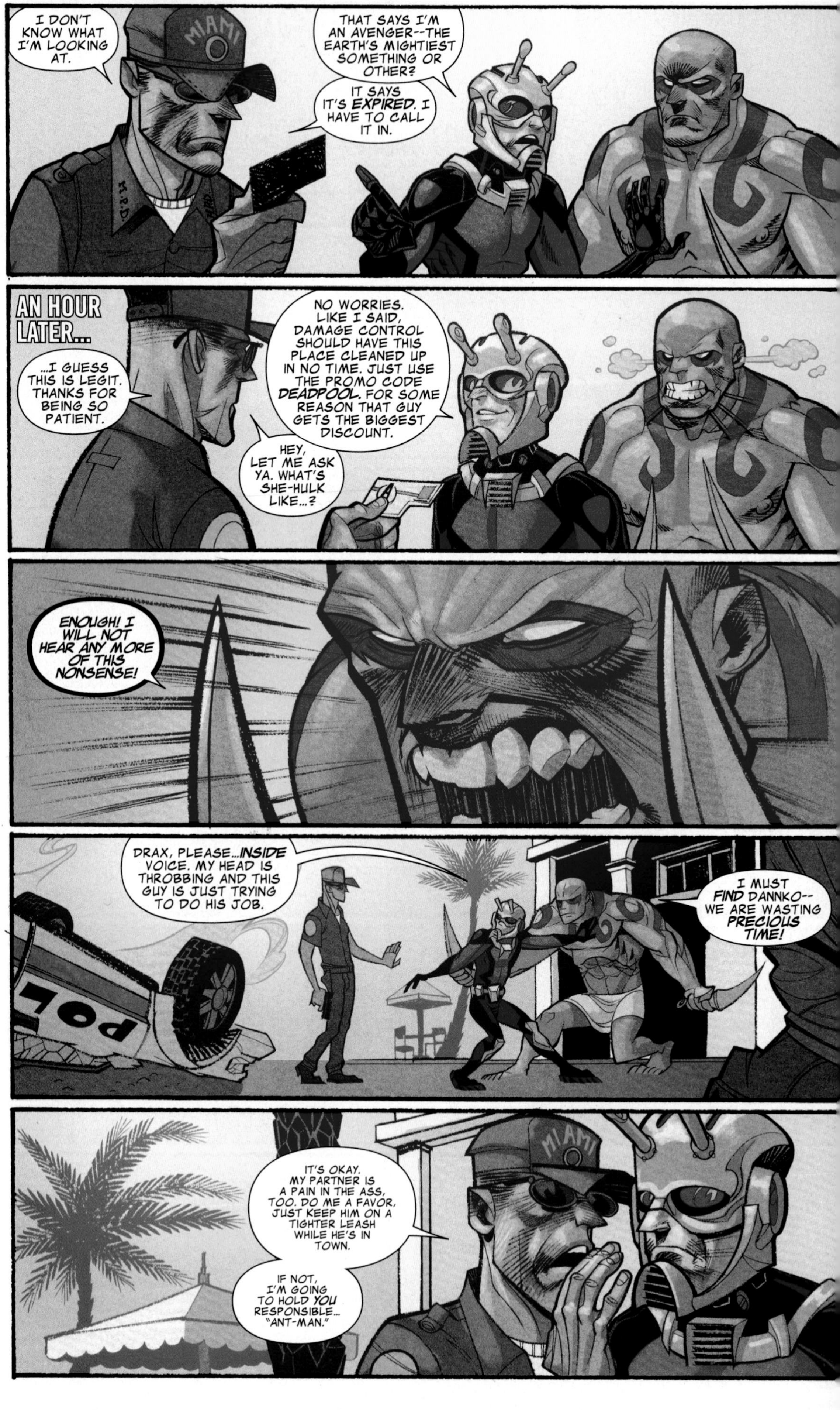
I DON'T KNOW WHAT I'M LOOKING AT.
THAT SAYS I'M AN AVENGER--THE EARTH'S MIGHTIEST SOMETHING OR OTHER?
IT SAYS IT'S EXPIRED. I HAVE TO CALL IT IN.
AN HOUR LATER...
...I GUESS THIS IS LEGIT. THANKS FOR BEING SO PATIENT.
NO WORRIES. LIKE I SAID, DAMAGE CONTROL SHOULD HAVE THIS PLACE CLEANED UP IN NO TIME. JUST USE THE PROMO CODE DEADPOOL. FOR SOME REASON THAT GUY GETS THE BIGGEST DISCOUNT.
HEY, LET ME ASK YA. WHAT'S SHE-HULK LIKE...?
ENOUGH! I WILL NOT HEAR ANY MORE OF THIS NONSENSE!
DRAX, PLEASE...INSIDE VOICE. MY HEAD IS THROBBING AND THIS GUY IS JUST TRYING TO DO HIS JOB.
I MUST FIND DANNKO--WE ARE WASTING PRECIOUS TIME!
IT'S OKAY. MY PARTNER IS A PAIN IN THE ASS, TOO. DO ME A FAVOR, JUST KEEP HIM ON A TIGHTER LEASH WHILE HE'S IN TOWN.
IF NOT, I'M GOING TO HOLD YOU RESPONSIBLE... "ANT-MAN."

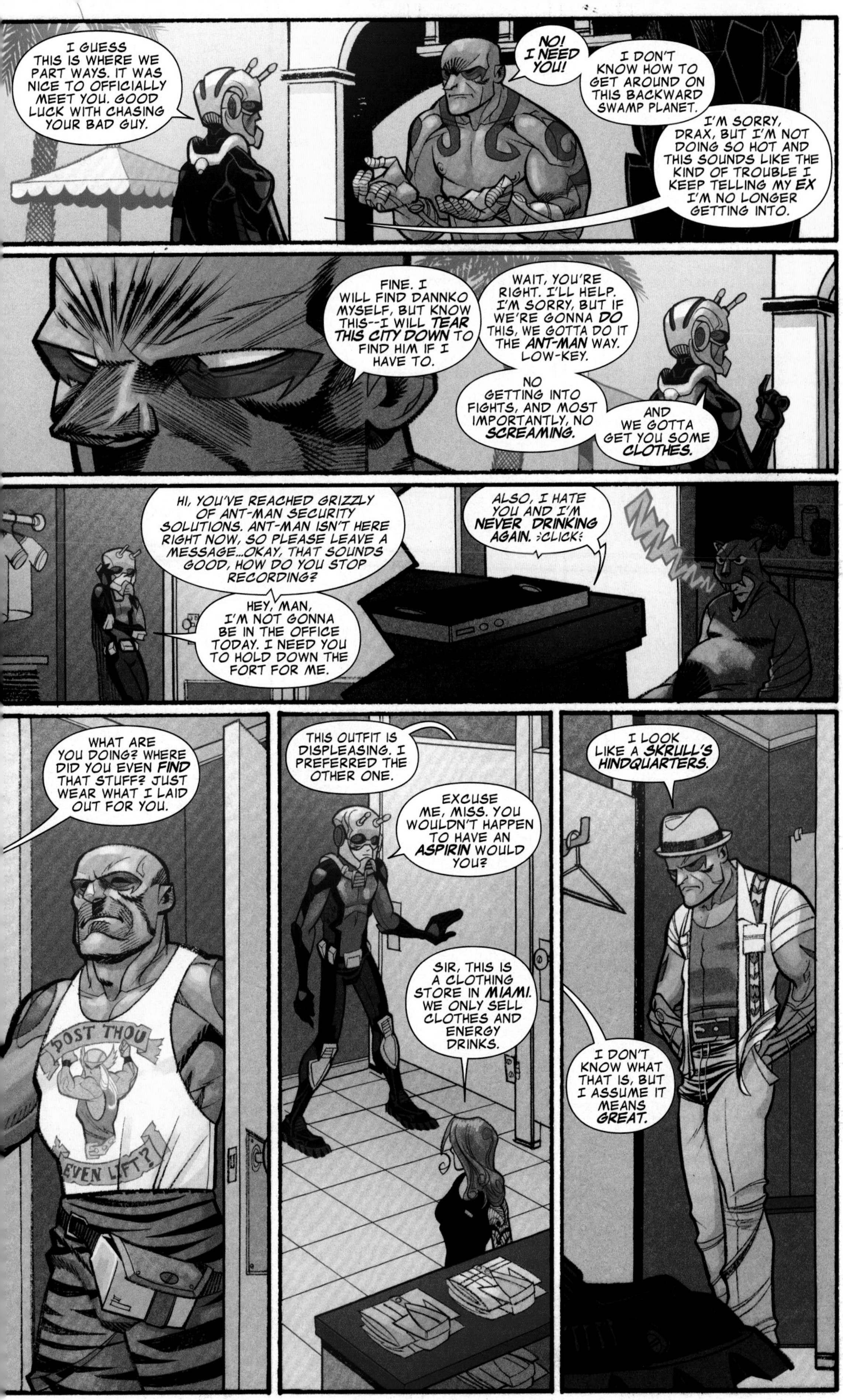
I GUESS THIS IS WHERE WE PART WAYS. IT WAS NICE TO OFFICIALLY MEET YOU. GOOD LUCK WITH CHASING YOUR BAD GUY.
NO! I NEED YOU!
I DON'T KNOW HOW TO GET AROUND ON THIS BACKWARD SWAMP PLANET.
I'M SORRY, DRAX, BUT I'M NOT DOING SO HOT AND THIS SOUNDS LIKE THE KIND OF TROUBLE I KEEP TELLING MY EX I'M NO LONGER GETTING INTO.
FINE. I WILL FIND DANNKO MYSELF, BUT KNOW THIS--I WILL TEAR THIS CITY DOWN TO FIND HIM IF I HAVE TO.
WAIT, YOU'RE RIGHT. I'LL HELP. I'M SORRY, BUT IF WE'RE GONNA DO THIS, WE GOTTA DO IT THE ANT-MAN WAY. LOW-KEY.
NO GETTING INTO FIGHTS, AND MOST IMPORTANTLY, NO SCREAMING.
AND WE GOTTA GET YOU SOME CLOTHES.
HI, YOU'VE REACHED GRIZZLY OF ANT-MAN SECURITY SOLUTIONS. ANT-MAN ISN'T HERE RIGHT NOW, SO PLEASE LEAVE A MESSAGE...OKAY, THAT SOUNDS GOOD, HOW DO YOU STOP RECORDING?
HEY, MAN, I'M NOT GONNA BE IN THE OFFICE TODAY. I NEED YOU TO HOLD DOWN THE FORT FOR ME.
ALSO, I HATE YOU AND I'M NEVER DRINKING AGAIN. CLICK
WHAT ARE YOU DOING? WHERE DID YOU EVEN FIND THAT STUFF? JUST WEAR WHAT I LAID OUT FOR YOU.
DOST THOU EVEN LIFT?
THIS OUTFIT IS DISPLEASING. I PREFERRED THE OTHER ONE.
EXCUSE ME, MISS. YOU WOULDN'T HAPPEN TO HAVE AN ASPIRIN WOULD YOU?
SIR, THIS IS A CLOTHING STORE IN MIAMI. WE ONLY SELL CLOTHES AND ENERGY DRINKS.
I LOOK LIKE A SKRULL'S HINDQUARTERS.
I DON'T KNOW WHAT THAT IS, BUT I ASSUME IT MEANS GREAT.

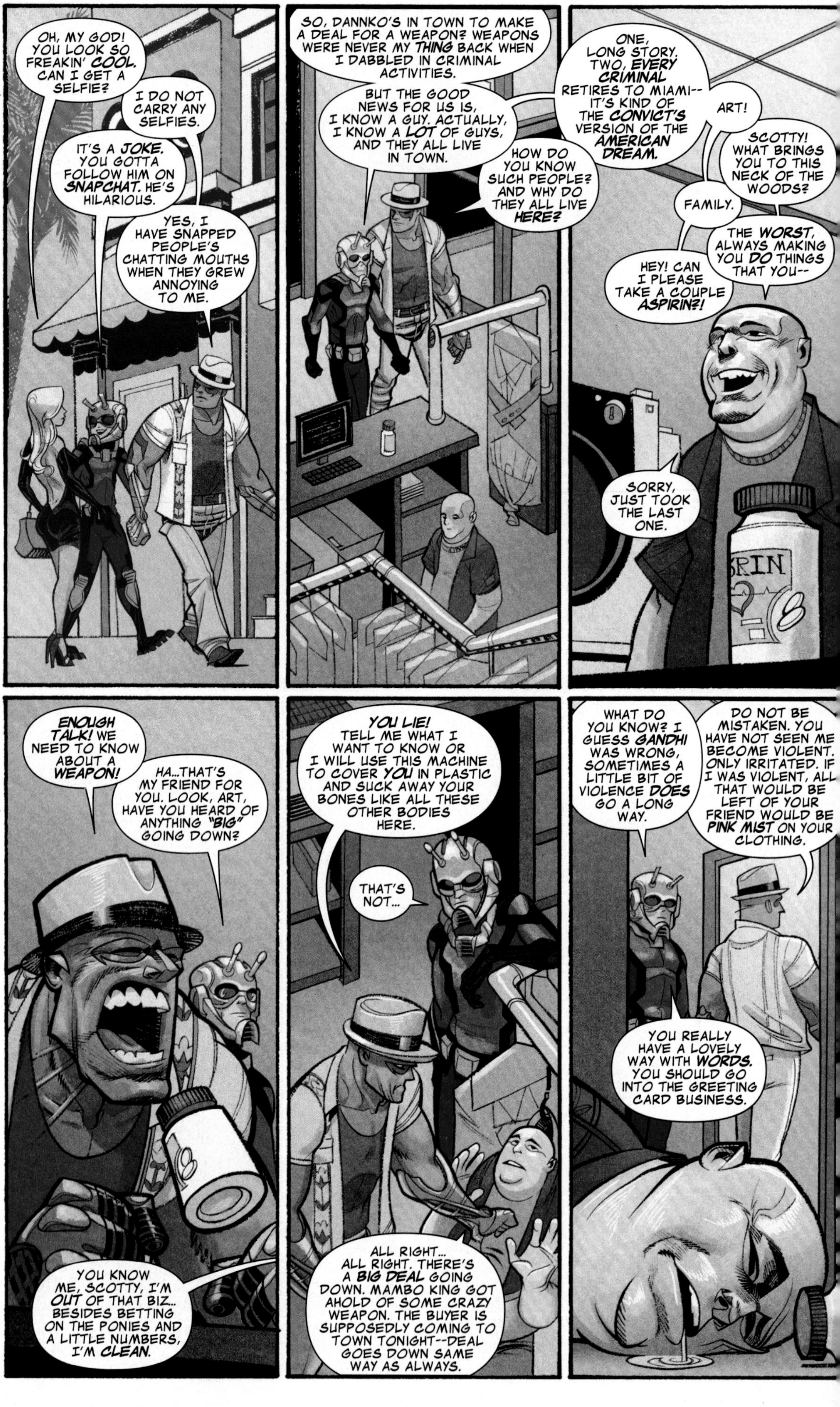
OH, MY GOD! YOU LOOK SO FREAKIN' COOL. CAN I GET A SELFIE?
I DO NOT CARRY ANY SELFIES.
IT'S A JOKE. YOU GOTTA FOLLOW HIM ON SNAPCHAT. HE'S HILARIOUS.
YES, I HAVE SNAPPED PEOPLE'S CHATTING MOUTHS WHEN THEY GREW ANNOYING TO ME.
SO, DANNKO'S IN TOWN TO MAKE A DEAL FOR A WEAPON? WEAPONS WERE NEVER MY THING BACK WHEN I DABBLED IN CRIMINAL ACTIVITIES.
BUT THE GOOD NEWS FOR US IS, I KNOW A GUY. ACTUALLY, I KNOW A LOT OF GUYS, AND THEY ALL LIVE IN TOWN.
HOW DO YOU KNOW SUCH PEOPLE? AND WHY DO THEY ALL LIVE HERE?
ONE, LONG STORY. TWO, EVERY CRIMINAL RETIRES TO MIAMI-- IT'S KIND OF THE CONVICT'S VERSION OF THE AMERICAN DREAM.
ART!
SCOTTY! WHAT BRINGS YOU TO THIS NECK OF THE WOODS?
FAMILY.
THE WORST, ALWAYS MAKING YOU DO THINGS THAT YOU--
HEY! CAN I PLEASE TAKE A COUPLE ASPIRIN?!
SORRY, JUST TOOK THE LAST ONE.
ENOUGH TALK! WE NEED TO KNOW ABOUT A WEAPON!
HA...THAT'S MY FRIEND FOR YOU. LOOK, ART, HAVE YOU HEARD OF ANYTHING "BIG" GOING DOWN?
YOU KNOW ME, SCOTTY, I'M OUT OF THAT BIZ... BESIDES BETTING ON THE PONIES AND A LITTLE NUMBERS, I'M CLEAN.
YOU LIE! TELL ME WHAT I WANT TO KNOW OR I WILL USE THIS MACHINE TO COVER YOU IN PLASTIC AND SUCK AWAY YOUR BONES LIKE ALL THESE OTHER BODIES HERE.
THAT'S NOT...
ALL RIGHT... ALL RIGHT. THERE'S A BIG DEAL GOING DOWN. MAMBO KING GOT AHOLD OF SOME CRAZY WEAPON. THE BUYER IS SUPPOSEDLY COMING TO TOWN TONIGHT--DEAL GOES DOWN SAME WAY AS ALWAYS.
WHAT DO YOU KNOW? I GUESS GANDHI WAS WRONG, SOMETIMES A LITTLE BIT OF VIOLENCE DOES GO A LONG WAY.
DO NOT BE MISTAKEN. YOU HAVE NOT SEEN ME BECOME VIOLENT. ONLY IRRITATED. IF I WAS VIOLENT, ALL THAT WOULD BE LEFT OF YOUR FRIEND WOULD BE PINK MIST ON YOUR CLOTHING.
YOU REALLY HAVE A LOVELY WAY WITH WORDS. YOU SHOULD GO INTO THE GREETING CARD BUSINESS.

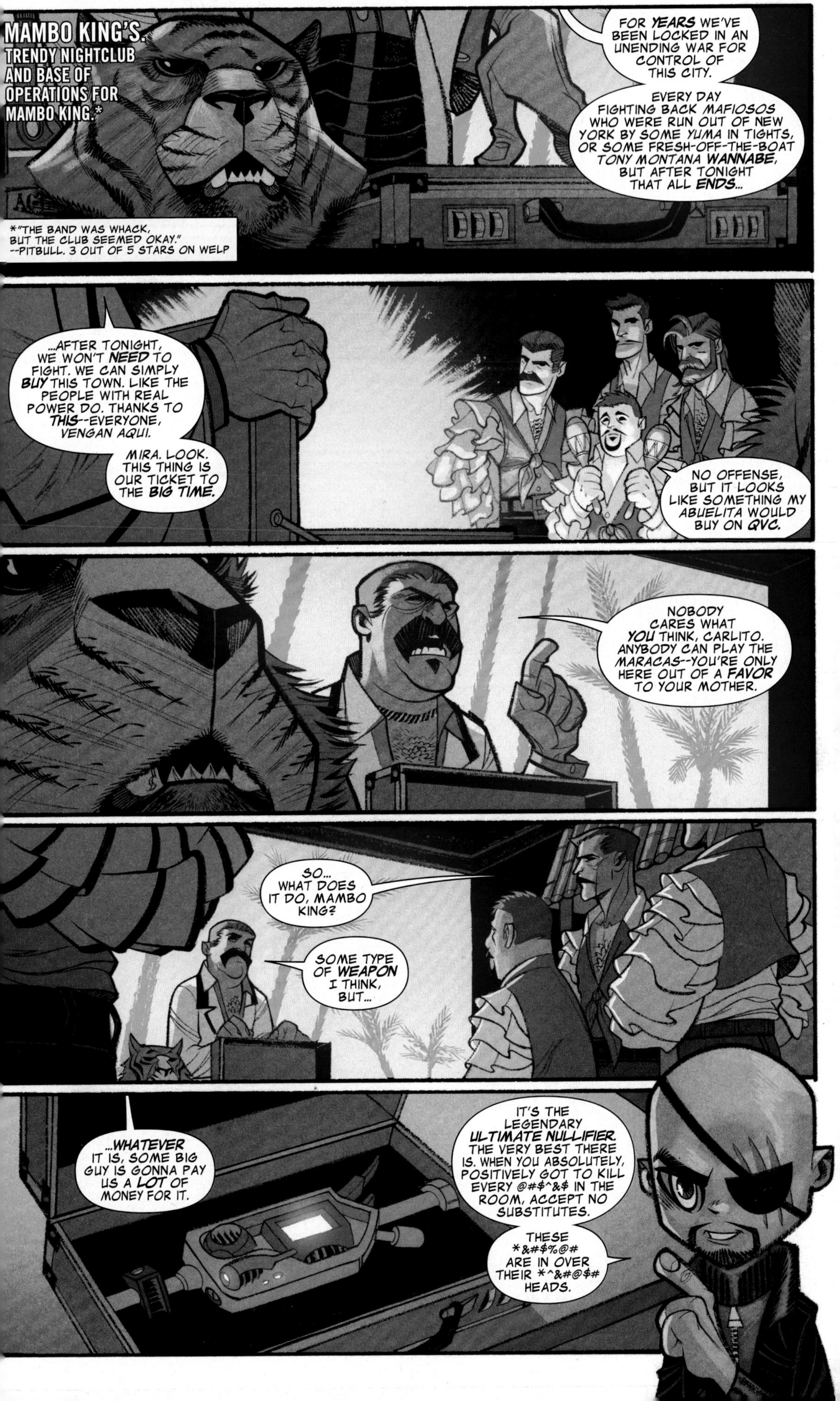

MAMBO KING'S. TRENDY NIGHTCLUB AND BASE OF OPERATIONS FOR MAMBO KING.*
FOR YEARS WE'VE BEEN LOCKED IN AN UNENDING WAR FOR CONTROL OF THIS CITY.
EVERY DAY FIGHTING BACK MAFIOSOS WHO WERE RUN OUT OF NEW YORK BY SOME YUMA IN TIGHTS, OR SOME FRESH-OFF-THE-BOAT TONY MONTANA WANNABE, BUT AFTER TONIGHT THAT ALL ENDS...
*"THE BAND WAS WHACK, BUT THE CLUB SEEMED OKAY." --PITBULL. 3 OUT OF 5 STARS ON WELP
...AFTER TONIGHT, WE WON'T NEED TO FIGHT. WE CAN SIMPLY BUY THIS TOWN. LIKE THE PEOPLE WITH REAL POWER DO. THANKS TO THIS--EVERYONE, VENGAN AQUI.
MIRA. LOOK. THIS THING IS OUR TICKET TO THE BIG TIME.
NO OFFENSE, BUT IT LOOKS LIKE SOMETHING MY ABUELITA WOULD BUY ON QVC.
NOBODY CARES WHAT YOU THINK, CARLITO. ANYBODY CAN PLAY THE MARACAS--YOU'RE ONLY HERE OUT OF A FAVOR TO YOUR MOTHER.
SO... WHAT DOES IT DO, MAMBO KING?
SOME TYPE OF WEAPON I THINK, BUT...
...WHATEVER IT IS, SOME BIG GUY IS GONNA PAY US A LOT OF MONEY FOR IT.
IT'S THE LEGENDARY ULTIMATE NULLIFIER. THE VERY BEST THERE IS. WHEN YOU ABSOLUTELY, POSITIVELY GOT TO KILL EVERY @#$^&$ IN THE ROOM, ACCEPT NO SUBSTITUTES.
THESE *&#$%@# ARE IN OVER THEIR *^&#@$# HEADS.

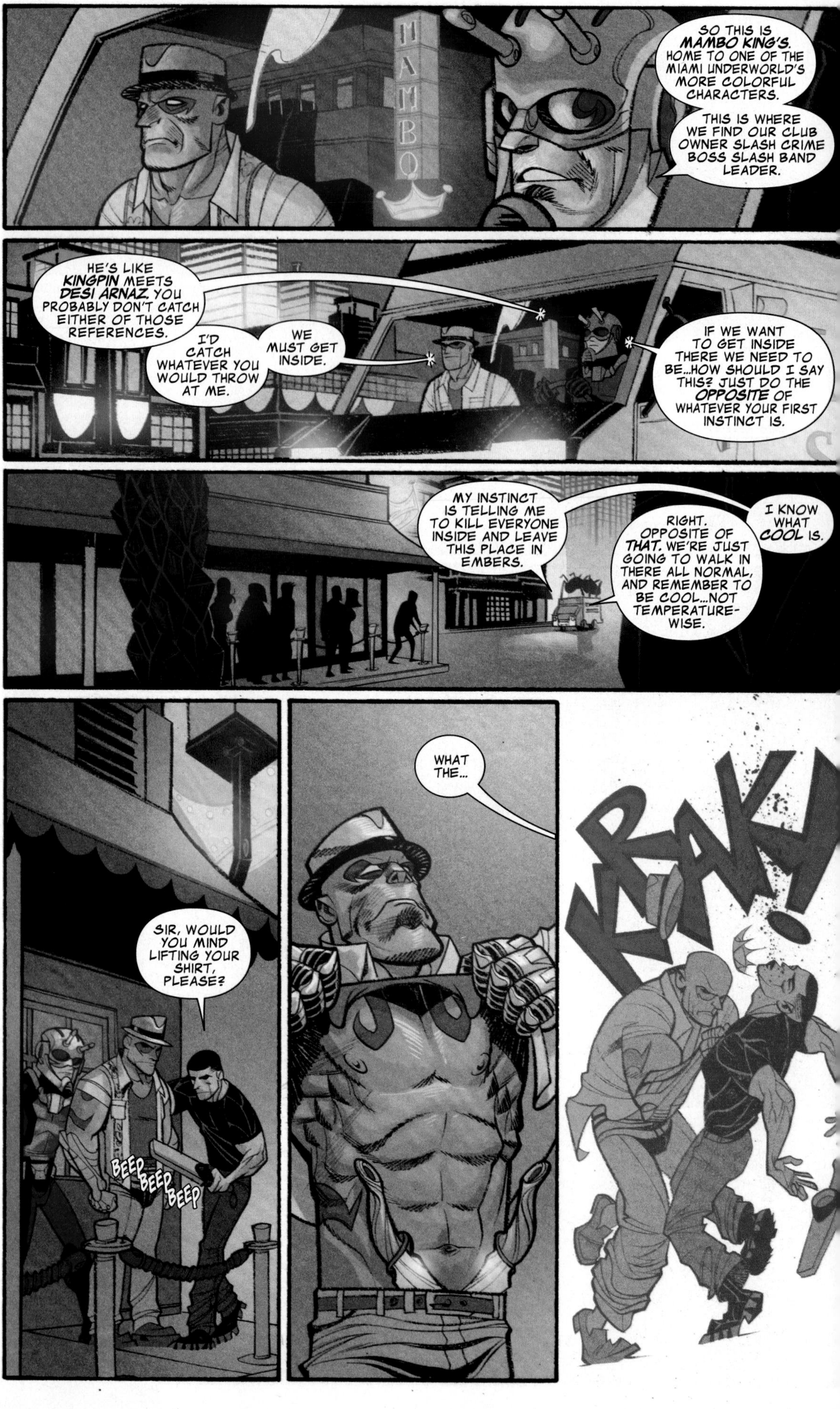

MAMBO
SO THIS IS MAMBO KING'S. HOME TO ONE OF THE MIAMI UNDERWORLD'S MORE COLORFUL CHARACTERS.
THIS IS WHERE WE FIND OUR CLUB OWNER SLASH CRIME BOSS SLASH BAND LEADER.
HE'S LIKE KINGPIN MEETS DESI ARNAZ. YOU PROBABLY DON'T CATCH EITHER OF THOSE REFERENCES.
I'D CATCH WHATEVER YOU WOULD THROW AT ME.
WE MUST GET INSIDE.
IF WE WANT TO GET INSIDE THERE WE NEED TO BE...HOW SHOULD I SAY THIS? JUST DO THE OPPOSITE OF WHATEVER YOUR FIRST INSTINCT IS.
MY INSTINCT IS TELLING ME TO KILL EVERYONE INSIDE AND LEAVE THIS PLACE IN EMBERS.
RIGHT. OPPOSITE OF THAT. WE'RE JUST GOING TO WALK IN THERE ALL NORMAL, AND REMEMBER TO BE COOL...NOT TEMPERATURE-WISE.
I KNOW WHAT COOL IS.
SIR, WOULD YOU MIND LIFTING YOUR SHIRT, PLEASE?
BEEP BEEP BEEP
WHAT THE...
KRAKK!

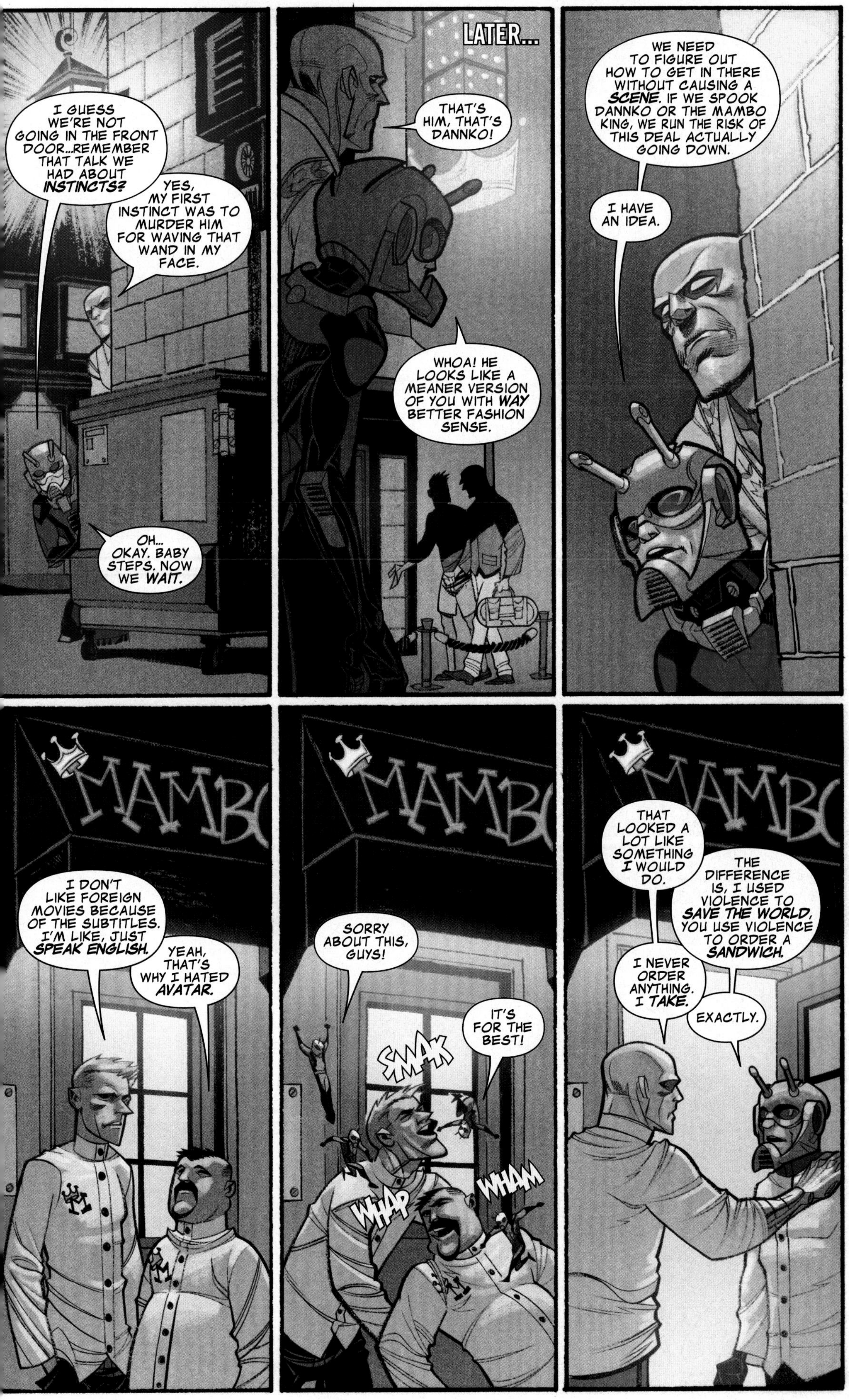

I GUESS WE'RE NOT GOING IN THE FRONT DOOR...REMEMBER THAT TALK WE HAD ABOUT INSTINCTS?
YES, MY FIRST INSTINCT WAS TO MURDER HIM FOR WAVING THAT WAND IN MY FACE.
OH... OKAY. BABY STEPS. NOW WE WAIT.
LATER...
THAT'S HIM, THAT'S DANNKO!
WHOA! HE LOOKS LIKE A MEANER VERSION OF YOU WITH WAY BETTER FASHION SENSE.
WE NEED TO FIGURE OUT HOW TO GET IN THERE WITHOUT CAUSING A SCENE. IF WE SPOOK DANNKO OR THE MAMBO KING, WE RUN THE RISK OF THIS DEAL ACTUALLY GOING DOWN.
I HAVE AN IDEA.
MAMBO
I DON'T LIKE FOREIGN MOVIES BECAUSE OF THE SUBTITLES. I'M LIKE, JUST SPEAK ENGLISH.
YEAH, THAT'S WHY I HATED AVATAR.
MAMBO
SORRY ABOUT THIS, GUYS!
IT'S FOR THE BEST!
SMAK
WHAP
WHAM
MAMBO
THAT LOOKED A LOT LIKE SOMETHING I WOULD DO.
THE DIFFERENCE IS, I USED VIOLENCE TO SAVE THE WORLD, YOU USE VIOLENCE TO ORDER A SANDWICH.
I NEVER ORDER ANYTHING. I TAKE.
EXACTLY.

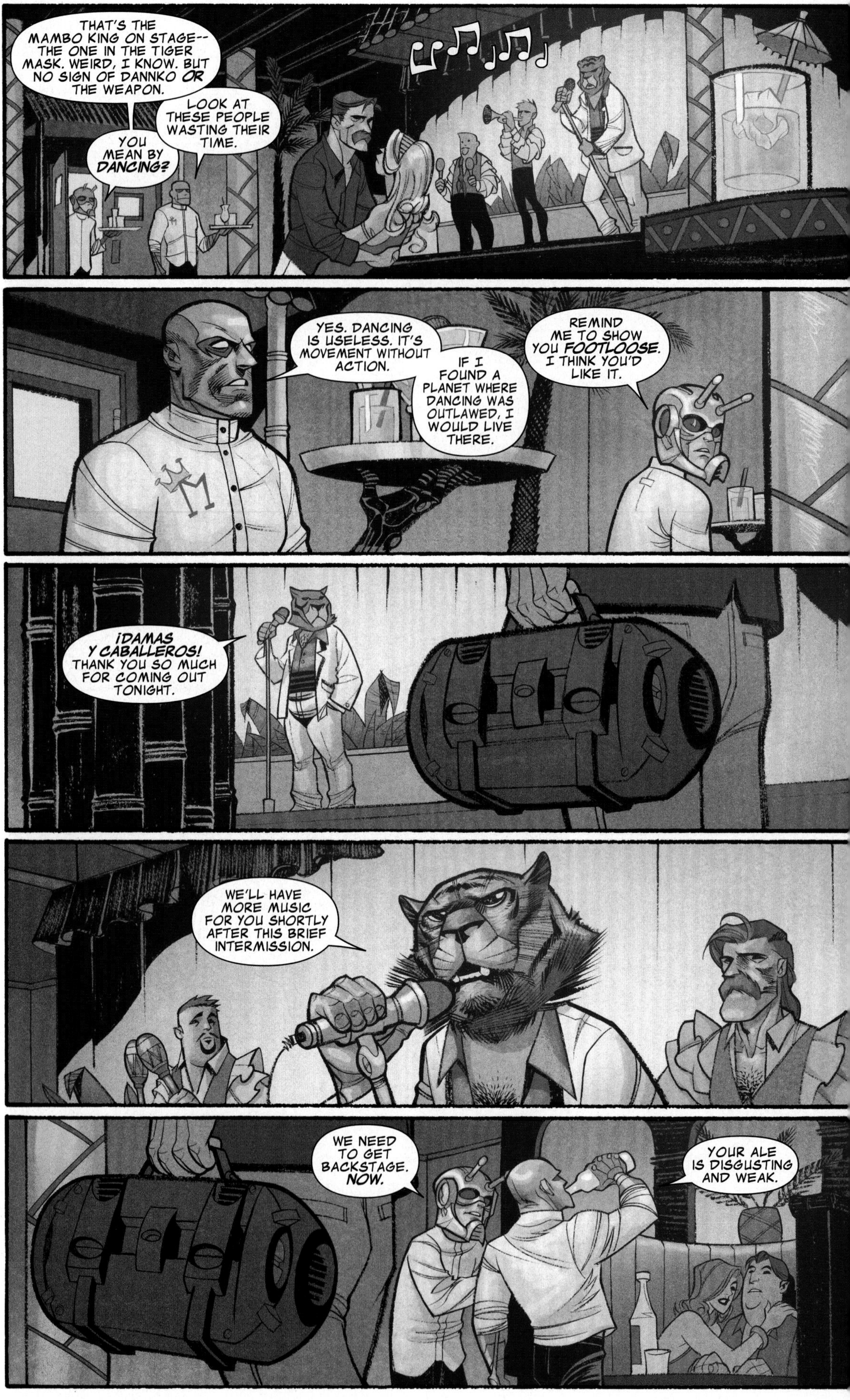
THAT'S THE MAMBO KING ON STAGE-- THE ONE IN THE TIGER MASK. WEIRD, I KNOW. BUT NO SIGN OF DANNKO OR THE WEAPON.
LOOK AT THESE PEOPLE WASTING THEIR TIME.
YOU MEAN BY DANCING?
YES. DANCING IS USELESS. IT'S MOVEMENT WITHOUT ACTION.
IF I FOUND A PLANET WHERE DANCING WAS OUTLAWED, I WOULD LIVE THERE.
REMIND ME TO SHOW YOU FOOTLOOSE. I THINK YOU'D LIKE IT.
¡DAMAS Y CABALLEROS! THANK YOU SO MUCH FOR COMING OUT TONIGHT.
WE'LL HAVE MORE MUSIC FOR YOU SHORTLY AFTER THIS BRIEF INTERMISSION.
WE NEED TO GET BACKSTAGE. NOW.
YOUR ALE IS DISGUSTING AND WEAK.

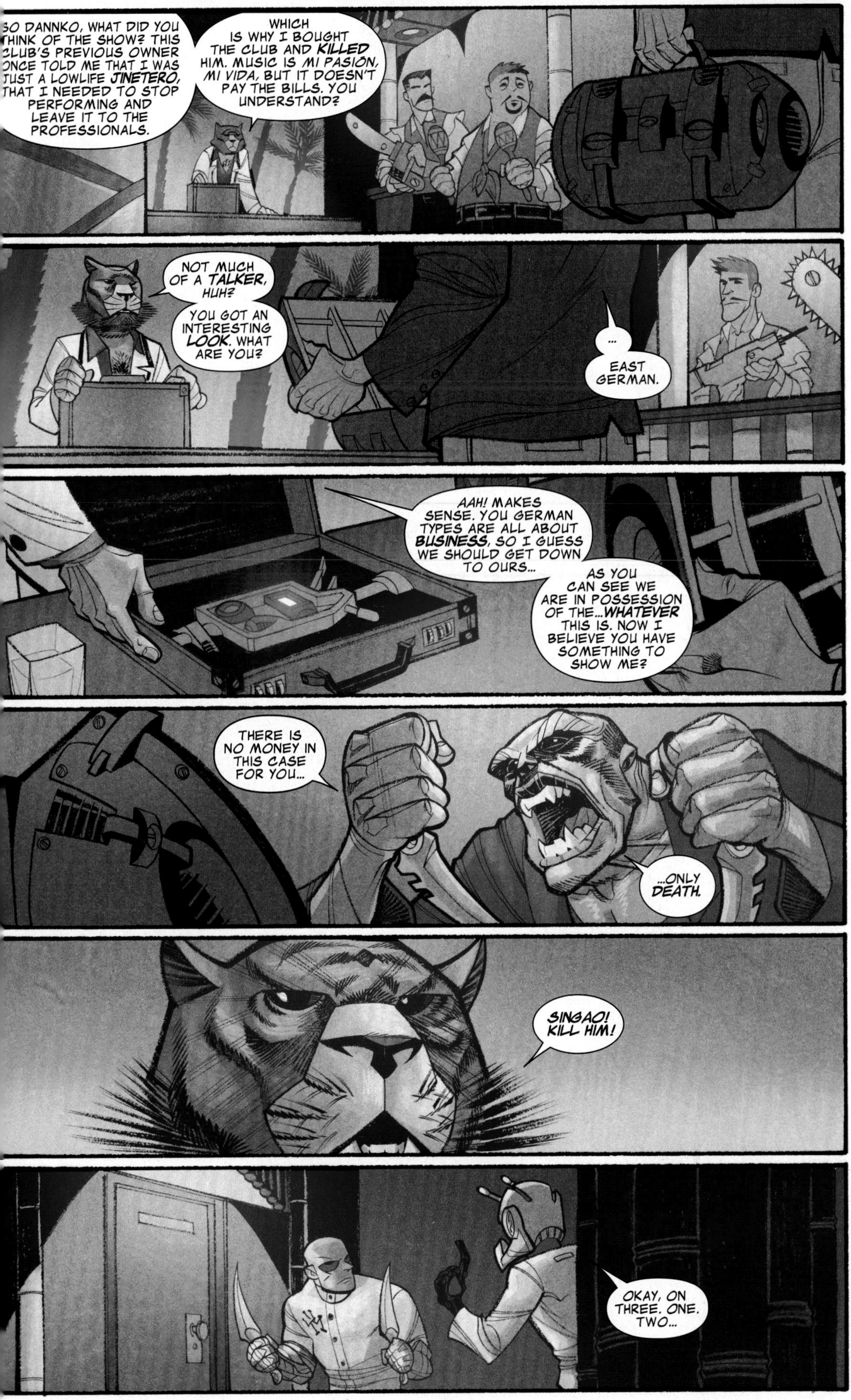
SO DANNKO, WHAT DID YOU THINK OF THE SHOW? THIS CLUB'S PREVIOUS OWNER ONCE TOLD ME THAT I WAS JUST A LOWLIFE JINETERO, THAT I NEEDED TO STOP PERFORMING AND LEAVE IT TO THE PROFESSIONALS.
WHICH IS WHY I BOUGHT THE CLUB AND KILLED HIM. MUSIC IS MI PASION, MI VIDA, BUT IT DOESN'T PAY THE BILLS. YOU UNDERSTAND?
NOT MUCH OF A TALKER, HUH?
YOU GOT AN INTERESTING LOOK. WHAT ARE YOU?
...
EAST GERMAN.
AAH! MAKES SENSE. YOU GERMAN TYPES ARE ALL ABOUT BUSINESS, SO I GUESS WE SHOULD GET DOWN TO OURS...
AS YOU CAN SEE WE ARE IN POSSESSION OF THE...WHATEVER THIS IS. NOW I BELIEVE YOU HAVE SOMETHING TO SHOW ME?
THERE IS NO MONEY IN THIS CASE FOR YOU...
...ONLY DEATH.
SINGAO! KILL HIM!
OKAY, ON THREE. ONE. TWO...

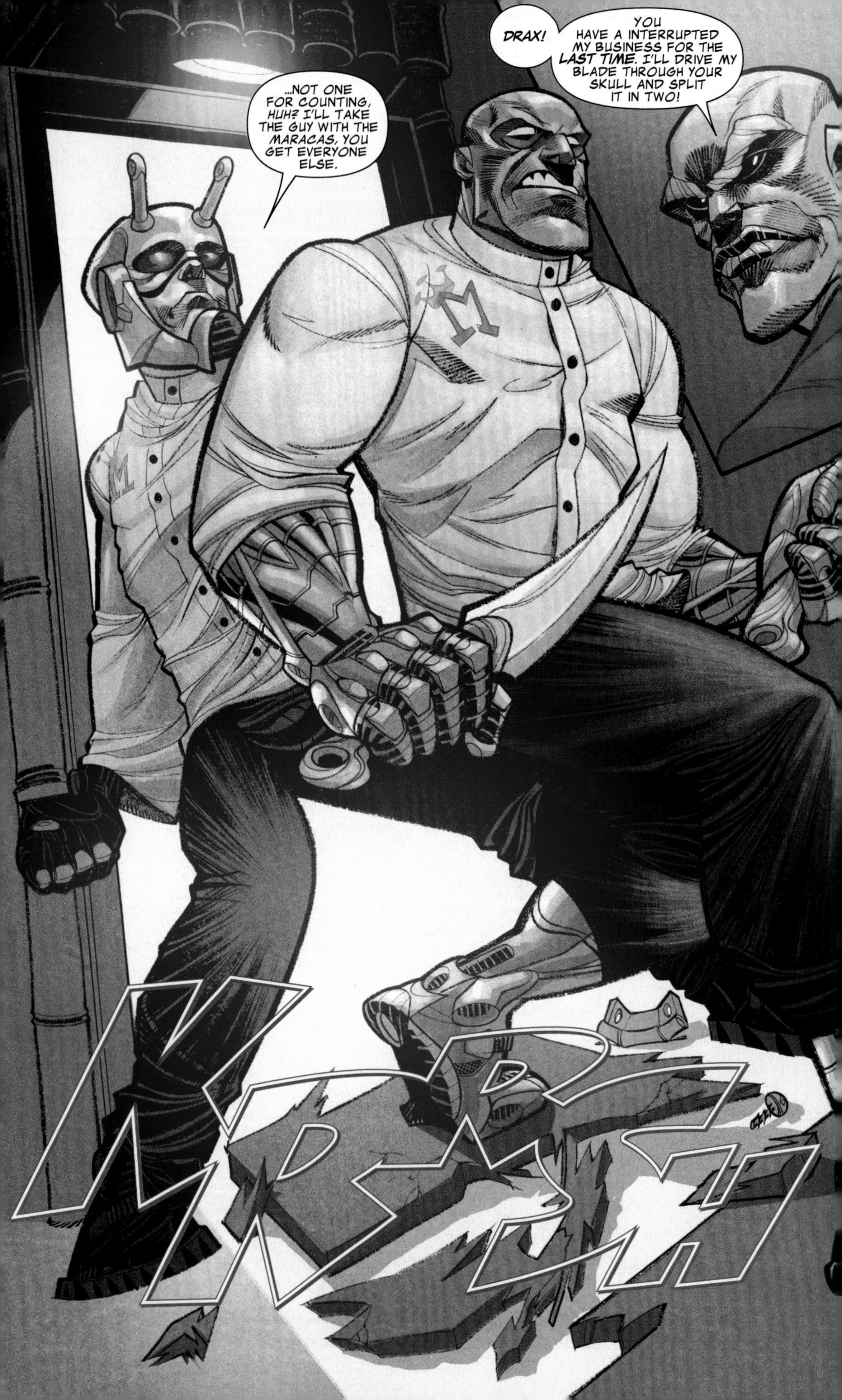
...NOT ONE FOR COUNTING, HUH? I'LL TAKE THE GUY WITH THE MARACAS, YOU GET EVERYONE ELSE.
DRAX!
YOU HAVE A INTERRUPTED MY BUSINESS FOR THE LAST TIME. I'LL DRIVE MY BLADE THROUGH YOUR SKULL AND SPLIT IT IN TWO!

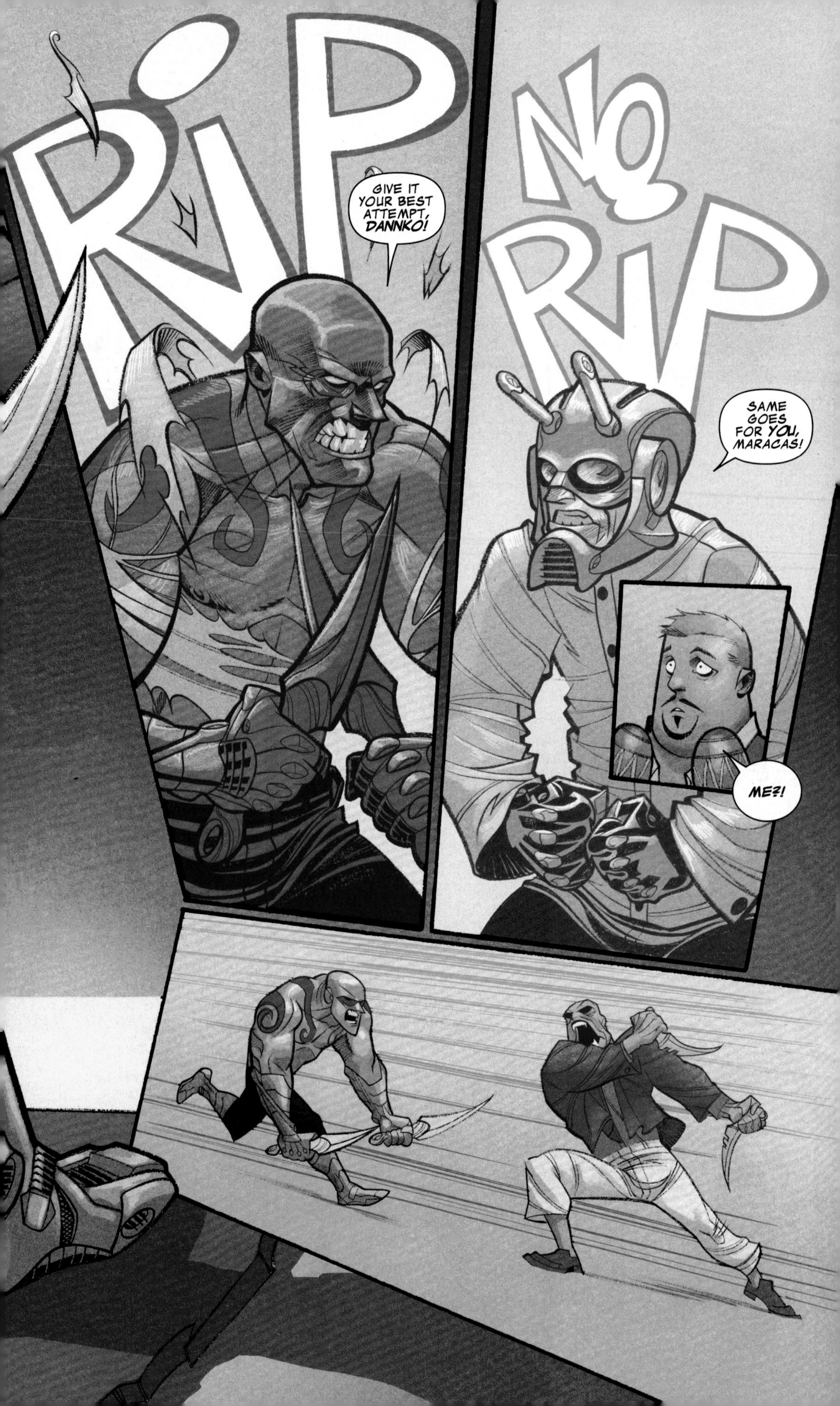
RIP
GIVE IT YOUR BEST ATTEMPT, DANNKO!
NO RIP
SAME GOES FOR YOU, MARACAS!
ME?!

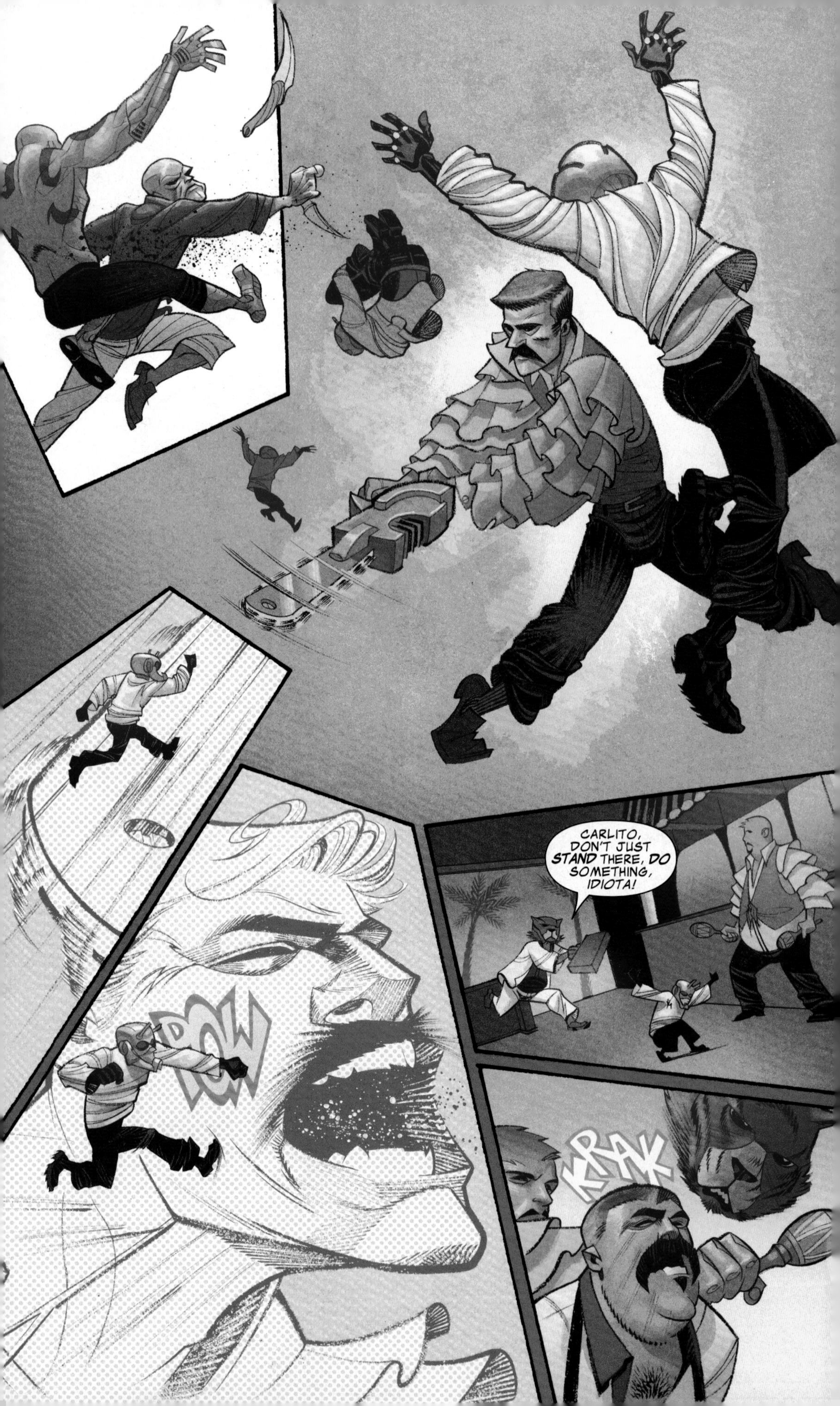
POW
CARLITO, DON'T JUST STAND THERE, DO SOMETHING, IDIOTA!
KRAK

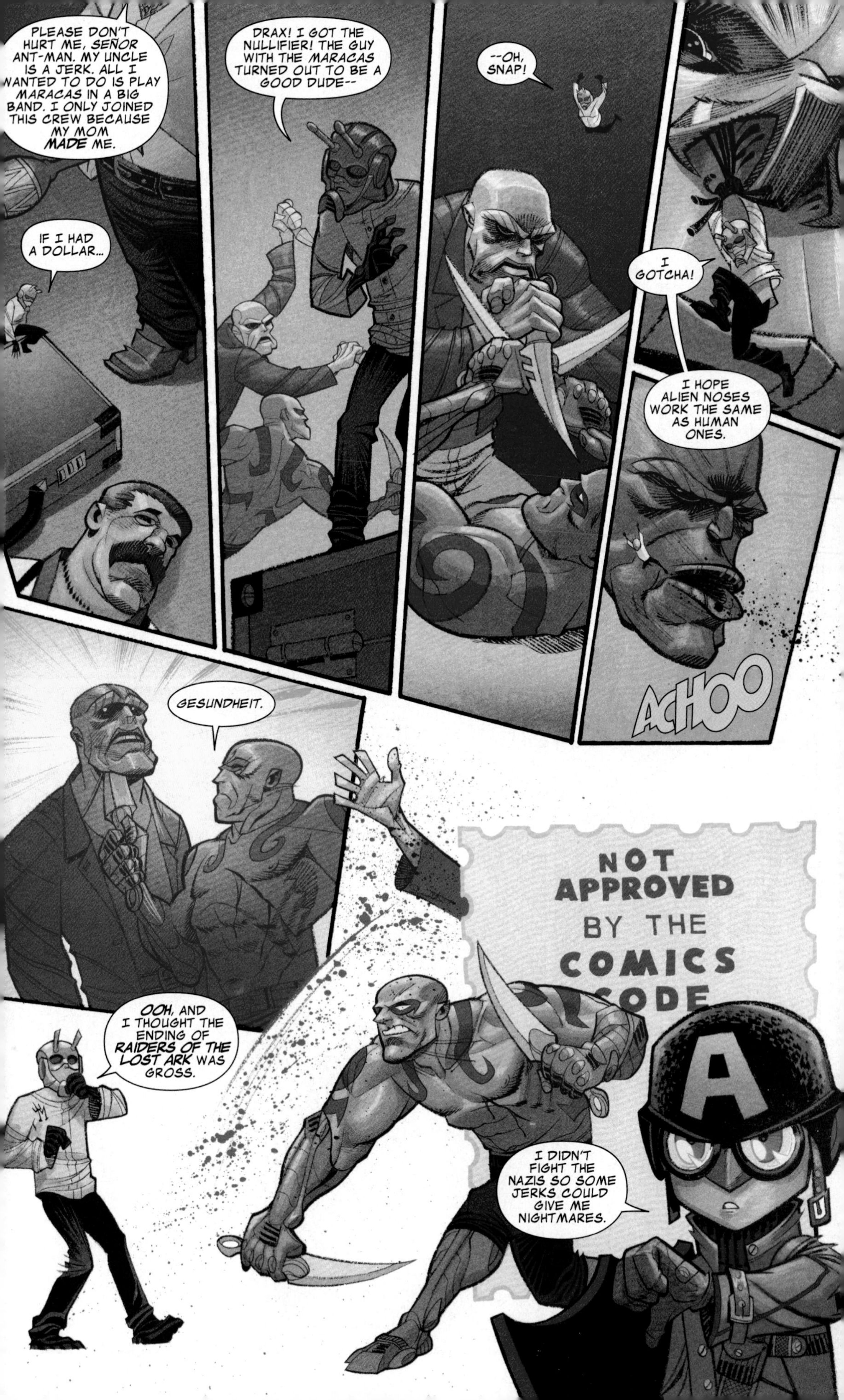
PLEASE DON'T HURT ME, SEÑOR ANT-MAN. MY UNCLE IS A JERK. ALL I WANTED TO DO IS PLAY MARACAS IN A BIG BAND. I ONLY JOINED THIS CREW BECAUSE MY MOM MADE ME.
IF I HAD A DOLLAR...
DRAX! I GOT THE NULLIFIER! THE GUY WITH THE MARACAS TURNED OUT TO BE A GOOD DUDE--
--OH, SNAP!
I GOTCHA!
I HOPE ALIEN NOSES WORK THE SAME AS HUMAN ONES.
ACHOO
GESUNDHEIT.
NOT APPROVED BY THE COMICS CODE
OOH, AND I THOUGHT THE ENDING OF RAIDERS OF THE LOST ARK WAS GROSS.
I DIDN'T FIGHT THE NAZIS SO SOME JERKS COULD GIVE ME NIGHTMARES.

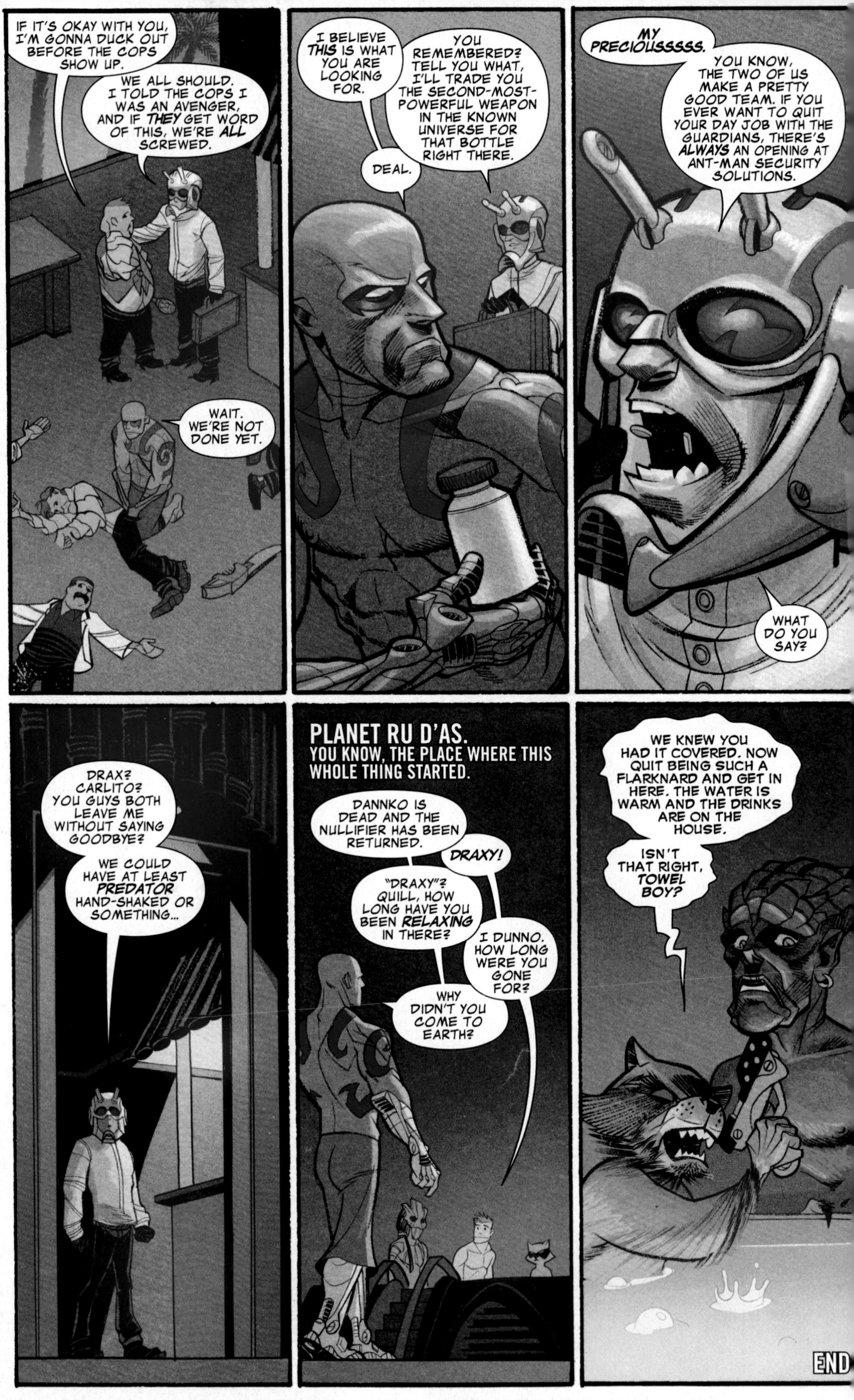
IF IT'S OKAY WITH YOU, I'M GONNA DUCK OUT BEFORE THE COPS SHOW UP.
WE ALL SHOULD. I TOLD THE COPS I WAS AN AVENGER, AND IF THEY GET WORD OF THIS, WE'RE ALL SCREWED.
WAIT. WE'RE NOT DONE YET.
I BELIEVE THIS IS WHAT YOU ARE LOOKING FOR.
YOU REMEMBERED? TELL YOU WHAT, I'LL TRADE YOU THE SECOND-MOST-POWERFUL WEAPON IN THE KNOWN UNIVERSE FOR THAT BOTTLE RIGHT THERE.
DEAL.
MY PRECIOUSSSSS.
YOU KNOW, THE TWO OF US MAKE A PRETTY GOOD TEAM. IF YOU EVER WANT TO QUIT YOUR DAY JOB WITH THE GUARDIANS, THERE'S ALWAYS AN OPENING AT ANT-MAN SECURITY SOLUTIONS.
WHAT DO YOU SAY?
DRAX? CARLITO? YOU GUYS BOTH LEAVE ME WITHOUT SAYING GOODBYE?
WE COULD HAVE AT LEAST PREDATOR HAND-SHAKED OR SOMETHING...
PLANET RU D'AS.
YOU KNOW, THE PLACE WHERE THIS WHOLE THING STARTED.
DANNKO IS DEAD AND THE NULLIFIER HAS BEEN RETURNED.
DRAXY!
"DRAXY"? QUILL, HOW LONG HAVE YOU BEEN RELAXING IN THERE?
I DUNNO. HOW LONG WERE YOU GONE FOR?
WHY DIDN'T YOU COME TO EARTH?
WE KNEW YOU HAD IT COVERED. NOW QUIT BEING SUCH A FLARKNARD AND GET IN HERE. THE WATER IS WARM AND THE DRINKS ARE ON THE HOUSE.
ISN'T THAT RIGHT, TOWEL BOY?
END